Researching Violence

Violence is a research topic that is fraught with difficulties. A notoriously sensitive subject, and one that is presumed to be largely hidden, researchers have long struggled with the question of how to measure its impact and how to explore its incidence. Arising from the ESRC's Violence Research Programme (VRP), *Researching Violence* is a practical guide both to these problems and to the obstacles encountered when negotiating this uneasy terrain. Comprising the reflections of researchers who have worked on diverse projects – from violence in the home to racial violence and homicide – this book demonstrates the ingenuity and at times courageous actions of researchers having to think on their feet. It also investigates the ethical and emotional issues arising from working with the victims and perpetrators of violence. This book will be indispensable for students and academics engaged in research projects on violence.

Raymond M. Lee is Professor of Social Research Methods at Royal Holloway, University of London. **Elizabeth A. Stanko** is Professor of Criminology at Royal Holloway, University of London, and Director of the ESRC Violence Research Programme.

Researching Violence

Essays on methodology and measurement

**Edited by Raymond M. Lee and
Elizabeth A. Stanko**

 Routledge
Taylor & Francis Group

LONDON AND NEW YORK

First published 2003
by Routledge
2 Park Square, Milton Park, Abingdon, Oxon OX14 4RN

Simultaneously published in the USA and Canada
by Routledge
711 Third Avenue, New York, NY 10017

Routledge is an imprint of the Taylor & Francis Group, an informa business

Typeset in Goudy by Rosemount Typing Services, Thornhill, DG3 5LS

British Library Cataloguing in Publication Data
A catalogue record for this book is available from the British Library

Library of Congress Cataloging in Publication Data
Researching violence : essays on methodology and measurement / edited by Raymond
M. Lee and Elizabeth Stanko.
       p. cm.
    Includes bibliographical references and index.
      1. Violence–Research–Methodology. I. Lee, Raymond M., 1946– II. Stanko,
Elizabeth Anne, 1950–

    HM1116 .R47 2003
    303.6'07'2–dc21

                                                                              2002028478
ISBN 0–415–30131–9 (hbk)
ISBN 0–415–30132–7 (pbk)

Contents

Figures and tables

Figures

Tables

Contributors

John E. Archer is a Reader in history at Edge Hill College of Education. He has published extensively on nineteenth-century rural crime and protest, and is currently working on violence in the north west of England.

Loraine Bacchus completed her Ph.D. on domestic violence in pregnancy at St George's Hospital Medical School, London in May 2002. Her research interests include domestic violence and health, and domestic violence interventions in maternity settings.

Christine Barter is a senior NSPCC Research Fellow with the Faculty of Health Care and Social Studies at Luton University. She has previously worked on a range of projects concerning the experiences of young people, including children who run away, protecting children from racial abuse, independent investigations into allegations of institutional child abuse and peer violence in residential children's homes.

Susan Bewley is a consultant obstetrician/maternal fetal medicine specialist and Clinical Director of Women's Health Services at Guy's and St Thomas' Hospitals, London. She has published on uterine Doppler, severe maternal morbidity, HIV, and legal and ethical issues in pregnancy.

Kate Cavanagh is a Senior Lecturer in social work at the University of Glasgow. She has published widely in the area of domestic violence. She is co-author with R. Emerson Dobash, Russell P. Dobash and Ruth Lewis of *Changing Violent Men* (2000) and is one of the co-investigators on the Homicide in Britain study. She is currently involved in an evaluation of the Protection from Abuse (Scotland) Act 2001.

Karen Corteen is a Lecturer in the Criminology Department of Edge Hill College. Her areas of research include sexuality and education.

Susan Creighton is Senior Research Officer at the NSPCC, where she has conducted research and written on the epidemiology of child abuse, and child deaths where abuse or neglect is implicated.

David Denney is Reader in Social and Public Policy at Royal Holloway, University of London. He has written in the areas of social services provision, race and criminal justice. He has published extensively and his books include *Racism and Antiracism in Probation* (1992) and *Social Policy and Social Work* (1998). He is currently writing a book on the relationship between risk and professional practices.

R. Emerson Dobash is a Professor in the Department of Applied Social Science at Manchester University. She has interests in studying violence and gender and collaborated with Kate Cavanagh, Ruth Lewis and Russell P. Dobash on an evaluation of perpetrators' programmes for domestically violent men; and co-authored *Changing Violent Men* with them. She has written numerous articles on domestic violence.

Russell P. Dobash is a Professor in the Department of Applied Social Science at Manchester University and, with Kate Cavanagh, R. Emerson Dobash and Ruth Lewis, co-authored *Changing Violent Men* (2000). He has interests in studying violence and gender and was involved with an evaluation of perpetrators' programmes for domestically violent men.

Kimmett Edgar was a Research Officer at the Centre for Criminological Research, University of Oxford, during the ESRC study.

Mary Ann Elston is a sociologist at Royal Holloway, University of London where she directs an M.Sc. programme in medical sociology. Her research interests are mainly related to health professions, the organisation of health care, gender and medical science and technology.

Julia Field was a Research Director at the National Centre for Social Research (formerly SCPR) for 25 years. Now retired, she continues to work for the centre as a consultant, retaining a particular interest in quantitative surveys on personally sensitive subjects, including the 1990 and 2000 National Survey of Sexual Attitudes and Lifestyles.

Steven Finch is Research Group Director in the National Centre for Social Research's Quantitative Research Department. He has managed a wide range of research projects, mostly in the fields of education, the family or socio-legal research.

Jonathan Gabe is Reader in Sociology in the Department of Social and Political Science, Royal Holloway, University of London. He has published widely in the areas of health care organisation, chronic illness and mental health, and was an editor of the international journal *Sociology of Health and Illness* from 1994 to 2000.

Deborah Ghate is co-director of the Policy Research Bureau. She has a strong track record in research on parenting and is the author of key texts in the field, including *Parenting in Poor Environments* (with N. Hazel, 2002). She provides expert advice on parenting policy, and is Visiting Professor in Social Policy Research at Royal Holloway, University of London.

Neal Hazel is Senior Research Fellow at the Policy Research Bureau. He specialises in research involving young people, including studies of youth justice and of parenting. His publications include *Parenting in Poor Environments* (with D. Ghate, 2002) and *Fathers and Family Centres* (with D. Ghate and C. Shaw, 2000).

Colin Knox is Professor of Public Policy in the School of Policy Studies at the University of Ulster. His most recent book is *Informal Justice in Divided Societies: Northern Ireland and South Africa* (with R. Monaghan, 2002).

Raymond M. Lee is Professor of Social Research Methods in the Department of Social and Political Science at Royal Holloway, University of London. He has written widely on a number of methodological topics including the problems and issues involved in research on 'sensitive' topics, research in dangerous environments, and on the impact of new technologies on the research process.

Mark Levine is a Lecturer in the Department of Psychology, University of Lancaster.

Ruth Lewis is a Lecturer in the Department of Sociology and Social Policy at Newcastle University. She has interests in studying violence and gender. She collaborated on an evaluation of perpetrators' programmes for domestically violent men and co-authored *Changing Violent Men* (2000) with Kate Cavanagh, R. Emerson Dobash and Russell P. Dobash.

Carol Martin was a Research Officer at the Centre for Criminological Research, University of Oxford, during the ESRC study.

Gillian Mezey is a Consultant and Senior Lecturer in Forensic Psychiatry based at St. George's Hospital Medical School in London. She has a particular research interest in the effects of sexual and physical violence and has recently completed research into domestic violence and pregnancy, battered women who kill their violent partners, and the psychological effects of murder on surviving family members.

Rachel Monaghan is a Lecturer in Human Geography at the University of Ulster. Her research interests include grassroots/community conflict resolution in comparative context (Northern Ireland and South Africa) and political violence undertaken by single-issue groups.

Leslie J. Moran is Reader in the School of Law at Birkbeck College, University of London. He has published extensively in the area of sexuality and law and hate crime. He is also involved in several gay and lesbian organisations doing work on violence.

Maria O'Beirne is a Research Officer in the Department of Social and Political Science, Royal Holloway. She has worked for ten years as a researcher on issues of social exclusion and more recently on work-related violence.

Ian O'Donnell is Research Fellow at the Institute of Criminology, University College, Dublin.

Larry Ray is Professor of Sociology at the University of Kent where he is currently head of the School of Social Policy, Sociology and Social Research. He previously taught at Lancaster University. He has published widely on social theory and social transformations and (with David Smith) on hate crimes and racist violence.

Emma Renold is a Lecturer in the School of Social Sciences, Cardiff University. Her research interests and publications include children's gender and sexual identities; gender-based bullying and sexualised harassment in the primary school; the impact of gender and sexuality on children's learned identities; violence between young people in residential children's homes; and researching sensitive topics.

Beverley Skeggs is Professor in the Department of Sociology, University of Manchester. She has written extensively on issues of class, gender and sexuality.

David Smith is Professor of Social Work at Lancaster University, where he has taught and researched since 1976. A former probation officer, he is currently researching the experiences of Black and Asian people on probation. He has published extensively on probation policy, youth justice and social exclusion.

Elizabeth A. Stanko was the director of the ESRC Violence Research Programme (1997–2002), and is a Professor of Criminology in the Department of Social and Political Science, Royal Holloway, University of London. She is the author of over 60 papers and books exploring gender and violence and the decision-making of public officials. Professor Stanko joined the Office of Public Services Reform in the Cabinet Office full time as a principal advisor in March 2002.

E. Kay M. Tisdall holds a joint post as Lecturer in Social Policy (University of Edinburgh) and Director of Policy & Research (Children in Scotland, the national membership agency of organisations working with children and their families). She convenes the MSc/Diploma in Childhood Studies and undertakes a range of research projects. Recent and current collaborative research include reviewing youth health policy in Scotland, children's views in family law, and integrated services for children and their families.

Paul Tyrer was Research Associate on the Violence, Sexuality, Space project from 1998 to 2000. He is currently research manager of the Northwest Forensic Academy Network.

Liz Wastell is a probation officer in Greater Manchester, and was the Research Officer for the project on racially motivated offending.

Introduction

Methodological reflections

Elizabeth A. Stanko and Raymond M. Lee

This volume contains the reflections of researchers who explored the nature and impact of violence in different contexts, under the umbrella of the UK's Economic and Social Research Council's Violence Research Programme (VRP). One of the few research programmes in the world devoted solely to the study of violence, the ESRC's VRP was funded for five years and supported 20 very different studies across the UK.[1] The research topics varied widely. Academics and professional researchers examined arenas such as conflict in prison, girls' experiences of violence, domestic violence during pregnancy, racist offending, homicide in Britain, and the prevalence of violent discipline of children in the home. The ESRC VRP embraced an interdisciplinary approach. Many social science disciplines – sociology, social policy, social psychology, geography, history, applied social studies and more – came together to examine the contemporary features of violence in the UK at the end of the twentieth century. The lessons learned are important for social science work throughout the twenty-first century. The dilemmas, difficulties and successes that researchers experienced while working with this research programme are worth sharing, across the individual projects and with many disciplines.

Debates about violence inevitably begin by deploring standard ways of measuring the impact of violence on different populations. Too much violence is hidden, it may be said. Findings based on 'seen' violence will, it is assumed, necessarily be distorted or biased. Too often, we suggest, many researchers are reluctant even to try to examine a phenomenon that is so quick to capture newspaper headlines or dinner party conversations, but presumed to be illusory to the researcher. Yet we challenge this assumption by asking: How can something so pervasive remain so elusive to research, and be allowed to remain so unexplored in a systematic way – by researchers or front-line workers – leaving decision-makers without evidence on which to base policies that might reduce violence? By way of an example, when the VRP took its findings to the UK's research and policy constituencies by hosting five regional seminars, we were struck by the first question that was inevitably raised by those present. How could we study a phenomenon that is so hidden? Ironically, the question was raised after the researchers presented their findings!

The ESRC VRP gathered an abundance of information on many forms of violence, collected via creative – albeit standard – methodological approaches from diverse research populations. Surveys and interviews took place in dance clubs, prisons, schools, homes, hospitals, vicarages, doctors' offices, sex workers' massage parlours, neighbourhood meetings and women's refuges (to name but a few of the locations where we found and spoke to our participants). Of course some of the participants were reluctant to share all of their experiences of violence. Many more, however, were willing to offer their insights about highly sensitive matters to the researchers. Yet audience after audience in our feedback seminars continued to think and speak of violence as hidden, as if the 'findings' presented to them in the seminars were not 'findings' at all.

Perhaps as a research community we are overly conscious that studying violence poses thorny dilemmas for researchers. And, of course, the researchers who contribute their thoughts to this volume ask questions similar to those asked by researchers who study sensitive subjects in other settings. For example, VRP researchers debated the following questions.[2]

- How do we 'measure' violence: does a physical injury help us to define its impact?
- Is psychological abuse violence?
- How does 'threat' work as a form of control when it does not result in a physical or sexual injury?
- How do our research participants affect the ways in which we document violence?
- Can we expect people to speak truthfully about violence (either as offenders or as victims)?
- Would people even answer questions about such a sensitive subject?
- Do researchers harm people further by asking them to recount traumatic incidents (whether they are victims or perpetrators)?
- Do we endanger people who answer our questions, or ourselves as researchers, if we explore aspects of life we know are dangerous?
- What is the overall emotional impact on us as researchers when we delve into the frightening, the damaging or the risky?

Such questions are ever-present when researching violence, threat and intimidation.

Researching violence as a sensitive topic

As a putatively 'sensitive' topic, investigating violence usually introduces into the research process contingencies less commonly found in other kinds of study. Sensitive topics raise difficult methodological and technical problems (Lee and Renzetti, 1990). Access is often problematic. The adequate conceptualisation of particular topics is sometimes inhibited (Hertzberger, 1990). Where research is threatening, the relationship between the researcher and the researched is likely to become hedged about with mistrust and concealment. Can we be sure as researchers that the information we collect under such circumstances adequately represents the phenomenon we are trying to study? Are the findings on violence in methodological terms, both reliable and valid? On top of these considerations, sensitive topics also raise wider issues related to the ethics, politics and legal aspects of research.

Lee and Renzetti define a sensitive topic as 'one which potentially poses for those involved a substantial threat, the emergence of which renders problematic for the researcher and/or the researched the collection, holding and/or dissemination of research data' (1990: 512). The kind of threat posed by a particular piece of research, as well as its level, is a highly contextual matter. In other words, the sensitive character of a piece of research inheres less in the specific topic and more in the relationship between that topic and the social context – defined both broadly and narrowly – within which the research is conducted. It is not unusual, for example, for the sensitive nature of an apparently innocuous topic to become apparent once research is under way, or for a researcher to approach a topic with caution only to find that initial fears about its 'sensitivity' have been misplaced. It may well be that a study seen as threatening by one group will be thought innocuous by another.

Be that as it may, research is often sensitive where it poses an 'intrusive threat', dealing with areas which are private, stressful or sacred. A second area of sensitivity relates to the study of deviance and social control and involves the possibility that information may be revealed by research participants which is stigmatising or incriminating in some way. Finally, research is often problematic when it impinges on political alignments, if 'political' is taken in its widest sense to refer to the vested interests of powerful persons or institutions, or the exercise of coercion or domination.

Although topics and activities regarded as private vary cross-culturally and situationally (Day, 1985), respondents often record misgivings or unease about questions directed to their private life. Other areas of personal experience are not so much private as emotionally charged. Research into such areas may be threatening to those studied because of the levels of stress that it may induce. An additional problem here, which also affects research into the private sphere, has to do with maintaining an appropriate demeanour in face-to-face contact with the researcher. Although it may be difficult to remain composed in trying circumstances, the ability to do so is socially prized (Goffman, 1957; Scheff, 1988). Doubts that one can maintain proper standards of poise when asked about sensitive matters may therefore make matters even more threatening. Of course, this is also frequently true for the researcher who may have to share feelings of unease, discomfort or emotional pain with those being researched.

The presence of a researcher is sometimes feared because it produces a possibility that illegal or deviant activities will be revealed. Where the members of some group to be studied are powerless or disadvantaged, they may fear exploitation or derogation, or be sceptical about the usefulness of research to better their own lives. Since research settings invariably exist inside a wider social, economic and political environment, that context often has repercussions. This is particularly true where the external environment is conflictual, producing fears that the results of the research may favour one faction rather than another, or that it might upset moves to resolve the conflict (Lee, 1995). Where power is capable of being used corruptly or in an illegitimate manner, researchers are an obvious liability to be excluded or hindered in their work (Punch, 1989). Even where this is not the case, elites, powerful organisations and governments are often sensitive to the way in which their image is portrayed. As a result, in an attempt to forestall what they regard as negative criticism they may be led to impugn a researcher's motives, methods and credibility (Beynon, 1988; see also Cohen and Taylor, 1977).

A further important point to make is that while the threat posed by research most obviously affects research participants it may also have an impact on others. These include the researcher, but also the family members and associates of those studied, the social groups to which they belong, the wider community, research institutions and society at large (Sieber and Stanley, 1988; see also Lee and Renzetti, 1990). As Jeffrey Sluka (1990) points out, the dangers that researchers face in the field are rarely discussed in a systematic way. Instead, the matter has traditionally been treated lightly, as a source of 'war stories' to be told informally, perhaps in a self-deprecating way, rather than as a methodological issue that needs to be addressed seriously. In line with a growing awareness of health and safety issues in a number of disciplines and professions (Lee, 1995), this lack of discussion is beginning to give way to an increasing level of informed awareness about the hazards of fieldwork.

It is possible to distinguish two kinds of danger that may arise for the researcher during the research process; the 'ambient' and the 'situational' (Lee, 1995). Ambient danger arises when the researcher is exposed to otherwise avoidable dangers simply from having to be in a dangerous setting for the research to be carried out. Whatever form they take, the risks posed by fieldwork in dangerous settings have a number of consequences. They shape research agendas by deterring researchers from investigating particular topics or working in particular regions. The strategies that researchers adopt to manage potential hazards, both to themselves and to those they study, are strongly implicated in the ethics and politics of field situations. Finally, awareness and understanding of the health and safety issues surrounding fieldwork have an impact on professional practice particularly in relation to professional socialisation. It is important not to assume that research in dangerous settings is impossible (Sluka, 1990). The risks inherent in researching dangerous social situations can be negotiated (Lee, 1995). They must, however, be approached with foresight and planning.

Sieber and Stanley (1988) observe that some researchers have dealt with the problematic aspects of studying sensitive topics by opting out of researching such areas altogether. This kind of approach – they argue – while personally convenient, is in effect an evasion of responsibility. If they are not to opt out, researchers need to find ways of dealing with the problems and issues raised by research on sensitive topics. The threats which research poses to research participants, to the researcher and to others need to be minimised, managed or mitigated, but without compromising the research itself or limiting the overall scope of research to address important features of contemporary society.

This volume

This collection demonstrates the way in which 12 projects of the Violence Research Programme engaged with many of the above dilemmas. Despite these, researchers indeed uncovered a wealth of information about violence. Moreover, many people the researchers spoke to, surveyed and observed agreed that the phenomenon of violence is important to examine.

Three contributions open our discussion. John Archer, an historian, challenges our thinking about method and measurement via an engaging essay on the debates about the way in which violence has been counted (and consequently accounted for) over time. Archer sketches the way in which English courts began to collect information about crimes of violence. The debate – about whether violence increased or decreased over time – is central to our view of the civilising process of modernity (see also Elias, 1978). Archer sets out the arguments of various influential historians who have tried to uncover the 'true' levels of homicides. What have been 'measured' and taken 'as measurement' of violence by most historians are the records of courts, which logged people, allegations, convictions and sentences, but rarely the gender of participants, circumstances of situations or social attitudes of the time. Yet it is in these spaces of the contexts of violence that we begin to understand that social tolerance of forms of violence has changed over time. For example, during the 1860s in London it was found that 80 per cent of all murder verdicts (in the coroners' courts) related to infants (Higgenbotham, 1989). But then, as now, stranger danger dominated the landscapes of popular print, ignoring the fact that the overwhelming majority of victims of recorded homicide were infants under the age of one. Today, the category at highest risk of homicide in England by age is that of infants under one year (Homicide Index, 2000). Aggregating homicides into one category, in the 1860s as now, masks its many patterns and types of victims.

Susan Creighton and her colleagues took a method of measurement – the Conflict Tactics Scale – used across the world to study violence, and creatively adapted it to examine parental conflict with children. The research team members carefully explain this adaptation, and share how this innovative study came to capture for the first time the prevalence of parental violence in the home. At the same time, the researchers captured the context within which discipline was used and the parents' attitudes towards its use. The researchers address some of the ethical problems that arose during the fieldwork. Supplemented by the qualitative understanding gleaned from focus groups and rigorous piloting, the research offers a baseline measurement for a highly controversial subject: child maltreatment in the home.

The final contribution to this section, by Ruth Lewis and her colleagues, reveals a novel approach to understanding homicide through the triangulation of three sources of information. Official homicide statistics, detailed analysis of inmates' casefiles and interviews with homicide offenders provide a unique way of exploring the situational contexts and risk factors for homicides in England, Scotland and Wales. As the researchers note, questions about the reliability and validity of data about homicide haunt its study. However, the researchers demonstrate the benefits of providing data that can specify different contexts of and for homicide. In this way, data collection links with the possibility of the prevention of homicide. Revealing these contexts enables an approach to homicide prevention that is empirically grounded. These data then challenge the view that homicides are 'just' spontaneous events, and that offenders differ in patterned ways. The researchers found that combined sources of the information lead to considerable continuity in observations about different offenders. These observations, and their differences, enable the researchers to paint a more complex picture of homicide events and homicide offenders.

Part II of the volume turns to ways of enhancing our collection of information on violence in order to anticipate the emotional harm to participants when exploring the sensitive topic of violence. Kimmett Edgar, Carol Martin and Ian O'Donnell discuss a useful tool for studying conflict in prison. Taking interviewees through a thorough and detailed account of a fight, the research team gathered information from both parties. Although most people assume that conflict – and physical assault in prison – is inevitable, the data reveal that many inmates do make decisions about when, and whether, to use violence to resolve what is often a long-simmering dispute (or, as the data reveal, a 'dispute waiting to happen'). Other researchers in the programme found this an intriguing approach to recording an incident of violence. As such, we suggest, this methodological tool might be applied to many other situations when violence occurs.

Two of the chapters in this section address children as informants to our thinking about violence. As the research suggests, children are more likely to be victims of violence than its perpetrators. Yet the imagery which links young people to violence regularly emphasises their unruliness and thuggery. This is especially true of young people who live in residential homes. In an honest and engaging essay, Christine Barter and Emma Renold share the problems and possible ways to resolve them experienced during a study of children living in residential homes in England. The children, many of whom have themselves been victims of abuse and neglect, are placed in such homes because their behaviour is often too challenging for foster carers. A study of peer violence within these homes presented a number of special dilemmas. First of all, there are few incentives for the children to participate in this research on violence. As Barter and Renold found, moreover, the children were highly protective of themselves, and with good reason. Opening up to researchers meant that the children had to reveal their vulnerability. These children have already experienced emotional traumas. It is this vulnerability that they must hide from their peers within the homes. Researchers did ask for participants to bare their souls about bullying and intimidation that they experienced from other children in the homes. And they had to find a safe way for them to do so. One way in which the children could avoid such vulnerability was not to participate at all. But this does not enhance the quality of the research. The balancing act between openness and harm is a delicate one, described in the chapter as an exhausting, emotional drain for the researchers as well as the children.

Although talk about violence is sensitive, it also leads to alternative ways of sharing anxiety and experience. Laughter, as Les Moran and his colleagues show, was laced throughout their focus group discussions on sexuality and safety. In a project exploring homophobic violence, the research team set up six focus groups to examine in depth issues of safety. Moran and his colleagues were struck by the extent to which laughter punctuated the talk of the groups. The team argues here that laughing plays a part in the emotional work involved in speaking about violence. In some ways, laughter enables the breaking of silences around how participants can articulate intricacies in the way violence works to intimidate them. In enabling a shared commentary, spontaneous eruptions and disruptions to the focus group facilitate and support a wider effective understanding about the way in which the focus group participants experience threat and attempt to talk about it. Achieving safety in the midst of threat meets, the participants reveal, with many awkward moments in their lives. Such awkward moments make visible some of the hidden features of the fear of violence.

Interrogating violence and its meanings through the use of the experimental method is rare. In his engaging chapter, Mark Levine describes three different experiments testing the interconnections between social identity of participants and a seemingly injured party. He shows that the willingness to help those in need of assistance does vary, and often varies with what people tell researchers they are willing to do. Levine argues that we social scientists always merge theory with our systematic studies. Choice of method in violence research may be linked to disciplinary preferences, he suggests, but remains theoretically an interrogation of power and how it works in social relations. His study set out to explore the webs of social identities, 'the power of the social' and its display in the willingness of others to intervene. His research project enables theoretical speculation about the importance of social identities for the prevention of violence. His research is also a haunting reminder of the social dynamics behind recent acts of genocide, for instance in Bosnia or Rwanda. Levine sets out a convincing case for the usefulness of the experimental method in challenging the way in which we conduct research on violence. He shows us that ordinary people do have the ability to reach out and overcome their reluctance to help. At the same time, he helps us to understand the power of social identity among those who may wish to do us harm.

Engaging participants, however, in studies about violence may lead to some unintended consequences. Using an explicit model of participation, the girls' understanding of violence project actively involved subjects in the process of analysis and the dissemination of findings. However, this participation produced a number of concerns. Did girls participate freely without the intrusion of their teachers or parents? Were the girls who participated in the dissemination of the findings too exposed to the media, who mostly distorted the findings? Kay Tisdall and her colleagues set out to keep girls within the framework of the research on violence as much as possible. But the investigators needed to be mindful and ever vigilant about their duty to protect under-aged girls from harm (or its risk). As a consequence, they could not guarantee absolute confidentiality to the young people who participated in their project. The researchers were also not able to protect the girls from the distorted limelight of the media. Throughout the four years of the Violence Research Programme, the media took an active interest in the study of violence and girls. The media desperately wanted the exclusive story that demonstrated that girls were 'becoming like boys' in the commission of violence. They urgently needed to find evidence of girl gangs to feed the headline frenzy. Although neither finding emerged from the study, the girls participating were not immune to the media's imagery. This proved to be a dilemma for the researchers, who found it almost impossible to challenge successfully the strong media interest in 'the violent female'. The media are but one contributor, and yet a significant one, to the context within which violence is understood, debated and studied.

In the final section of the collection, the social context of researching violence is explored in greater depth. Just as earlier chapters emphasised the importance of measuring levels and degrees of violence, these chapters place the discussion about research on violence in context to ponder the impact of institutional support and political stability on the research outcome. Does it matter where we 'are' (whether it be a 'safe' or 'risky' environment) and does it affect the way in which we ask questions about the nature of violence?

Colin Knox and Rachel Monaghan begin with reflection on the study of punishment beatings in Northern Ireland and vigilantism in South Africa. Researchers had to walk a fine line when gaining access to victims. The very subject matter – paramilitary 'punishments' in Northern Ireland and vigilante retaliation to perpetrators of crime in South Africa – is rife with volatility. Speaking to victims of such horrific attacks caused anxiety on the part of both victim and researchers, despite the willingness of victims to share their stories. The visual impact of wounds, the fragility of peace and security, and the political landscape all contributed to a never-ending balancing act between research and its political implications. Every gatekeeper had a political reputation at stake. Every gatekeeper wanted the research to show how 'harmed' he or she was. The researchers cannot escape from the context; they both live and work in Northern Ireland. Studying vigilantism in South Africa enabled a contrast with their own political situation. The researchers' abilities to step back and to reflect on these recent experiences provide the reader with much to contemplate. As with many other research projects in the Violence Research Programme, media interest and media distortion of the findings contributed to additional distress of the researchers.

Maria O'Beirne and her colleagues explored the meanings and the prevalence of violence in three professional groups: clergy, doctors and probation officers. They asked: how does the social positioning of these professionals affect the way in which they speak about violence? Much work on violence in the workplace, for example, demonstrates how little of it is reported to managers and other colleagues. Although violence, and in particular the emotional abuse accompanying bullying, are frequent topics in debates about workplace culture, few speculate about whether such debates might have an impact on the way in which people speak about violence. This chapter reminds the reader that we as individuals hold many identities simultaneously. When we are interviewed 'as professionals' who have experiences of violence, the self and the professional may be at odds. The researchers set out an engaging challenge to the way we collect and measure violence in many workplaces, and elsewhere. Keeping in mind the contribution of our multiple selves to thinking and speaking about violence is a useful lesson for other researchers.

Loraine Bacchus, Gill Mezey and Susan Bewley discuss their study of the prevalence of domestic violence towards pregnant women. The project was equally an experiment in enabling health workers – in this case midwives – to incorporate questions about domestic violence during their routine antenatal clinic care. The authors share in detail how difficult it is to enlist overworked health care workers in an ever-shifting institutional environment to change their clinical practice. There is a great debate about the usefulness of health care workers in intervention within domestic violence situations. This chapter contributes to this discussion and shows that the organisational context does matter. Constant change in work patterns and responsibilities is disruptive. It is especially disruptive to research that depends on the health care providers to supply the raw data for any study of prevalence. The authors end pessimistically, clearly frustrated by the way in which institutional practices undermine potential beneficial clinical practices which might lead not only to better and healthier babies, but to a lessening of domestic violence.

Larry Ray, David Smith and Liz Wastell report how disclosures of racist violence have an institutional framework as well. Their study of racist violent offenders took place in the wider climate of greater willingness to confront racism in the UK. The lessons of this project are applicable in a context wider than the particular institution under study – the probation service. The lessons address the ability of any organisation to reach beyond stereotypes about violence. A typical assumption about racist offending, for instance, is that hate crime offenders are especially motivated to target any member of the disfavoured 'group' and that they are 'specialists' in 'hatred'. Gatekeepers may presume that the wider public readily understands such motivation. The problem for the researchers was that few violent offenders were identified by the probation department as violent racist offenders. More often, victims of racist attacks name the violence as linked to racial abuse. Moreover, the image that a racially violent offender has connections to right-wing groups is misleading. These and other researchers continue to confirm that offenders are more likely to know the victim than not. Ray and his colleagues share an honest account of their difficulties and frustrations in dealing with an organisation 'open' to challenging racism. The problem was that the kind of racism professionals think they know about might not be readily identifiable as racially violent offending.

Researching violence: concluding thoughts

It is possible to research violence responsibly. It is crucial that we begin to embrace a willingness and reflective methodologies to do so. We firmly believe that violence is often preventable. Without good information, we fail to use social science inquiry to challenge the impact and the consequences of violence.

Before closing this introduction, it is worth mentioning again the effect of conducting research on a topic that is continuously in the spotlight of the media. The dominant image of violence portrays it as 'random', wanton, and the intentional acts of evil folk. Researchers have tried recently to challenge this imagery. Joel Best, in *Random Violence*, goes as far as to state that the term 'random violence' 'ignores virtually everything criminologists know about crime' (1999: xiii). Henry Brownstein (2000), in another attempt to inject 'evidence' into the debate about violent crime, decries the way in which violence inevitably comes to portray a struggle between good and evil. All this imagery sets the stage for the way in which research findings will be received by the wider society as well as by policy-makers. After all, incidents of violence can undermine the credibility of government to deliver public safety.

As the researchers from the VRP will readily share, this imagery loomed above the researchers, who pondered how their information could be disseminated without distortion. Indeed, one of the major tasks Stanko had to deal with during her tenure as Director of the ESRC Violence Research Programme was managing media interest in the programme. Reporters wanted to shadow the researchers in bars, on the street while interviewing sex workers, or in the schools when discussing bullying. Newscasters wanted exclusive stories to feature in the morning or evening shows. Talk show hosts were constantly on the lookout for the novel. On most occasions, we refused to co-operate. Although many of these projects were eventually featured in newspaper and television reports, many researchers approached the popular dissemination of their findings with unease. There were some exceptions. Mark Levine (see Chapter 7) was able to reproduce his experimental intervention project in front of BBC cameras, and to show to a wide audience the approach to understanding the factors involved in bystander intervention into violence. That said, engagement with the media was often unsatisfactory for the researchers. Investigators complained bitterly of distortion by the media, of twisted facts and of gross sensationalism (see, for instance, Knox and Monaghan, and Tisdall). Some of the projects' findings were also featured in heated political debates, with lots of column inches devoted to various opinions one way or the other. No doubt, historians of the future might think that during this time there was a miniature violent crime wave, as so many of the projects made headline after headline.

Media attention to research on violence, we suggest, should be anticipated and included as part of the research strategy as much as is practicable. What is important is that the media not interfere with the research once it is in progress. Ethical issues, confidentiality and the avoidance of further harm should be thought through in advance and included as a prime consideration in any research on violence. After all, violence is preventable. The more we gather knowledge about it, the better off we are to contribute to its minimisation in society. We hope that this volume contributes to the debate and helps to prepare others for this work.

Notes

1   Economic and Social Research Council's Violence Research Programme, www.rhul.ac.uk/socio-politicalscience/research/vrp/htm
2   See, for example, *British Journal of Criminology*, vol. 41, no. 3, (2001). .

References

Best, J. (1999) *Random Violence: Talk About New Crime and New Victims*. Berkeley, CA: University of California Press.

Beynon, H. (1988) 'Regulating research: politics and decision making in industrial organizations' in A. Bryman (ed.) *Doing Research in Organizations*. London: Routledge.

British Journal of Criminology (2001), vol. 41, no. 3.

Brownstein, H. H. (2000) *The Social Reality of Violence and Violent Crime*. Needham Heights, MA: Allyn and Bacon.

Cohen, S. and L. Taylor (1977) 'Talking about prison blues' in C. Bell and H. Newby (eds) *Doing Sociological Research*. London: Allen and Unwin.

Day, K. J. (1985) 'Perspectives on privacy: A sociological analysis'. Unpublished Ph.D. thesis, University of Edinburgh.

Elias, N. (1978) *The Civilizing Process*. Oxford: Basil Blackwell.

Goffman, E. (1957) 'Alienation from interaction', *Human Relations*, 10: 47–59.

Hertzberger, S. D. (1990) 'The cyclical pattern of child abuse: a study in research methodology', *American Behavioral Scientist*, 33: 529–45.

Higgenbotham, A. (1989) '"Sin of the age": Infanticide and illegitimacy in Victorian London', *Victorian Studies*, Spring.

Homicide Index for England and Wales (2000) London: Home Office.

Lee, R. M. (1993) *Doing Research on Sensitive Topics*. London: Sage.

—— (1995) *Dangerous Fieldwork*. Thousand Oaks, CA: Sage.

Lee, R. M. and C. M. Renzetti (1990) 'The problems of researching sensitive topics: an overview and introduction', *American Behavioral Scientist*, 33: 510–28.

Punch, M. (1989) 'Researching police deviance: a personal encounter with the limitations and liabilities of fieldwork', *British Journal of Sociology*, 40: 177–204.

Scheff, T. J. (1988) 'Shame and conformity: the deference–emotion system', *American Sociological Review*, 53: 395–406.

Sieber, J. E. and B. Stanley (1988) 'Ethical and professional dimensions of socially sensitive research', *American Psychologist*, 43: 49–55.

Sluka, J. A. (1990) 'Participant observation in violent social contexts', *Human Organization*, 49: 114–26.

Part I

Documenting violence

Counting and accounting for violence

1 Researching violence in the past
Quantifiable and qualitative evidence

John E. Archer

This chapter proposes to examine and review historical studies and debates of English interpersonal violence, especially those focused on homicide, and for the purposes of this chapter homicide includes both murder and manslaughter. Such studies have had to address problems and issues which confront all historians of violence; not least, can we quantify violence over long periods? Or is the accuracy of the statistical data so questionable as to invalidate any conclusions drawn from quantitative analysis? In reviewing possible drawbacks to this statistical quantifying approach to studies both of homicide and of non-lethal forms of violence, this chapter will examine alternative approaches which draw on qualitative data. Such material provides context and detail surrounding violent incidents which quantitative evidence cannot. Historians can also glean some insights into conflicting attitudes and perceptions of violent behaviour which, though classified as illegal by the authorities, may well have been regarded as wholly legitimate and customary by significant numbers of people within a community. In reviewing possible drawbacks to the statistical studies, this chapter will draw on evidence collected in a recent study on violence between 1850 and 1914 in the north-west of England.[1] This industrial and urbanised region was thought by contemporaries to be one of the most violent areas of the United Kingdom but, according to official statistics, it experienced a decline in reported and prosecuted violence in the second half of the nineteenth century.

Historians of violent crime have until recently attempted to address and answer the 'big question': was the past more violent than the present? A corollary to this was the additional question: did crimes of interpersonal violence fluctuate, were there highs and lows, and if so, why? Answers to the question 'was the past more violent?' have relied on and been constrained, to a large extent, by what has left a trace or 'footprint' in surviving documents and records. Court records for the period and, since the early nineteenth century, judicial annual statistical returns collected by parliament have provided historians with most of their sources of evidence. Quantifying incidences of criminal behaviour prior to the nineteenth century presents historians with many problems. First, it is as well to note that crime, processed by the judicial system, and recorded in the form of assize and quarter sessions indictments and calendars held at the Public Record

Office or in the local county record offices, has left the most voluminous records and even then some areas of England and Wales are better provided than other areas. Lower level crime such as common assault would have been dealt with, if at all, at the local magistrates' or petty sessions courts. Records emanating from such forums of justice have, in most instances, not survived.[2] From 1810 data relating to the number of males and females committed for indictable offences in England and Wales were collected and published annually by parliament. Throughout the nineteenth century various modifications, improvements and additions were made to these annual statistics – not least the inclusion of the numbers of women and men brought before magistrates on summary jurisdiction for less serious offences, and the numbers of indictable offences known or reported to the police, whether or not they resulted in a prosecution. Finally, further changes were introduced in 1893 which can complicate historians' tasks in creating long-time series for criminal offences of various kinds. The most important change concerns the year in which the data were recorded and counted. For example, until 1893 police returns had a year end of 30 September, and prison returns ended on 31 March. Both sets of returns were then standardised and ran from 1 January to 31 December. Historians have, therefore, at their disposal a reasonably consistent set of national data on crimes known to the police dating from 1857. Thus comparisons and trends can be made for most crimes of interpersonal violence for the past 150 years, although it would be unwise – perhaps even foolish – of historians to place too much trust, meaning or significance in changes over time for some of these crimes. This is especially true of violence relating to women and children, for example, which was and is notoriously under-reported.

Quantifying homicide: debates on long-term trends

Historians have for the most part argued that one particular crime of violence, namely murder, can be quantified or counted reasonably accurately and over a long period. Comparisons with the present are thus possible and conclusions may be reached on the relative violence of specific periods in history. Whether the crime of murder can be taken as a measure of a society's propensity to violence is, however, a moot point. The initial and arguably the seminal study on crimes of homicide was that put forward by Gurr (1981). He argued that of all data relating to incidences of violent crime, those which relate to homicide are probably the most accurate and fully reported. The more serious the crime, the greater the likelihood that it will be reported. Murder, he contended, possesses the smallest 'dark figure' of unrecorded crime. Moreover, most homicides have been committed by persons known to their victims, and as a consequence, clear-up rates for murder were and are relatively high. This high degree of reportage was, it has been argued, better than that for other crimes of violence, as sudden deaths have been reported and investigated by coroners since the Middle Ages (Havard 1960: 11–27). Historically, dead bodies have been investigated. Thus murder and manslaughter are more likely to have left an historical trace in the records. And, as a bonus for historians, the legal definition of murder has been relatively stable in England and Wales since the sixteenth century, allowing like to be compared with like.

Drawing on regional county studies by Hanawalt (1976) and Samaha (1974) for the medieval period, and Cockburn (1977) and Beattie (1974) for the early modern, Gurr was able to identify a long downward trend in homicides since the mid-fourteenth century. The rate, which is measured as the number of homicides per 100,000 of the population, declined from about 20/100,000 in 1200 to about 1.5/100,000 in 1800.[3] Using the more accurate national figures from the nineteenth century, and also the more accurate census returns on which to base the ratio of murders to population, the murder rate continued to drop throughout the nineteenth century and the first half of the twentieth, reaching an all-time low of 0.3/100,000 in both 1931 and 1951. Only in the last 30 years of the twentieth century has the rate begun to creep up to just 1.0/100,000 in 1981. Gurr has, as a result, concluded that English homicide rates have declined dramatically from about AD1200 and that rates of violent crime were 'probably 10 and possibly 20 or more times higher' in medieval and early modern England than in the twentieth century (1981: 312).

While all historians accept that the homicide rate has declined over the past 500 years or so, not all have been in agreement as to the timing of this decline. In a short interpretative essay in *Past and Present* and a rejoinder, Stone (1983 and 1985) argued that the decline was 'especially rapid between 1660 and 1800'. In response Sharpe (1985) accepted the downward trend in homicides but introduced a note of caution in so far as the measurement of homicide rates per 100,000 fails to tell us about how violence was perceived. Quantitative studies cannot, in Sharpe's opinion, answer the more profound and challenging questions and issues such as whether society was fearful or not, whether it was conscious of living in a violent age, and just 'how violent is a "violent society"?' (Sharpe 1985: 215).

When Cockburn (1991) entered the scholarly affray between Sharpe and Stone he did so not as a peacemaker but as a 'powder monkey', providing ammunition for both parties. His paper went far beyond his modest and self-effacing claims as it came to represent one of the most complete studies of homicide over a long period. Taking the county of Kent as his focus, Cockburn was able to present a continuous homicide rate from 1559 to 1971, and add a number of refinements, not least the changes in methods of killing and the use of weapons over time. Moreover, he confronts difficult methodological problems which affect all historical studies of homicide. Do we, for example, count in infanticide and concealment of births? Should attempted murders be included in the later decades under scrutiny since improvements in medicine have led to better survival chances? And what of unlawful killings on the public highway? Some of these questions, according to Eric Monkkonen, are capable of resolution. He has estimated that 50 per cent of New York's victims of homicide, for example, would have been saved from death nowadays due to improvements in medicine (2001b: 18). The upshot of this empirical research is that English and Welsh society by the turn of the millennium would appear to be indisputably less violent than it was, say, 300 years ago, if murder is taken as the yardstick to measure violence. Most historians would argue that the decline in murder in particular, and in homicide in general, which shows up in the surviving records, represents a real decline as many factors have existed since the nineteenth century which would have increased reportage of violent deaths. The introduction of the 'new' police from 1829 onwards, the growing 'sensitisation to violence' and the necessity of registering deaths from 1837 are just three examples which would have made reportage more probable.

This conclusion, based on statistical data, that the present is less violent than the past, may seem somewhat commonplace to today's students. However, Gatrell, in one of the most influential and thought-provoking studies for 20 years observed that 'it has become one of the more widely accepted axioms of our age that an increasing crime rate is the invariable price of material progress' (1980: 238). Through the analysis of official statistics issued between 1857 and 1914 Gatrell has concluded that all forms of interpersonal violence, sexual violence excepted, declined in the second half of the nineteenth century (1980: 286). This conclusion also held good for property crime, and consequently historians have come to regard the second half of the nineteenth century as experiencing an 'English miracle'. It would appear that 'modernisation' or progress need not necessarily result in increased criminality.

In what has come to represent the most profound challenge to the reliability of quantitative data, Howard Taylor, in 'Rationing Crime' (1998) has offered a radical revision of the accepted historical consensus on the declining homicide rate of England and Wales. In examining the official statistics of the higher courts, Taylor noted a peculiar pattern. After a huge increase in the number of trials for indictable crime between 1805 and 1842, the growth stopped thereafter until the twentieth century. Offences known to the police, which were collected from 1857, remained constant, varying by only 20 per cent either side of the norm, until 1925 when they began to move upwards. This stagnation in crime, in both recorded and prosecuted crime, occurred in the context of national population growth, which meant that in effect crime and prosecutions were actually falling. This was all the more remarkable given that the country had police forces in every town and county whose job it was to record and investigate crime.

How does this relate to the study of homicide? Taylor found a similar pattern for murder in England and Wales. Between 1880 and 1966 murders averaged 150 a year with a variation within 20 per cent either side of the average. This pattern would appear to hold good with one or two exceptions back to the mid-1860s (1998: 569–71). Explanations for this surprising and, some would argue, shocking pattern lay, according to Taylor, in the costs of investigation and prosecution. He goes so far as to argue that murders were 'among the most strictly rationed of all crimes', and that consequently 'most murders and suspicious deaths went uninvestigated' (1998: 588). Apart from calling into question the veracity of official statistical data on even the most reported of all crimes – murder – Taylor's thesis also brings to our attention the way in which official criminal statistics were constructed and how homicides and sudden deaths were examined and decided upon. An initial reading of Taylor would suggest that some conspiracy involving chief constables, coroners and the office of the Director of Public Prosecutions was involved. Other questions arise out of his argument: not least, was the rise in suicides from 1,314 in 1856 to 5,054 in 1939 related in any way to the contemporaneous stagnation or decline in murders? Was a finding of suicide a disguised murder or secret homicide? He cites a number of medical practitioners who certainly thought this to be the case. And what is so significant about this figure of 20 per cent either side of the average? Surely such an enormous variation actually allows for wide differences in the amount of reported crime. The press certainly become very excited nowadays if crime rises by just 5 per cent over a previous year, and the government is quick to claim credit for single-figure percentage falls in crime.

In one of the first responses to Taylor, Robert Morris, in an article which plays on Disraeli's aphorism for its title, 'Lies, Damned Lies and Criminal Statistics' (2001), picks up on the 20 per cent variation which he regards as a highly volatile degree of variation. In addition he argues that to keep the annual murder figures to 150 a year it would have required a sophisticated conspiracy of over 100 police forces. Dismissing this scenario as unlikely, he concludes that 150 was an 'arithmetical accident'. However, it might be possible to argue that no conspiracy was required in as much as each police force would have been given a budget and once that budget was met, the chief constable would have then reinterpreted some cases and even downgraded some murders to manslaughter, suicide, accidents or assaults. Therefore the number of murders taking place in any given geographical area of the country would have been the result of bureaucratic, administrative and budgetary forces which need not have involved an annual target of murders being set by anyone in the Home Office. The size of the budget in effect defined the number of murders per year, and any variation depended on whether a murder was an easy one to solve or not. Whether one accepts Taylor's 'conscious manipulation of the figures' conspiracy because of budgetary considerations, or Morris's more prosaic explanation which emphasises the complacency of the police, their lack of effectiveness and the shortcomings of forensic science, both sides agree that official data on homicides are deeply flawed.

To what extent do the annual criminal returns underestimate the real number of murders in England and Wales over the past 150 years? The American historian Eric Monkkonen, while not engaging directly in the Taylor debate, has argued that the murder figures for both the United States and England were probably underestimates of the true amount. By employing 'capture–recapture' or the Chandra–Sekar–Deming technique which is normally used for counting wild animals, Monkkonen has recalculated the homicide figures for the cities of New York, Liverpool and London in the nineteenth century (2001a: 151–79, 2001b: 10–11). The official returns probably underestimate the homicide rates by no more than 10 per cent.

Qualitative approaches: homicides

The sophisticated quantitative data analysis employed by Monkkonen can only take our understanding so far. Historians need to combine the quantitative approach with qualitative analysis, and Monkkonen is an excellent exemplar of the approach with his recent study *Murder in New York City* (2001a). By examining individual cases through court depositions held at the Public Record Office and newspaper reports of the initial incident, the coroner's inquest and any subsequent trial arising out of the case, historians start to build a fuller picture of each murder. Context, detail and the supposed motive behind the killing add new dimensions to our understanding of homicides in the past. Work by Knelman (1997) and more recently by Martin Wiener (1999 and 2001), for example, bring to the fore the relationships between the murderer and victim and the social dynamics of the event. Wiener's research has shown, and will show in a future study on wife killing and domestic homicide, that the prosecution and trials of murders were cultural processes. No amount of quantitative data will bring to light the attitudes of police and the public to different types of killings or explain why some homicides were prosecuted as murders and others as manslaughter.

The qualitative approach to the history of homicide can be important in providing specific documentary evidence which may or may not support Taylor's arguments. If, as he has claimed, most murders went unrecorded by the police then such events as suspicious and sudden deaths may have left a trace in other sources and records, not least the coroner's court papers (where they exist) or more probably the local newspapers. In examining a sample of the Manchester and Liverpool newspapers between 1850 and 1910 it has been possible to identify reports of numerous 'suspicious' and 'mysterious' deaths which did not appear in the police and judicial statistics.

The most substantial group of 'victims', and one largely underplayed by Taylor and uncounted by Monkkonen, concerns infants under one year of age. As a group they have been vulnerable to homicide, especially those children branded as illegitimate. The Act of 1624 on infanticide was especially harsh to unmarried mothers who could be hanged if convicted of killing their children (Jackson 1994). In practice this law was rarely enforced, a fact recognised in 1803 when the charge of concealment of birth was introduced to cover most cases of infanticide. All through the nineteenth century coroners and police authorities continued to under-record the murder of infants even though children under one year of age constituted the largest group of homicide victims. In the Liverpool Coroner's Court Register for the period between 1852 and 1865 there were 182 murders recorded, of which 63 per cent related to children under one year of age.[4] During the 1860s in London it was found that 80 per cent of all murder verdicts (in the coroners' courts) related to infants (Higginbotham 1989: 321).

While such findings suggest that young babies were being killed in large numbers it is undoubtedly true that the recorded numbers of illegal killings are a gross underestimate of the true extent of infant murder. Coroners' court verdicts of 'stillborn', 'found suffocated', 'suffocated in bed', 'accidentally smothered' or the open verdict of 'whether stillborn or born alive no evidence' suggest either that the courts were not prepared to investigate too closely or that forensic science was unable to determine the cause of death. Infanticide was clearly a matter of interpretation rather than hard 'fact'. This can be seen in the case of Edwin Lankester, coroner of Central Middlesex. In 1862, immediately prior to his appointment, infanticide within his jurisdiction numbered just seven cases or 5.6 per cent of the national total of infanticides. Twelve months later infanticide had risen to 40 cases in Central Middlesex or 24 per cent of the national total. In later years it rose to 71 cases whereas a heavily urbanised county such as Lancashire returned just 12 cases of infanticide. Clues as to their differences in interpretation can be found in the open verdicts: for example, Lancashire returned 506 'found dead' verdicts whereas Central Middlesex returned just nine (Behlmer 1979: 409–10). Reports in the press do raise one's doubts and suspicions. For example, in one case where the confinement of the mother was overseen by her mother and a neighbour, the infant died of suffocation but the coroner's court could find no evidence to show by what means death had occurred (*Liverpool Mercury*, 26 November 1873).

Doubts must also be placed on the coroner's jury verdict of 'stillborn'. In one particularly revealing case the mother was visited shortly after the alleged stillbirth by an unregistered midwife. The mother told the midwife that she did not want the bother of a coroner's inquest whereupon the midwife gave her a certificate to bury it as a stillborn child. The certificate, however, was stopped by the registrar's beadle, and an examination of the body was made. Medical evidence suggested that it had been born alive and had died from exposure and want of attention at birth (*Liverpool Mercury*, 16 December 1868). Such an example suggests that midwives could have played a key role in misleading the authorities and that some of the 644 stillbirths buried in four Liverpool cemeteries in 1868 were cases of infanticide (Rose 1986: 131).

Even where the evidence to modern eyes looks conclusive, there are instances in which the charge of either murder or manslaughter was not found. Such is the case of 19-year-old unmarried Louisa Brough. Complaining of feeling unwell, she took to her bed where she gave birth to a female baby. A day later suspicions were aroused in the household that she had given birth, but the child had by this time died of suffocation. The doctor who attended Brough gave evidence that she was in a 'weak and exhausted state' when he visited her and that she answered his questions 'in a mechanical way'. She did not, he maintained, fully understand the consequences of what she admitted, namely that the baby had been born alive, that it had cried and that she had suffocated it. His evidence crucially allowed for a 'get-out' clause when he concluded by saying that 'she might have accidentally suffocated it when, on hearing it cry, she tried to attend to it' (*Liverpool Mercury*, 24 November 1894). It was decided that she had understood neither the questions put to her nor the answers which she had given so soon after the birth, and that her mind was temporarily unhinged soon after the trauma of giving birth.

While infant deaths such as the one above undoubtedly formed the bulk of unrecorded homicides, there were many examples of suspicious deaths of adults which also went unrecorded and even uninvestigated by the police. One could almost go so far as to say there was a kind of hierarchy of corpses. Those that were deemed to be foreign, out of town or friendless do not appear to have detained the authorities for very long. The attitude was, no doubt, that public order was not endangered and that it was a needless expense to ratepayers to investigate people who were either not missed or did not possess an identity. The River Mersey and the dock basins attached to it acted as a kind of conduit for the disposal of bodies, perhaps of sailors leaving port. It was reported that many ships set sail from Liverpool on which drunken brawls and fights took place about which captains preferred to keep silent. Men found dead in the streets were similarly ignored, as in the case of a reportedly sober man, found lying on the ground with a wound behind his left ear and who died without regaining consciousness (*Liverpool Mercury*, 11 September 1871). The coroner's jury returned a verdict of 'died of injuries received, but no evidence', and there the matter ended.

Contradictory or inconclusive evidence led either to prime suspects being discharged or to the police ignoring the case altogether. Take the mysterious death of 3-year-old Ann Concannon who was found head-first in a privy at 11 o'clock one night in August 1892. Initial reactions in the press and from the police suggested that she had been murdered by suffocation. Her mother reported that she had dressed the little girl with nearly new boots and gold-plated earrings and witnesses reported seeing her with a group of women early in the evening. Between that last sighting and when she was found dead Ann had had the boots and earrings taken from her. Both the police and the coroner chose to believe that someone had stolen her clothes and then returned her alive to the privy where she slipped head-first and became stuck. But the evidence which really brings the historian up short came from one of the surgeons at the inquest who, in a final throw-away remark, stated that 'they also found marks which led them to believe that she had been improperly dealt with'. This allusion to sexual assault suggested that violence had been perpetrated against the girl at some point in her short life but that it had not contributed to her death. Neither her death nor the alleged sexual assault would have been included in any police statistics (*Liverpool Mercury*, 4, 5, 6 and 18 August 1892).

Poisoning, the classic method of killing which frequently evaded police detection, was clearly suspected in a number of cases relating to young people.[5] In many cases open verdicts were arrived at by coroners' juries. At one inquest, that of 5-year-old Ellen Fairclough, the Liverpool Coroner's Register cites the victim as having died of narcotic poisoning but gives no evidence of how this was administered. The newspaper report, however, provides considerably more detail. Her young brother told the coroner's court how two young men had placed something resembling 'white soda' or 'raw potato' in both their mouths and forcibly made them swallow. He survived only because he was sick immediately but Ellen lingered for 24 hours despite the best efforts of the chemist (*Liverpool Mercury*, 7 March 1862). Where medical evidence as to the cause of death was disputed by medical expert witnesses, for example between natural causes and violence, courts would often favour the defendant and give them the benefit of the doubt. The police added homicides to their annual statistics only after the cases had been successfully tried in court or where, 'in the opinion of the head constable', a successful prosecution would have taken place had an arrest been made. This allowed enormous leeway to head constables to undercount crime within their jurisdictions.

Forensic medical investigation was not able to determine the cause of death of Elizabeth Porter at the hands, or rather feet, of her 45-year-old husband, Thomas, at Hindley, near Wigan, Lancashire. Because of her ill-health – she suffered from heart disease and bronchitis and was recovering from a paralytic stroke – the grand jury had reduced the charge from wilful murder to grievous bodily harm. Three medical witnesses brought conflicting evidence to the trial and were asked to provide opinions as to whether the discolouration on her body was a result of the alleged kicking which both the deceased and a neighbour claimed to have occurred, or whether it came from natural causes. Mr Justice Wills, clearly exasperated, said in his summing up, 'that when medical opinion was required Wigan ought to be disfranchised. How could a jury settle a difference of opinion between private medical men? The result would be that in the gravest cases such as the present one, there would continually be a danger of either an innocent man being convicted or of a guilty man going free. Such contradictory medical testimony was of no value for the purpose of a court.' The jury acquitted Thomas Porter (*Liverpool Mercury*, 22 November 1894).

It would appear from the examples cited above that Taylor's thesis that many murders went uninvestigated is credible. However, less certainty can be placed on his explanation which emphasises costs: cost of detection and investigation, and cost of prosecution. Many factors no doubt account for the relatively low murder figures, not least the lack of forensic knowledge in the period, and legal and social conventions which did not regard suspicious infant deaths as homicides. In addition, social and cultural conventions may well have saved numerous men from the gallows where domestic or partner killings were concerned. If the female victim was castigated in court as a drunk or 'poor' wife while the husband was able to provide character references then it was more than likely that he would escape a charge of murder. Finally, and by way of emphasising the fact that murder was to some extent a social construct rather than a legally fixed certainty, where the victim was unknown, friendless, or an outsider and where the deaths did not challenge or unhinge the social and moral fabric, or where possible suspects were deemed 'respectable', then the killings were put down as accidents or left open. The recent events in south Manchester where Dr Harold Shipman has been practising both medicine and killing should serve as warning to any quantifying historians in the future.[6]

Non-lethal crimes of violence

If the most serious crimes of interpersonal violence, such as murder and manslaughter, went under-reported and unprosecuted then it is reasonable to assume that less serious crimes of violence were even more under-reported.

Quantitative analysis of non-fatal crimes of interpersonal violence would appear therefore to have serious deficiencies, one might almost say fatal drawbacks, for the statistically minded historian. Nowhere is this more apparent than for the period prior to the official collection of national statistics. John Beattie, the doyen of eighteenth-century crime history, believes it is impossible to measure violence (1985: 36–42, and 1986: 74–6) even though other documentary sources suggest a decline in brutality among the English. Another equally authoritative student of the eighteenth-century courts, Peter King, noted that crimes of violence were virtually ignored by the courts. In fact, anyone wishing to study violence through the evidence of the quarter sessions and the assize courts would assume either that English society was remarkably tolerant or peaceful or that there were other ways of seeking redress. It would appear that physical violence was a more 'accepted' and 'legitimate' way of solving disputes (King 1996: 43) and that if an injured party wished to seek redress this could be achieved through civil action or private recompense. This latter method was true even of rape cases in which the assailant paid 'damages' to the husband, father or male 'protector' of the female victim (Conley 1986: 534). In such examples history clearly shows how attitudes towards and tolerance of violent actions have changed over time.

The downgrading of criminal charges was also common in cases where armed or unarmed men fought with each other. Such clashes were deemed almost 'natural' and were regarded as legitimate defences of masculine honour. Duelling, for example, continued to be practised, albeit infrequently, up to the mid-nineteenth century, especially between military officers (Simpson 1988), whereas unarmed combat, using fists, was deemed to be the English way of fighting by the majority of men. This kind of mindset lingered on into the early twentieth century even among magistrates (Archer 2000). At the Liverpool Police Court a Spanish seaman, Manuel Martinez, was charged with assaulting the aptly named George Smiter of the Royal Navy. It was reported that Martinez had tried to use a knife, which was regarded as an underhand foreign method of fighting, but that he had been overpowered and given into custody. In court the stipendiary magistrate asked an interpreter to tell Martinez that 'if he wants to attack a British sailor he had better take a dozen men with him on the job. Tell him, also, it is very fortunate that the sailor did not give him a good thrashing.' Addressing Smiter, the magistrate concluded the case, 'You behaved very well, indeed. If you had punched his head, I don't think I would have said anything to you about the matter – not officially, at any rate' (*Liverpool Mercury*, 3 December 1901).

This kind of contextual detail is lost when dealing with mere numbers although quantification is not wholly unrewarding. Vic Gatrell, working with the official statistics for the years 1857–1914, argued that most forms of interpersonal violence declined in the second half of the nineteenth century (1980: 286). By relating these figures for offences against the person to convictions for drunkenness, for example, it may also become possible for historians to identify when 'the spirit of lawlessness' was worst. The criminal registrar reported in 1899 that the years 1872–6 were the worst of the second half of the nineteenth century when there were 423.78/100,000 offences against the person. By 1897–9 this figure had dropped to 233.34/100,000. It was, perhaps, no coincidence that prosecutions for drunkenness were high at exactly the same time (British Parliamentary Papers 1901: 37). The criminal statistics may also suggest other trends, and in Liverpool, for example, the proportion of women tried summarily in the lower courts was remarkably high, being twice the national average. For crimes of violence this figure was even higher, being closer to 30 per cent. Such conclusions and findings beg further questions, however. How reliable are these numbers? What about the huge dark figure of unrecorded crime and its relationship to recorded crime? Are the drunkenness convictions simply a reflection of heightened police activity brought about by parliamentary concern and so forth?

Whether the statistics bear any relationship to real incidences of crimes of interpersonal violence is in some ways unimportant since they can contain within themselves many different meanings which historians can identify and interpret through the use of other sources. Both Gatrell and more recently Sindall (1990) argue that the crime statistics, while not being an accurate reflection of criminal behaviour, were nevertheless believed at the time to be a true and accurate guide. Consequently the authorities and the middle-class public who believed in their veracity responded to them and acted on them. The statistics, in other words, do not have to be accurate for them to have significance. Consequently historians can, for example, identify social or moral panics such as the London garotting scare of 1862–3 in which the crime figures suddenly leap for a couple of years before returning to their previous levels (Davis 1980).

The annual figures also reflect changes in public and police attitudes towards certain forms of criminal behaviour such as sex crimes perpetrated on children and assaults on children in general. It would appear that prior to 1891 there was little or no cruelty to children, but between then (when it gained a separate heading in the criminal register) and 1899, trials for such offences almost doubled. Public sentiment, outrage even, and the growth of societies such as the National Society for the Prevention of Cruelty to Children whose role it was to prosecute cases of ill treatment to children, and changes in the law contributed to this apparent growth (Jackson 2000). The job of the historian is therefore to move from the statistical to the qualitative evidence, taking with her or him a host of new questions relating to changes in public attitude and sentiment concerning the unacceptability of violence to children. Both quantitative and qualitative evidence, in other words, have a part to play in our understanding of violence. Neither one nor the other can be employed separately.

However, when it comes to domestic violence the quantitative evidence is particularly unhelpful (Hammerton 1992, D'Cruze 1998). Although a new law on the aggravated assault of women was passed in 1853, many male partners were prosecuted, if at all, under the law covering common assaults.[7] There is no way of knowing how large was the problem of domestic violence. In 1881, in Manchester with a population of 462,000, there were only 64 cases of aggravated assault. In Liverpool in 1880 there were a mere 60 charges but by contrast there were 1,073 cases of common assault brought before the courts. How many of them were for attacks on women there is no way of knowing since the statistics fail to identify the gender of victims. The only way of finding out is by going to the magistrates' court registers (where they have survived), which list every case or, maybe, by taking a sample of the cases reported in the police court columns of the local newspapers. This latter approach is fraught with problems since the press had a tendency to have occasional crusades against particular crimes and these crusades tended to exaggerate the true extent of the crimes. Thus, in the 1880s domestic violence was perceived to be a particular issue which needed highlighting and eradicating, and consequently newspapers presented long and detailed descriptions of that crime. It is doubtful whether wife beating was any more prevalent in this decade than   in earlier ones. Even then historians are provided with hints that the cases which they read about represent only the tip of a much larger problem. In a report on the North Dispensary, a cheap and popular medical centre for the working classes in the north end of Liverpool, it was noted that the centre treated 100 cases of wounding a week, not one of which was prosecuted (*Liverpool Review*, 9 October 1886).

Historians have been moving steadily away from questions arising out of quantification. Studies now revolve around the social meanings of violence, the representations of violence and popular attitudes towards violence. In these circumstances qualitative evidence, most commonly the local press, has provided the most rewarding source material since it can supply the context in which the events took place, how neighbours and other witnesses responded to the events and how the incidents were then written up and reported in the press. Historians are clearly hamstrung by various imponderables, not least the questions of truth and fact where the evidence in a court case is concerned. Did the events happen in the way in which witnesses say they happened, for example? We all know that lies are told, and that witnesses are mistaken, but even the most post-modern of post-modernists will extract some meaning and significance from the language and representation of the crime report. When all is said and done, the historians have only a limited amount of evidence at their disposal and their best methodological approach would appear to be a combination of the quantitative and qualitative, with the emphasis on the latter. Only then can we fully understand how violence has changed over time, how and why there have been fluctuations in the amounts of prosecuted violence and why some societies were more violent than others.

Notes

1 Some of the evidence cited in this chapter is based on material drawn from the project 'Violence in the North West with Special Reference to Liverpool and Manchester 1850–1914', funded by the Economic and Social Research Council (award number: L133251004) as part of the Violence Research Programme. I wish to extend my thanks to Jo Jones, the research project officer, and to Andrew Davies for his helpful advice and comments. Weekly and daily newspapers from Liverpool and Manchester were consulted for the period 1850–1914. See also my article (1999).

2　Only from 1857 do we have annual returns on summary offences in England and Wales. Up to the 1840s magistrates could hold their petty courts where they liked, even in their own homes. The general informality of such courts suggests that official record keeping was kept to a minimum, if it took place at all.

3　Homicide figures for the medieval period show wide variation between counties, ranging from 9/100,000 in Norfolk to 23/100,000 in Kent. Oxford, on the other hand, returned an unlikely 110/100,000 in the 1340s which would make contemporary American cities such as New York with a homicide rate of 27/100,000 havens of tranquillity (Stone 1985: 224). See also Monkkonen (2001b) for the problems of 'spotty knowledge' on individual localities which may or may not have been representative. His appendix of homicide rates in US cities of more than 100,000 population in 1996 should act as a warning to all historians and criminologists using statistics.

4　The Coroner's Register from January 1852 to September 1865 for Liverpool can be found in the Liverpool Record Office, 347 COR 1.

5　The poisoning of children was thought to be extensive during the nineteenth century in the north west of England where babies were put on opiates from a very early age (Havard 1960: 51–5).

6　It is unlikely that we will ever know the total number of patients killed by the general practitioner Dr Harold Shipman who worked in Todmorden and Hyde between 1975 and 1998. An inquiry, currently meeting, is investigating the sudden deaths of about 450 of his patients. In January 2000 he was convicted of 15 murders (*The Independent*, 9 October 2001).

7　An aggravated assault involved the use of a dangerous or deadly weapon and/or the inflicting of injuries. Men could be summarily convicted and imprisoned for up to six months under the 1853 Act.

References

Archer, J.E. (1999) ' "The Violence We Have Lost"? Body Counts, Historians and Interpersonal Violence in England', *Memoria y Civilización*, 2, 171–90.

— (2000) ' "Men Behaving Badly"?: Masculinity and the Uses of Violence, 1850–1900' in S. D'Cruze (ed.) *Everyday Violence in Britain, 1850–1950: Gender and Class*. Harlow: Longman.

Beattie, J. (1974) 'The Pattern of·Crime in England, 1660–1800', *Past and Present*, 62, 47–95.

— (1985) 'Violence and Society in Early Modern England' in A. Doob and E. Greenspan (eds) *Perspectives in Criminal Law*. Ontario: Canada Law Books.

— (1986) *Crime and the Courts in England 1660–1800*. Oxford: Oxford University Press.

Behlmer, G.K. (1979) 'Deadly Motherhood: Infanticide and Medical Opinion in Mid-Victorian England', *Journal of the History of Medicine and Allied Science*, 34, 403–27.

British Parliamentary Papers (1901) *Criminal Statistics for England and Wales 1899*, Vol. LXXXIX, Cd 659.

Cockburn, J.S. (1977) 'The Nature and Incidence of Crime in England, 1559–1625: A Preliminary Survey' in J.S. Cockburn (ed.) *Crime in England, 1550–1800*. London: Methuen and Co Ltd.

— (1991) 'Patterns of Violence in English Society: Homicide in Kent 1560–1985', *Past and Present*, 130, 70–106.

Conley, C.A. (1986) 'Rape and Justice in Victorian England', *Victorian Studies*, 29, 519–36.

Davis, J. (1980) 'The London Garotting Panic of 1862: A Moral Panic and the Creation of a Criminal Class in Mid-Victorian England' in V. Gatrell, B. Lenman and G. Parker (eds) *Crime and the Law: A Social History of Crime in Western Europe since 1500*. London: Europa.

D'Cruze, S. (1998) *Crimes of Outrage: Sex, Violence and Victorian Working Women*. London: UCL Press.

Gatrell, V.A.C. (1980) 'The Decline of Theft and Violence in Victorian and Edwardian England' in V. Gatrell, B. Lenman and G. Parker (eds) *Crime and the Law: A Social History of Crime in Western Europe since 1500*. London: Europa.

Gurr, T.R. (1981) 'Historical Trends in Violent Crime: A Critical Review of the Evidence', *Crime and Justice: An Annual Review of Research*, III, 295–353.

Hammerton, A.J. (1992) *Cruelty and Companionship: Conflict in Nineteenth-Century Married Life*. London: Routledge.

Hanawalt, B.A. (1976) 'Violent Death in Fourteenth- and Early Fifteenth-century England', *Comparative Studies in Society and History*, xviii, 297–320.

Havard, J.D.J. (1960) *The Detection of Secret Homicide: A Study of the Medico-legal System of Investigations of Sudden and Unexplained Deaths*. London: Macmillan.

Higginbotham, A. (1989) '"Sin of the Age": Infanticide and Illegitimacy in Victorian London', *Victorian Studies*, Spring.

Jackson, L.A. (2000) *Child Sexual Abuse in Victorian England*. London: Routledge.

Jackson, M. (1994) 'Suspicious Infant Deaths: the Statute of 1624 and Medical Evidence at Coroners' Inquests' in M. Clark and C. Crawford (eds) *Legal Medicine in History*. Cambridge: Cambridge University Press.

King, P. (1996) 'Punishing Assault: the Transformation of Attitudes in the English Courts', *Journal of Interdisciplinary History*, 27/1, 43–74.

Knelman, J. (1997) *Twisting in the Wind: the Murderess and the English Press*. Toronto: University of Toronto Press.

Monkkonen, E.H. (2001a) *Murder in New York City*. Berkeley: University of California Press.

— (2001b) 'New Standards for Historical Homicide Research', *Crime, History and Societies*, 5/2, 5–26.

Morris, R.M. (2001) '"Lies, Damned Lies, and Criminal Statistics": Reinterpreting the Criminal Statistics in England and Wales', *Crime, History and Societies*, 5/1, 111–27.

Rose, L. (1986) *Massacre of the Innocents: Infanticide in Great Britain 1800–1939*. London: Routledge & Kegan Paul.

Samaha, J. (1974) *Law and Order in Historical Perspective: The Case of Elizabethan England*. New York and London: Academic Press.

Simpson, A. (1988) 'Dandelions on the Field of Honour: Duelling, the Middle Class and the Law in Nineteenth-century England', *Criminal Justice History*, 9, 99–155.

Sindall, R.S. (1990) *Street Violence in the Nineteenth Century: Media Panic or Moral Danger?* Leicester: Leicester University Press.

Sharpe, J.A. (1985) 'The History of Violence in England: Some Observations', *Past and Present*, 108, 206–15.

Stone, L. (1983) 'Interpersonal Violence in English Society 1300–1800', *Past and Present*, 101, 22–33.

— (1985) 'A Rejoinder', *Past and Present*, 108, 216–24.

Taylor, H. (1998) 'Rationing Crime: the Political Economy of Criminal Statistics since the 1850s', *Economic History Review*, LI, 3, 569–90.

Wiener, M.J. (1999) 'The Sad Story of George Hall: Adultery, Murder and the Politics of Mercy in Mid-Victorian England', *Social History*, 24, 174–95.

—— (2001) 'Alice Arden to Bill Sikes: Changing Nightmares of Intimate Violence in England, 1558–1869', *Journal of British Studies*, 40, 184–212.

2 Putting the Conflict Tactics Scale in context in violence from parent to child

Susan Creighton, Deborah Ghate,
Neal Hazel, Julia Field and Steven Finch

Introduction

The national study of parents, children and discipline[1] was the first study to include a national random probability survey to be conducted with British parents. While its initial focus was on violence by parents towards their children, the survey placed this in the wider context of the discipline that parents used with their children. The research team wanted to take advantage of a unique opportunity of interviewing a nationally representative sample of parents, to look at the factors that influence and surround a particular disciplinary strategy. Factors such as beliefs and attitudes towards discipline and punishment, parenting style and the parent–child relationship, the immediate and distal stresses affecting the family, and the child's attributes, were all included.

Central to the survey was the measurement of the incidence and prevalence of the use of various parental responses to conflict with children, including violence. The tool that was devised for this measurement was the Misbehaviour Response Scale (MRS). The MRS was developed from the Conflict Tactics Scale (CTS). This chapter covers the methodological issues and ethical dilemmas involved in designing and carrying out the survey. In particular, it looks at past criticisms of the CTS and how these were addressed and overcome in the study of parents, children and discipline.

Background to the Conflict Tactics Scale

The CTS was developed by the Family Violence Research Group in New Hampshire, US in the mid-1970s (Straus, 1979; Straus *et al.*, 1980). It is now probably the most widely used scale for measuring intra-familial violence in the world. In the field of parent to child violence it has been used in countries as diverse as Sweden (Gelles and Edfelt, 1986), Canada (MacMillan *et al.*, 1997), Egypt (Youssef *et al.*, 1998), Hong Kong (Lau *et al.*, 1999), Korea and China (Kim *et al.*, 2000) and Italy (Bardi and Borgogni-Tarli, 2001), as well as in the USA and the UK.

The developers of the scale drew on conflict theory (Coser, 1956; Dahrendorf, 1959; Adams, 1965; Straus, 1979) as their theoretical underpinning. All human relationships, and, in particular, the parent–child one, may inevitably involve conflict. Resolving those conflicts may, or may not, include the use of physical force by one participant on the other. The original CTS was designed for use with adult couples. It included a list of various behaviours that may be used in response to interpersonal conflict. The behaviours ranged from non-violent reasoning items such as 'calm discussion', through psychologically aggressive items such as 'threatening to hit', to actual physical assaults. These were divided into 'minor' and 'severe' physical assaults. Minor physical assault included items such as 'slapping or spanking' and 'pushing and grabbing'. In the parent–child context these could be classified as corporal punishment. Severe assault behaviours included 'hitting with something', 'burn or scald' and 'threatening with a knife or gun'.

In addition to the actual behaviours used, the scale measured how frequently they had been used in the past year (i.e. a measure of chronicity), and whether they had ever been used (the lifetime prevalence). Incidence of the behaviour during the past year ranged from once to 20+ times. The incidence of physical assaults measured in this way has been correlated with age (Gelles and Straus, 1988; Wolfner and Gelles, 1993), sex (National Center on Child Abuse and Neglect, 1988), social position (Wolfner and Gelles, 1993), race and ethnicity (Hampton and Gelles, 1991). The correlations between physical assault and age, sex and social position, have led to social stress being posited (Gelles, 1993) as one of the main underlying mechanisms involved in the use of violence between spouses and in other family relationships.

Criticisms of the Conflict Tactics Scale

The emphasis of the CTS on behavioural acts out of context of what led up to or caused the conflict has drawn criticism (for example, Breines and Gordon, 1983; Dobash *et al.*, 1992), particularly from family violence researchers using a feminist perspective (Yllo, 1993; Kurz, 1993). These critics say that the scales make no allowance for the context in which these assaultive behaviours take place. They take no account of the purpose or severity of the assault, or of its outcome in terms of physical injuries. The history of the relationship, the relative powers of the two individuals (both physical and psychological), the cultural norms and expectations about family relationships condition both these more immediate initiators and sequelae.

Though our study proposed to utilise a CTS-style approach in relation to measuring violence between parents and children, it is worth considering the objections of those researching spousal violence, since they illustrate some of the wider complexities of the measurement of interpersonal conflict. In relation to the respective roles of husbands and wives, feminist theorists (for example, Yllo, 1993) have argued that cultural expectations of masculine and feminine behaviour, and how these interact within marriage and the family, are largely socially constructed. Furthermore, this social construction is aimed at creating and maintaining male power within the family and the wider society. Dobash and

Dobash (1979) and Schecter (1982) have described male violence as a means of exerting social control over women in general. Official crime statistics, the extreme end of the physical assault spectrum, show that women are much more likely to be victims of violence at the hands of men than men are at the hands of women. By contrast the Family Violence Surveys (Gelles and Straus, 1988; Straus and Gelles, 1986), using the CTS, had shown similar rates of physical assault by wives on husbands as by husbands on wives. In the US the National Crime Victimization Survey of 1982 found that husbands, or ex-husbands, were responsible for over 90 per cent of all violent crimes between spouses.

The 1996 British Crime Survey showed that women were twice as likely as men to have been injured by a partner in the past year, and three times as likely to have suffered frightening threats (Mirrlees-Black, 1999). Women were also more likely than men to say they had suffered domestic violence at some time in their lives and were over twice as likely to have been assaulted on three or more occasions. The British Crime Survey is a periodic random probability survey of adults living in private households in England and Wales to measure the extent of household and personal crime, whether or not it was reported to the police. The 1996 survey interviewed over 16,000 people and included a special section on domestic violence. This covered both physical and psychological assaults between partners, including incidents that would not have been classified as 'crimes' either by the police or by the victim. However, although the 1996 British Crime Survey showed that women were more likely than men to be harmed by domestic violence, it also showed that the same percentage of men as of women had been physically assaulted by a current or former partner in the past year. These latter findings of the British Crime Survey support both those of the Family Violence Surveys and those of researchers concerned with the outcomes of domestic violence.

In contrast to the use of violence by husbands as a method of social control, wives who use violence against their husbands largely attribute this to self-defence (Saunders, 1989) or to anger, frustration or retaliation against their partner's dominating or violent behaviour (Emery et al. 1989). The use of weapons or implements by women on their partners (i.e. *severe* assaults on the CTS) has been argued as a means of equalising the inherent power imbalance between men and women. There have been some recent high-profile appeals against murder convictions in England and Wales by women such as Sara Thornton and Kiranjit Ahluwalia, who had been driven to stab or set fire to their partner after prolonged physical and psychological assaults by him. These women said that they were driven to these assaults in a final effort to defend themselves, rather than as a method of control. Eagly and Steffen (1986), in a meta-analysis of research on differences in aggression, found that women were less likely than men to use aggression if the behaviour was likely to cause harm. However, the CTS was not designed to take into account the reasons, both immediate and distal, for initiating a physical assault or the consequences of that assault. It records the actual occurrence, and frequency of occurrence, of particular behaviours including physical assault.

Relevance of CTS debate to current study

Power, dominance and social expectations of family roles within intimate relationships are as applicable in studying violence by parent to child as they are in studying violence between spouses. Parents are both physically and psychologically more powerful than their children (at least, in relation to younger children), and are expected by society to exert influence over their child's behaviour. Allied to this, the spread of the human rights movement, and the children's rights movement in particular, may have complicated current social expectations of the relative roles of 'parent' and 'child', making parenting (an already difficult job) even more challenging in the modern world. Therefore our research was designed to explore not only the disciplinary behaviours, including violent behaviours, that parents in Britain were using with their children, but also their beliefs and attitudes towards what they felt they should be achieving. The relationship between parent and child, the stresses affecting the family, the distal and immediate factors that had escalated into conflict, and the resolution and outcome of that conflict would be examined to provide further context to the actual behaviours.

Overall design of the current study on parents, children and discipline

The study comprised a nationally representative quantitative survey of 1,249 parents of children aged 0–12 years in Britain. This was followed up by qualitative depth interviews with a sub-sample of 20 parents who had taken part in the quantitative survey. Interviews were also conducted separately with their children. The study explored the occurrence of violence, in the context of discipline, by parents to children in their home. The qualitative sub-sample of parents was chosen to represent the differing use of physical force in disciplining children, and differing attitudes to child discipline, among the whole sample. The interviewed child was aged 8 or more to facilitate a wider consideration of the context surrounding particular incidents. A further eight focus group discussions were held with groups of children aged 8–12 years old to get the children's perspective on parental disciplinary techniques. Although some research had been carried out with children in other countries (Sariola and Uutela, 1992; Ritchie and Ritchie, 1981), British children's perspectives on physical punishment have been largely excluded from the debate so far. By studying matched pairs of parents and children, as well as conducting group discussions with children, the study would give children, as well as parents, an opportunity to contribute to the current debate on how parenting practices impact upon children.

This chapter is largely concerned with the use of the MRS in the quantitative survey, but the addition of qualitative information from both parents and children helped to clarify some of the context explored in the survey.

The development of the Misbehaviour Response Scale

The first objective of the survey was to provide normative data on the extent and frequency of parental violence to children in British homes. Physical violence was defined in this study as any act with a reasonable probability of causing physical pain or injury. Physical punishment comprised acts involving the use of force or violence following perceived misdemeanours by the child. Discipline, as applied by parents to their children, is a broad concept not only encompassing 'teaching' and 'setting rules' but also shaping and guiding the child's behaviour more informally. Discipline might include physical punishment but would also include positive methods such as praising and encouraging good behaviour. The main instrument used for measuring parental disciplinary behaviours was the MRS, a version adapted for use in Britain of the revised parent–to–child version of the CTS, the Conflict Tactics Scales Parent to Child (CTSPC) (Straus *et al.*, 1998). The MRS incorporated new information on British parents' punitive behaviours (Smith, 1995; Nobes *et al.*, 1999), and was set in the context of the child's misbehaviour or the parent's responses to the child's behaviour (see 'make you upset' in introductory wording to Table 2.1). The MRS (see Table 2.1) was designed to measure the incidence and prevalence of use of 26 parental responses to the behaviour or misbehaviour of a randomly selected 'index' child.

Table 2.1 The Misbehaviour Response Scale

Children often do things that are wrong, disobey or make their parents annoyed or upset. Please look at this list of some of the things that parents may do in these situations. Please say how often you have done any of these things with your child in the past year (12 months). The questions cover a wide age range of children, but please answer each question as best as you can, even if you are not absolutely certain, or a question seems daft!

A Discussed the issue calmly/explained why the behaviour was wrong
B Gave child something else to do, instead of what they were doing wrong
C Moved something dangerous or tempting out of child's way
D Brought someone else in to help sort things out
   (If child is age 2 or over)
E Made child take 'time out' to think about their behaviour – e.g. sent child to bedroom, made them sit on a 'naughty stair', etc.
F Gave child a chore or something unpleasant to do:
G 'Grounded' or stopped child going out, or took away treats (e.g. sweets, TV)
   (All)
H Walked out on child, or left the room or house
I Refused to talk to child/gave child 'the silent treatment'
J Shouted, yelled *or* swore at child
K Said *you* wouldn't love child, or you would send them away, or *you* would go away or leave them
L Threatened to smack or hit child (but did not actually do it)
M Smacked child's bottom
N Smacked or slapped child on hands, arms, or legs
O Smacked or slapped child on the face, head or ears
P Grabbed, pushed, or handled child roughly
Q Shook child

Table 2.1 continues

Table 2.1 continued

R   Punched or kicked child
S   Bit or pinched child
T   Hit child with something like a slipper, belt, hairbrush or other hard object
U   Pulled child's ears or hair
V   Washed child's mouth out with something (e.g. soap) or make them swallow something unpleasant
W   Beat child up (that is, hit child over and over again as hard as you could)
X   Burned or scalded child on purpose
Y   Grabbed child round the neck, or choked them

The response frequencies offered were:
    More than 20 times in the past year
    About 11–20 times in the past year
    About 3–10 times in the past year
    Once or twice in the past year
    Not in the past year, but has happened before
    This has never happened

The title 'Misbehaviour Response' and the introductory wording to the scale are perhaps somewhat less threatening to respondents than the CTS. The implication was that the parental response was provoked by the child rather than the parent, even if the child did not intend to provoke conflict. This approach enables both 'blame' and 'no blame' situations to be captured. While the child-abuse literature contains many examples of unprovoked parental attacks on helpless and vulnerable infants and children, few parents are likely to admit to such behaviour. The MRS enabled parents to describe responses they had made and to do so in a morally neutral manner. The study was designed to provide data on the full extent of parental violence to children in the home. The naming of the scale, the introductory wording to the scale and the gradually decreasing social acceptability of behaviours were designed to 'give permission' for parents to admit to using behaviours that they may have condemned as unacceptable in an earlier part of the questionnaire.

The MRS responses were divided into five groups including two physically non-violent (non-aggressive and psychologically aggressive), and three physically violent (minor, severe and very severe). These groups were chosen specifically in order to maintain comparability with surveys on violence by parents to children conducted in other countries that had used the CTS.

Supplying the context to the Misbehaviour Response Scale

As we have noted, CTS-type approaches to the measurement of family violence have inherent limitations, in that they measure acts of violence but not the contexts in which that violence occurs. Thus, the second objective of our study was to explore the contexts for the use of violent physical responses by parents to children. These included both the immediate trigger factors and the more distant background factors that may have influenced the conflict. The background factors explored included:

- parent's own childhood experience of discipline, including physical discipline, and judgement of it;
- parent's beliefs and attitudes to discipline in child rearing in general, and the use of physical punishment in particular;
- parenting style and the parent–child relationship: for example, warmth, hostility, communication and supervision;
- stresses affecting the family: personal relationships and support, physical, mental or material disadvantage and stressful life events;
- child's behaviour in general and those behaviours which parents found especially provoking.

All these factors are thought to affect the use of physical violence by parents towards their children. They constituted the distal or background context.

The immediate, proximate or trigger factors for the conflict included the location, the time of day and week, the type of behaviour displayed by the child and the parent's mood immediately prior to the incident. The respondent was also asked why they thought the child was behaving in a provoking manner. These constituted the 'immediate' context.

Outcomes were explored by asking about any marks or bruises caused by the physical response, the child's behaviour afterwards and the parent's feelings about the incident. These included immediate feelings and a general retrospective judgement on the effectiveness of the response and how 'well' they had handled the situation.

The qualitative data from parents and children also provided further contextual information to the study as discussed elsewhere (Ghate *et al.*, forthcoming). By exploring all these background and immediate factors surrounding the use of physical violence by parents to children, the study intended to both employ the adapted CTS and to supply the context to the behavioural responses. It would '*put the CTS in context in violence from parent to child*'.

Methodological issues

The main methodological issues involved in carrying out the quantitative stage of the study, and in particular supplying the context to the MRS, were:

- the reliability and validity of the MRS and other scales used in the questionnaire;
- ensuring the fullest and frankest responses to sensitive questions;
- focusing on a particular incident in order to concentrate on immediate context.

Reliability and validity of the Misbehaviour Response Scale

The CTS as a scale has good concurrent and construct validity (Straus and Hamby, 1997). The revised CTSPC (Straus et al., 1998) was designed to increase the CTS's internal consistency reliability. The MRS was tested for internal reliability using the data gained from the first Computer Assisted Personal Interview (CAPI) pilot. A test-retest experiment was conducted on parts of the questionnaire, including the MRS, to assess external reliability. A sample of parents was asked to complete the same sections of the questionnaire on two occasions, one week apart. The internal reliability yielded an average Cronbach's *alpha* of 0.88 for the MRS, indicating good internal consistency. The external reliability from the test-retest experiment gave a Spearman's *rho* of 0.87, an acceptable measure.

Ensuring full and frank responses

The best method of ensuring the participation and honest answers of potential respondents is to convince them of the importance of the subject being surveyed and reassure them of the confidentiality of their responses. Once this has been achieved, the skill of experienced interviewers and the robustness and sensitivity of the survey instrument used can encourage full and frank responses.

The role of the skilled survey interviewer is to engage the potential respondent on the doorstep, interest them in the survey being undertaken and encourage them to respond. We took the view that it was vital to greet all responses in a neutral and empathetic manner and to make the whole interview as enjoyable and unthreatening as possible for the respondent. The interviewers used in this study were from the experienced field force of the National Centre for Social Research (NatCen). NatCen is a leading independent research institute with some 30 years of experience in survey work, exclusively in the public sector, academic and grant-funded social policy research. High proportions of NatCen's interviewers have worked for them for many years and have built up substantial expertise in survey research, including research on such sensitive topics as the National Survey of Sexual Attitudes and Lifestyles.

The questionnaire administered by the interviewers also needs to engage and interest the respondent so that they want to complete it as fully as possible. It should flow smoothly and for a reasonable time, and where sensitive information is being sought the ordering of questions should lead up to this gradually. It should be clear why information is being requested, so that questions do not seem overly intrusive. The wording of the questions, particularly the sensitive ones, was designed to 'give permission' to admissions of socially stigmatised behaviour and the opportunity to show that more socially acceptable acts had preceded the less socially acceptable. Information vital to the survey should, ideally, be in the earlier part of the questionnaire in case the interview has to be ended early. The respondent should be left feeling satisfied with the interview so the final questions should be reasonably 'upbeat'.

Thorough piloting both of the questionnaire and of the ways of presenting it were required. The questions had to be clear and unambiguous and the whole questionnaire completed in a reasonable time. In the event three pilots were undertaken, one pre-pilot using paper questionnaires and two dress-rehearsal pilots using computerised versions of the questionnaire.

The first pre-pilot used a qualitative 'cognitive interviewing' (Willis, 1994) approach with different sections of the questionnaire. This approach is designed to get respondents to recount and explain how they understood the questions and how they had answered them. It is a particularly useful technique for making questions clear and unambiguous. It was also helpful in establishing which parts of the questionnaire were particularly sensitive or distressing for respondents. Following this pre-pilot some of the wording of the questions, and the order in which they were presented, was changed. An example would be the section on the respondent's own experience of being parented. This had initially been placed early on in the questionnaire as a logical way of leading into their own parenting behaviour. In the pre-pilot this section had proved distressing for some respondents and had affected their subsequent responses so was moved to a later position in the questionnaire.

The method used to administer the questionnaire can also affect the willingness of respondents to answer as comprehensively as possible. Computer Assisted Personal Interview (CAPI) is now widely used in survey methodology and offers significant advances in terms of data quality. Computer Assisted Self-Interviewing (CASI) has been shown to be superior to self-completed paper questionnaires in getting answers to sensitive issues (Tourangeau and Smith, 1996; Turner et al., 1998). The questionnaire is programmed into a laptop computer, which the trained interviewer operates, keying in either numeric answers or verbatim transcript. The programme routes the questions in response to the previous answers so that no item is inadvertently missed out, as can happen with a paper questionnaire. For the most sensitive parts of the interview the interviewer hands the computer over to the respondent to self-complete (the CASI part). Some practice questions are provided to familiarise the respondent with the completion process. The interviewer will then demonstrate how the program keeps their answers to this section completely confidential, by 'locking' the data within the computer so that they cannot be viewed again until downloaded for editing and analysis by the central field controllers.

Turner et al. (1998) found a threefold increase in admissions of same-sex encounters and use of drugs and violence in adolescent boys, using CASI technology, compared with the use of self-completed paper questionnaires. In the present survey the arrangement of topics within the questionnaire that resulted in the best flow of questions involved the use of two CASI sections. This had the added advantage of providing breaks and changes of pace within a relatively long interview. The majority of the respondents had no difficulty in using the computer themselves. Only 20 (2 per cent of the whole sample) preferred the interviewer to input their responses, and only one because they disliked using a computer.

The second pilot, the first CAPI dress rehearsal with the re-structured questionnaire, tested the questionnaire, the screening and selection process and the introductory literature. For the main survey nearly 11,000 households had to be screened in order to obtain just over 2,000 households containing a parent of a child aged 0–12 years. The first CAPI pilot led to some restructuring of the programme, which was tested out in a second CAPI pilot prior to the main fieldwork.

The interviewers who carried out the pilots were able to confirm that the process by which potential respondents were found worked; the introductory material had engaged them and they were interested and co-operative in completing the questionnaire.

The experiences from these pilots were used to inform the careful briefing of interviewers conducting the main fieldwork. Eight day-long briefing sessions were held with groups of interviewers in different parts of the country. The topics covered during these sessions included the background to the study, the screening and interviewing procedures, how to introduce the survey, and how to reassure respondents of the confidentiality of their answers, as well as how to administer (with practice in administering) the questionnaire in a neutral, encouraging manner.

The design of the questionnaire, the use of the latest computer technology, thorough briefing and the skill of the survey interviewers all helped to ensure full and frank responses from the parents interviewed.

Focus on a particular incident

Exploring the immediate context to a specific disciplinary incident was the most difficult part of the survey to design. Although this was an area that could be explored using qualitative techniques, it was thought essential to get quantitative data as well. The difficulty lay in trying to measure, cross-sectionally, what is actually a process, rather than a single event, using standard survey techniques. Discipline and conflict also tend to take place in an aroused affective state, which may make it even harder to establish the sequence of events. It was decided to focus on the 'most recent incident when the parent had disciplined the child'. This incident should be the easiest for the respondent to remember, including the context in which it arose as well as the details of the sequence of behaviours that ensued. It also provided a method of achieving a random sample of disciplinary incidents rather than trying to focus on a particular type of incident.

The questions focusing on the most recent incident were designed to provide as rich and explanatory a context to a particular behaviour as was possible in a quantitative survey. Both parents who had, and parents who had not, used physical disciplinary measures in the past year, answered this section, allowing contrasts between the two groups. Since we were particularly interested in physical discipline, the computer displaying their answers to the original MRS prompted those parents who had used some form of physical discipline in the past year. They were asked to check which of these they had used on the most recent occasion, and when this had been. Further information was confined to incidents occurring in the previous six months as it was felt that recall prior to this would be less reliable. Within these parameters the majority of the incidents captured in the survey had occurred within the past month.

The most recent incident was explored in relation to:

- place and time
- triggering behaviours
- emotions at time
- alternative strategies employed.

Figure 2.1 outlines the factors included and processes explored, in looking at disciplinary responses relating to the most recent incident.

Some of the questions we were attempting to answer included:

Place and time

Are there times of the week or day that are particularly stressful and lead to conflict between parents and their children? Do disciplinary incidents mainly occur in private with just the parent and child present or are other children, relatives or adults present?

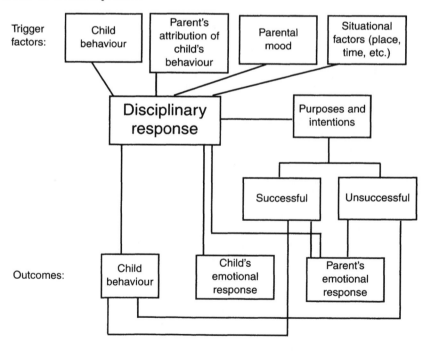

Figure 2.1 The processes involved in investigating a disciplinary response

Triggering child behaviours

How was the child behaving that had upset or annoyed the parent? Were the child behaviours that provoked the most recent incident the same in practice as had been described in principle?

Parental emotions and attributions

Had the mood of the parent rather than the behaviour of the child precipitated the conflict? Had they been feeling tired or stressed before the incident? Why did they think the child was behaving in the annoying manner? Did they think that the child was behaving 'normally' or being deliberately defiant? And why had they responded in that particular fashion? Was it a response aimed at immediate child compliance or more long-term consequences? Was it designed to change the child's behaviour or relieve the parent's frustration?

Outcomes

Outcomes to the most recent disciplinary incident included an assessment of how the child had behaved afterwards and how the parent had felt. Lastly, the parent's view of the effectiveness of the discipline was ascertained, by asking them their views on it having prevented similar misbehaviour by the child in the future, and how they felt they had handled the situation.

Alternative strategies employed

It was important to discover if those parents who had used physical methods on the most recent occasion had also tried non-physical disciplinary techniques at the same time. This would suggest an escalation of the conflict rather than a repertoire of disciplinary techniques confined to physical responses.

The insights gained from the answers to the questions focusing on the most recent disciplinary incident were followed up and extended in the qualitative interviews with individual parents and their children.

Ethical and methodological considerations

In any study examining sensitive topics, which may include destructive or illegal practices, there are two main ethical dilemmas. The first is the duty of any ethical research to safeguard the rights and feelings of the individuals being researched. Denscombe (1998) has outlined how this can be done. Respondents need to be assured of the confidentiality of their responses, not deceived, and the impact of recalling and reporting distressing or stressful events should be minimised. It is only by applying such ethical standards that researchers can hope to maximise the potential respondent's confidence in the study so that they feel able to answer questions as honestly and candidly as possible.

The second ethical dilemma is how to respond to answers or practices that are patently dangerous and may affect other vulnerable individuals. In a study on parents, children and discipline the second dilemma is particularly relevant as the behaviour revealed could be harmful, and even life-threatening, for the child concerned. Both dilemmas were made more salient by the involvement of the NSPCC (National Society for the Prevention of Cruelty to Children) as one of the organisations undertaking the research. The NSPCC is a national children's charity covering England, Wales and Northern Ireland, with a remit to prevent cruelty to children. It has been established for over a century, and is the only voluntary organisation in the UK with a statutory right to remove a child from an abusive home, and to bring legal proceedings against a parent for abusing their child. The study researchers considered that they had an ethical responsibility to inform all potential respondents about who was funding and carrying out the research and about its main aims. However, there was some concern that the inclusion of the NSPCC's name might well deter some respondents from taking part in the study, particularly those parents who were conscious of using most violence against their children. For those who did agree to participate (and particularly those whose parenting styles were unusually strict or harsh), the NSPCC's name might lead to less than completely frank answers to some questions. We cannot assess the extent of bias that may have been introduced in this way, though responses to the NSPCC's involvement at the pilot survey stage were exclusively positive, suggesting that, on balance, the reputation of the organisation was a positive rather than a negative aspect of the survey.

The introductory letter (see Appendix) was framed to balance the respondent's right to know who was involved in the research with getting the fullest and most honest answers. The introductory letter was shown to potential respondents by the interviewer at their first contact. It explained the aims of the study and who was carrying it out and funding it, in accordance with research ethics. It also stressed the confidential nature of the responses. The letter included the fact that the NSPCC was one of the organisations carrying out the research, but placed emphasis on the complete confidentiality of the answers given.

The impact on respondents of recalling and reporting distressing or stressful events had been addressed in the design and piloting of the questionnaire and the briefing of the interviewers. An additional anxiety, at the time of the main fieldwork, was the widespread media coverage of the abduction and murder of 8-year-old Sarah Payne. Parental concerns about roving homicidal paedophiles were heightened. The screening process for the survey essentially involved strangers enquiring about the presence of young children in the house. The problem of allaying any such concerns was addressed by using the skills of the interviewers, the provision of contact names and phone numbers of the study researchers of the Policy Research Bureau (PRB) and NatCen for further enquiries, and the knowledge of the local police. It is standard fieldwork practice for interviewers to inform the local police about any study they are carrying out in the area. This information includes the purpose of the study, the interviewer's name and car registration number and when they would be interviewing parents in the area, and contact details for NatCen's Operations Department. The purpose was to establish the interviewer's bona fides both with the local police and with any householder or potential respondent who might contact the police about the study. In the aftermath of the Sarah Payne murder this aspect of practice was thought particularly important.

The methods used in the survey to engage respondents, reassure them of the confidentiality of their responses, and keep their interest and confidence in the survey, can be judged to be successful by the number who agreed to participate in a possible follow-up. Some 91 per cent of the respondents said they were willing to be contacted later.

The second dilemma was how to respond to evidence of child abuse within the respondent's home if we uncovered any. The research team carefully considered this ethical dilemma. We decided that, in this study, strict confidentiality must be promised to the respondents, since otherwise the main purpose of the study – to obtain national 'benchmarking' data – could be compromised. The sample was a normative one of parents from the general population and the interviewers from NatCen were bound by the social survey research principle of confidentiality. All parents would, however, be given an information leaflet listing sources of advice and support for those experiencing difficulties with their children. Similarly, for those children taking part in the study, a 'child-friendly' leaflet on sources of support or services for children would be provided. Information leaflets of this kind had been used successfully by the applicants in previous normative general population studies on adults (Creighton and Russell, 1995) and children (Ghate and Daniels, 1997).

Conclusions

This chapter has outlined some of the methodological issues and ethical dilemmas involved in mounting the first nationally representative survey of the disciplinary measures employed by parents with their children aged 0–12 in Britain. The development of the MRS from the CTS means that the extent and severity of the use of violence on their children by British parents can now, for the first time, be compared with the international body of work collected in other countries.

The innovative methods used to capture information on violence to children based on the 'most recent incident' model enabled us to identify the situations and contexts most likely to lead to violent conflict. These can be used to develop recommendations for prevention and early intervention to prevent violence to children. The combination of quantitative survey data from parents with qualitative data from children has developed a method for successfully capturing the sophistication and complexity of young children's views on the effectiveness, acceptability and appropriateness of a range of violent and non-violent disciplinary tactics. The incorporation of attitudes to, and beliefs about, disciplining children in the survey provided national data on community definitions of 'abusive' as opposed to 'normal' violence. The qualitative interviews with parents were able to probe the difficulties parents face in reconciling their beliefs about discipline with their actual actions, in the day-to-day management of their children.

Finally, the study was successful in developing a robust questionnaire, which was acceptable and interesting to parents, and can be used to monitor future trends in the parental disciplining of children. Full details of the design and content of the quantitative and qualitative surveys and their findings will be covered in Ghate *et al.* (forthcoming).

Note

1   The national study of parents, children and discipline was conducted by the Policy Research Bureau, the NSPCC, and the National Centre for Social Research. It was funded by the Economic and Social Research Council as part of their Violence Research Programme, award number L133251021.

Appendix

Introductory letter shown by interviewers to potential respondents when describing the study

---

National Centre for Social Research
Operations Department
100 Kings Road
Essex CM14 4LA
01277 200 600
Our ref: P1756

POLICY ● RESEARCH   B U R E A U

2a Tabernacle Street
London
EC2A 4LU
0171 256 6300

Spring 2000

Bringing Up Children: A National Study Of Parents In Britain

Everyone knows that being a parent is one of the hardest jobs there is. There is a lot of debate in the media about this subject but parents' views are rarely asked for. This study gives parents across Britain a chance to say what they think. The results will be useful for planning better services for families and children.

The study is about bringing up children and how parents try to manage their children's behaviour. We are interested in what parents do, and their views on 'what works' and what is acceptable when guiding or managing children's behaviour. We want to learn more about the pressures parents face these days and we are also exploring parents' views about how they were brought up, to see if families are changing over time. The study is being carried out by independent researchers at the National Centre for Social Research, the Policy Research Bureau, and the NSPCC. It is being funded by the Economic and Social Research Council.

We are talking to 1,200 parents all over the country and your address has been selected at random from a list of addresses to which the Post Office delivers mail. It is important that everyone who has been selected agrees to take part so that we can be sure the picture we get is reliable. Interviews will take around an hour, at a time that suits you. We think you will enjoy taking part.

Your answers will be confidential. Nothing you say to the interviewer will be passed to anyone outside the research team in any way that could identify you or your family and you will not have to answer any questions you would rather not. All interviewers working on the study carry an identity card from the National Centre for Social Research.

If you have any queries please call Heather Clements, who is the Project Controller at the National Centre, on 01277 200 600.

We hope you will feel able to help with this important national study.

STEVEN FINCH
Research Group Director
National Centre for Social Research

Dr DEBORAH GHATE
Co-Director
Policy Research Bureau

References

Adams, B.N. (1965) 'Coercion and Consensus Theories: Some Unresolved Issues', *American Journal of Sociology*, 71, pp. 714–16.

Bardi, M. and Borgogni-Tarli, S.M. (2001) 'A Survey on Parent–Child Conflict Resolution: Intrafamily Violence in Italy', *Child Abuse and Neglect*, 6, pp. 839–53.

Breines, W. and Gordon, L. (1983) 'The New Scholarship on Family Violence', *Signs*, 8, pp. 490–531.

Coser, L. (1956) *The Functions of Social Conflict*. New York: Free Press.

Creighton, S.J. and Russell, N. (1995) *Voices from Childhood: A Survey of Childhood Experiences and Attitudes to Child Rearing among Adults in the United Kingdom*, London: NSPCC.

Dahrendorf, R. (1959) *Class and Class Conflict in Industrial Society*. London, England: Routledge and Kegan Paul.

Denscombe, M. (1998) *The Good Research Guide*. Buckingham: Open University Press.

Dobash, R.E. and Dobash, R.P. (1979) *Violence Against Wives: A Case Against the Patriarchy*. New York: Free Press.

Dobash, R.E., Dobash, R.P., Wilson, M. and Daly, M. (1992) 'The Myth of Sexual Symmetry in Marital Violence', *Social Problems*, 39, pp. 71–91.

Eagly, A.H. and Steffen, V.J. (1986) 'Gender and Aggressive Behavior: A Meta-Analytic Review of the Social Psychological Literature', *Psychological Bulletin*, 100, pp. 309–30.

Emery, B., Lloyd, S. and Castleton, A. (1989) *Why Women Hit: A Feminist Perspective*, paper presented at the annual meeting of the National Council on Family Relations, New Orleans.

Gelles, R.J. (1993) 'Through a Sociological Lens: Social Structure and Family Violence' (1993) Ch. 2 in R.J. Gelles and D.R. Loseke (eds), *Current Controversies in Family Violence*. Newbury: Sage.

Gelles, R.J. and Edfelt, A. (1986) 'Violence Towards Children in the United States and Sweden', *Child Abuse and Neglect*, 10, pp. 501–10.

Gelles, R.J. and Straus, M.A. (1988) *Intimate Violence: The Causes and Consequences of Abuse in the American Family*, New York: Simon & Schuster.

Ghate, D. and Daniels, A. (1997) *Talking about my Generation: A Survey of 8–15 Year Olds Growing up in the 1990s*, London: NSPCC.

Ghate, D., Hazel, N., Creighton, S., Finch, S. and Field, J. (forthcoming) *Parents, Children and Discipline: A National Study of Families in Britain*.

Hampton, R.L. and Gelles, R.J. (1991) 'A Profile of Violence Toward Black Children', in R.L. Hampton (ed.) *Black Family Violence: Current Research and Theory*. Lexington, MA: Lexington Books.

Kim, D-H., Kim, K-I., Park, Y-C., Zhang, L.D., Lu, M.K. and Li, D. (2000) 'Children's Experience of Violence in China and Korea: A Transcultural Study', *Child Abuse and Neglect*, 24, pp. 1163–73.

Kurz, D. (1993) 'Physical Assaults by Husbands: a Major Social Problem', Ch. 5 in R.J. Gelles and D.R. Loseke (eds), *Current Controversies in Family Violence*. Newbury: Sage.

Lau, J.T., Liu, J.L., Yu, A. and Wong, C.K. (1999) 'Conceptualization, Reporting and Underreporting of Child Abuse in Hong Kong', *Child Abuse and Neglect*, 23, pp. 1159–74.

MacMillan, H.L., Fleming, J.E., Trocme, N., Boyle, M.H., Wong, M., Racine, Y.A., Beardslee, W.R. and Offord, D.R. (1997) 'Prevalence of Child Physical and Sexual

Abuse in the Community', *Journal of the American Medical Association*, 278 (2), pp. 131–5.

Mirrlees-Black, C. (1999) *Domestic Violence: Findings from a new British Crime Survey Self-completion Questionnaire*, Home Office Research Study 191. London: Home Office.

National Center on Child Abuse and Neglect (1988) *Study Findings: Study of National Incidence and Prevalence of Child Abuse and Neglect: 1988.* Washington, DC: US Department of Health and Human Services.

Nobes, G., Smith M., Upton P. and Heverin A. (1999) 'Physical Punishment by Mothers and Fathers in British Homes', *Journal of Interpersonal Violence*, Vol. 14, No. 8, pp. 887–902.

Ritchie, J. and Ritchie, J. (1981) *Spare the Rod.* Sydney: Allen & Unwin.

Sariola, H. and Uutela, A. (1992) 'The Prevalence and Context of Family Violence against Children in Finland', *Child Abuse and Neglect*, 16, pp. 823–32.

Saunders, D.G. (1989) *Who Hits First and Who Hurts Most? Evidence for the Greater Victimization of Women in Intimate Relationships*, paper presented at the 41st Annual Meeting of the American Society of Criminology, Reno, NV.

Schecter, S. (1982) *Women and Male Violence: The Visions and Struggles of the Battered Women's Movement.* Boston: South End.

Smith, M.A. (1995) *A Community Study of Physical Violence to Children in the Home, and Associated Variables.* Poster presented at International Society for the Prevention of Child Abuse and Neglect, 13–16 May, Oslo, Norway.

Straus, M.A. (1979) 'Measuring Intrafamily Conflict and Violence: The Conflict Tactics Scale', *Journal of Marriage and the Family*, 41, pp. 75–88.

Straus, M.A. (1993) 'Physical Assaults by Wives: A Major Social Problem', Ch. 4 in R.J. Gelles and D.R. Loseke (eds), *Current Controversies in Family Violence.* Newbury: Sage.

Straus, M.A., and Gelles, R.J. (1986) 'Societal Change and Change in Family Violence from 1975 to 1985 as Revealed by Two National Surveys', *Journal of Marriage and the Family*, 48, pp. 465–79.

Straus, M.A., Gelles, R.J. and Steinmetz, S.K. (1980) *Behind Closed Doors: Violence in the American Family.* Garden City, NY: Anchor/Doubleday.

Straus, M.A., Hamby, S.L., Finkelhor, D., Moore, D.W. and Runyan, D. (1998) 'Identification of Child Maltreatment with the Parent–Child Conflict Tactics Scales: Development and Psychometric Data for a National Sample of American Parents', *Child Abuse and Neglect*, 22, pp. 249–70.

Straus, M.A. and Hamby, S.L. (1997) 'Measuring Physical and Psychological Maltreatment of Children with the Conflict Tactics Scales', in G. Kaufman Kantor and J.L. Jasinski (eds), *Out of the Darkness: Contemporary Research Perspectives on Family Violence*, pp. 119–35. Thousand Oaks, CA: Sage.

Tourangeau, R. and Smith, T.W. (1996) 'Asking Sensitive Questions: The Impact of Data Collection Mode, Question Format and Question Context', *Public Opinion Quarterly*, 60, pp. 27–34.

Turner, C.F., Ku, L., Rogers, S.M., Lindberg, L.D., Pleck, J.H. and Sonenstein, F.L. (1998) 'Adolescent Sexual Behavior, Drug Use, and Violence: Increased Reporting with Computer Survey Technology', *Science*, 280 (no. 5365), pp. 867–73.

Willis, G.B. (1994) *Cognitive Interviewing and Questionnaire Design: a Training Manual.* Hyattsville, MD: National Centre for Health Statistics.

Wolfner, G. and Gelles, R.J. (1993) 'A Profile of Violence Toward Children', *Child Abuse and Neglect*, 17, pp. 197–212.

Yllo, K.A. (1993) 'Through a Feminist Lens: Gender, Power, and Violence', Ch. 3 in R.J. Gelles and D.R. Loseke (eds), *Current Controversies in Family Violence*. Newbury: Sage.

Youssef, R.M., Attia, M.S. and Kamel, M.I. (1998) 'Children Experiencing Violence I: Parental Use of Corporal Punishment', *Child Abuse and Neglect,* 22, pp. 959–73.

3   Researching homicide

Methodological issues in the exploration of lethal violence

Ruth Lewis,[1] R. Emerson Dobash,
Russell P. Dobash and Kate Cavanagh

Introduction

This, the first national study of murder in Britain, aims to develop a typology of murder and to use three different sources of data to develop a more empirically informed understanding of lethal violence. The specific aims of the Homicide in Britain study are to identify various types of murder; to examine each type in terms of risk factors, situational contexts and lethal intentions; and to make relevant comparisons across and within these types. This study addresses a highly complex and sensitive subject and poses many methodological questions about how to develop meaningful, valid, empirical data to inform a theoretical understanding of this phenomenon. In this chapter, we discuss the data collection techniques used in the Homicide in Britain study and locate these within the context of some of the traditional approaches used to investigate violence and crime. In particular, we consider the value of combining official statistics, in-depth interviews and documentary analysis for investigating murder. We argue that research which adopts a context-specific approach and uses triangulation to generate qualitative and quantitative data can make an important contribution to an empirically and theoretically informed understanding of lethal violence and the situations and circumstances in which it occurs.

Methodologies for investigating violence

There is considerable debate among social scientists about the methodological and epistemological aspects of studying violence. The debates tend to be argued within disciplines with relatively little cross-fertilisation across disciplinary boundaries (Dobash and Dobash, 1998). This research draws on and adds to some of the long-standing debates within the social sciences about the collection and uses of qualitative and quantitative data and about different approaches to data collection, from the survey to ethnography. It also draws on methods less frequently used in the social sciences, such as documentary analysis.

Ethnography has been used widely in the study of crime, violence and drugs. Since the early studies of crime and 'deviance' at the Chicago School in the first half of the twentieth century, countless social scientists in the US and Britain have been eager to participate in and/or observe a range of criminal activities (Becker, 1963; Bourgois, 1995; Fielding, 1981; Hobbs and May, 1993; Maher, 1995). Work in this tradition has ranged from studies that exhibit careful, nuanced, scholarly examinations of a range of serious and sensitive issues to approaches that tend to 'sensationalise' crime and violence and emphasise 'dangerous' encounters that valorise the researcher and perpetrators in a style more characteristic of tabloid journalism than scholarly social science.

Other social scientists, particularly those in North America, have relied almost solely on quantitative data from official records (e.g. homicide statistics and police records). For example, in the United States, most research on homicide has relied on data from the Uniform Crime Reporting (UCR) of the FBI which contains a limited amount of information about all reported homicides in the US since the 1920s (Riedel, 1999). Studies based on these data have provided valuable information about patterns, distributions and socio-economic correlates of homicide across time and over geographic areas. For this kind of research, methodological concerns focus on issues about the reliability of the data and statistical techniques for analysis of large datasets (Smith and Zahn, 1999). While findings based on such data are useful in providing information about broad patterns of homicide based on a large number of cases over a long period, they suffer from the limited amount of information available about each of these cases. The advantages of an *extensive* database are balanced against the lack of *intensive* information about each case (situations, contexts, personal history, etc.) that would allow for a more comprehensive examination of the differential patterns of homicide and more adequate conceptualisation and theoretical explanations of homicide.

In the general area of crime and violence, large-scale victim surveys have added immeasurably to the understanding of crime and victimisation (Johnson, 1998, 1996; Tseloni, 1995; Mirrlees-Black, 1994). Obviously, victim surveys have a limited utility in the study of homicide although recent work has used this approach to interview victims of 'near' homicides and compare them with similar cases in which there was a homicide (Campbell, 2001).

Overall, in the study of violence and crime, there has been a tendency to rely on a single data collection technique rather than an integration of qualitative with quantitative data, which generates the associated advantages of such integration. The Homicide in Britain study used both qualitative and quantitative data from three different sources (official statistics, official documents and interviews). It is our contention that if the aim is to better understand and explain any social issue, then the use of different methods with their respective strengths and weaknesses provides a more fruitful approach than relying solely upon a single data collection technique.

When it comes to the study of 'sensitive topics' such as violence, there has been an assumption, which in some cases has been elevated to the level of an axiom, that the in-depth interview is the most valuable and perhaps even the only data collection method that can yield information that counts as 'truth'. For example, some feminist researchers have claimed that the in-depth interview is the only way to 'give voice' to women who have been ignored, misrepresented or misinterpreted in 'traditional' social science. Indeed, something of an orthodoxy has developed whereby much of feminist research is associated with hostility towards quantitative methods in pursuit of a singular preference for qualitative methods and in-depth interviews, particularly with women respondents. While challenges to this orthodoxy are not new (Dobash and Dobash, 1979, Dobash and Dobash, 1998: 6; Cavanagh and Lewis, 1996; Kelly *et al.*, 1994; Reinharz, 1992; Yllo, 1988), this commitment persists among many feminist social scientists.

Scholars investigating violence face particular methodological dilemmas about ethics, data collection, confidentiality, safety, empathy, 'emotionality'[2] and values. Within the study of violence, the examination of violence against women provides something of a paradigm for honing methodological practice. For example, conceptualising and measuring lethal and non-lethal violence against women has demonstrated the importance of a keen understanding of its context, meaning and consequences (Dobash and Dobash, 1983; Dobash *et al.*, 1997; Dobash *et al.*, 1992; Nazroo, 1995) and the effect of different methods on the reporting of experiences of violence (Johnson, 1998). The in-depth interview has clearly been an invaluable tool in addressing many of these issues in the study of violence against women. It has primarily been used in the study of women as survivors of physical and sexual violence but has also been extended to the study of men as the perpetrators of this violence (Dobash *et al.*, 2000; Cavanagh and Lewis, 1996; Scully, 1990; for an early example of in-depth interviews with violent men see Toch, 1969).

The Homicide in Britain study is located at the intersection of many disciplines within the social sciences with their respective methodological preferences but it extends beyond traditional disciplinary boundaries and methodological orthodoxies. The research does not rely on a single data collection technique or argue for the value of one form of data over another. Instead, the study uses several data collection techniques (triangulation) in order to produce a variety of qualitative and quantitative data. Taken together, these data provide detailed and extensive information about murder that may, in turn, be used to provide a better understanding of its nature and of the contexts in which it occurs. The three datasets include official statistics (Homicide Indexes for England/Wales and Scotland), case file documents from 866 instances of murder, and interviews with 200 men and women currently serving life in prison for murder. These different types of data were used in an effort to obtain a more comprehensive picture of the murder event and its context. Below, we consider in some detail the nature of two of these methods (the interview and documentary analysis) before examining how they were used in the Homicide in Britain study.

The interview

Although not without its shortcomings, the interview is clearly an extremely valuable and productive method for eliciting data that can contribute to empirically and theoretically informed knowledge about violence and murder. Interviews can provide rich, meaningful insights into participants' experiences and the meanings they attach to them, their feelings, attitudes and values. They can tell us about the discourses and language – verbal and non-verbal – which people use to construct their lived realities. Unlike non-interactive forms of data collection, they provide an opportunity to probe a participant in order to gain further insight and clarity. There is no doubt that interviews have made a major contribution to our understanding of the social world.

However, Lee (2000) reviews the criticism of the interview and notes how it may create as well as measure attitudes, may elicit atypical responses and may be limited to those who are accessible and amenable to participation. Accounts given at interview are inevitably partial and may reflect socially desirable responses from respondents who may underplay their own negative involvement in events. Such concerns are of particular relevance when the sample group is made up of perpetrators of lethal violence who have reason to minimise their culpability. Others have expressed concern about the possible impacts of interviews on respondents who may be emotionally aroused and/or 'provoked' into certain behaviours (Brannen, 1988; Burman *et al.*, 2001; Kennedy Bergen, 1993). Such concerns have generated discussion about the impacts of the language used in the interview, the relationship between interviewer and interviewee, the characteristics of the interviewer, the ordering of questions, and the emotional effects on both interviewer and interviewee.

Moreover, some criticisms go further as some post-modernists regard the interview as a 'topic' rather than a resource. From this perspective, information collected from interviews cannot reflect material and social reality but, rather, reflects only the subjective interaction between the interviewer and interviewee. Post-modernists are particularly interested in the language and discourses used in interviews but do not see these discourses as reflecting anything other than this subjective interaction. While criticism of research methods is essential to the continued development of social scientific good practice, it is vital to remember that all data collection techniques have their shortcomings. Views that imply that there is a superior, or even a perfect, technique impede rather than advance social science. Views that conclude that all data are simply a narrative, a fiction that can tell us about nothing more than the construction of the data through negotiated interaction between social actors, place such activities outside the boundaries of social science. Furthermore, this offers no means upon which to build social change, social policy or intervention.

While all methods are fallible, the fallibilities vary across methods. Using different methods that complement each other can minimise the impact of the fallibilities and narrow the gaps in knowledge (Lee, 2000). Such triangulation of sources has a long and respected history in the social sciences (Webb *et al.*, 1981). It avoids the well-worn and stagnant arguments about the supposed dichotomy of qualitative and quantitative methods. Moreover, using a variety of data sources can improve knowledge and understanding as the interpretation of one source aids the examination and interpretation of another. Bosworth (2001: 439) makes this point in relation to her archival study of the imprisonment of women, 'I was able to make sense of the documents, written in a different time and in another language, in part because of my experiences of research with women in contemporary prisons.' As we will go on to argue, the use and understanding of a variety of data sources in our own research about murder benefited from this kind of interactive approach.

Documentary analysis

Another source of information about murder is documentary evidence. While classical sociologists such as Marx, Durkheim and Weber relied on documentary investigation (Scott, 1990), this method has been relatively neglected by contemporary social scientists. In his discussion of 'human documents', Plummer (1983) makes the point that the collation and analysis of documents is rarely recognised as a valid method, or discussed in terms of what it can offer to the advancement of knowledge about the social world. For the most part, detailed documentary analysis has tended to be used by historians who have long recognised and valued the 'seduction of the archive' and the potential of documents to illuminate details about private lives and past events (Bradley, 1999). According to Bradley (1999: 108), the archive is a 'slippery concept' and is variously defined. Archival research, documentary research, and unobtrusive and non-reactive methods all include the examination of documents for the study of the social and/or historical world and there is a wide range of sources for such research. Plummer (1983) refers to 'human documents' such as letters, diaries, photos, memos, graffiti, suicide notes and tombstone memorials. Scott (1990) defines documents as 'physically embodied texts where the containment of the text is the primary purpose of the physical medium'. Others refer to archives that comprise 'records, documents, photographs, film, video and all the minutiae on which culture is inscribed' (Featherstone, 2000: 161), or 'personal diaries, account books, notarial documents, council minutes, or personal letters' (Milner, 1999: 90). Closer to our own topic of study, Gresswell and Hollin (1992) explore a 'new methodology' of using case material to explore attempted multiple murder.

These variously defined sources can shed light on private lives, past events, official perspectives. They are invaluable for historians and in many cases provide the only source of information about past eras. Consequently, a healthy debate has emerged about what these documents can tell us, and how historians do and should use such an important resource. Contrary to recent suggestions that there is a historical tradition of using documents in an empiricist, positivistic way as if they simply 'reveal' past reality, historians have long recognised the role played by interpretation and analysis. For example, Evans (1997) disputes the 'newness' of the post-modern critique about 'meaning', arguing that 'An awareness of the multiple meanings of texts, and their relative autonomy from the intentions of the author, has long been part of the stock-in-trade of the author' (Evans, 1997: 103). That is, historians have acknowledged that, rather than simply being read as straightforward, factual accounts, documents must be analysed, interpreted and contextualised in the processes of their production. But that analysis is not arbitrary or endless; it is limited by the text itself and awareness of the context in which it was written. Interpretation is not 'everything' as some post-modernists would have us believe. Evans (1997: 89) likens the process to the piecing together of a jigsaw:

> We imagine the contours, ... and have to speculate on quite a bit of detail; at the same time, however, the discovery of the existing pieces does set quite severe limits on the operation of our imagination. *If they only fit together to produce a picture of a steam-engine, for instance, it is no good trying to put them together to make a suburban garden: it simply will not work.* The fragmentary nature of the traces left to us by the past is thus no reason for supposing that historians' imagination is entirely unfettered when it comes to reconstructing it. [*Our emphasis*]

Similarly, when using documents to study murder, the information, ideas and the interpretations of events contained within them should not be treated as mere fictions with no objective reality. Such an approach seems particularly crass with respect to events involving violence and death and the documents about them. Instead of containing words that can be interpreted simply as 'discourse', such documents are dealing with a social and material reality that has real meanings, impacts and consequences.

While documents have been a key resource for historians, even within historical scholarship, the tendency has been to use them qualitatively. By contrast, in the Homicide in Britain study, documents were used to generate both qualitative and quantitative data for analysis. This integration of qualitative and quantitative data enables us to conduct both extensive analysis of patterns of murder and intensive analysis of descriptions, meanings and interpretations of such events and other related factors.

Whatever the form of data extracted from documents, there are always the questions about validity and reliability, and some historians have specifically addressed these issues. To ensure that interpretation of documentary evidence is valid, Scott (1990) suggests that researchers assess their data according to four criteria: *authenticity* (is the evidence of genuine or unquestionable origin?); *credibility* (is the evidence free from error or distortion?); *representativeness* (is evidence typical of its kind, or is extent of untypicality known?); *meaning* (is evidence clear and comprehensible?). Such a systematic, thorough and careful use of documents as a data source acknowledges both their value and their limitations, questions that must also be addressed when examining documents about murder.

The Homicide in Britain study

This is the first national study of Homicide in Britain and the first of its kind in Europe. The purpose of the study is to examine contexts, motivations and intentions of different types of murder. It provides a unique collection of data from three sources, the Homicide Index from England/Wales and from Scotland, casefile documents of men and women convicted of murder, and interviews with men and women serving life in prison for murder. We shall provide a brief description of each source of data but focus primarily on the documents and interviews and consider their contributions to furthering knowledge and understanding of this form of violence.

Official statistics: homicide index

The homicide indexes for the two major jurisdictions in mainland Britain (England/Wales and Scotland) provide information about every homicide event known as such to the police. Compiled from police information, the indexes contain a small number of variables (about 27 for England/Wales and 19 for Scotland) about each case. Most of the North American research on homicide relies on datasets such as these. These *extensive* datasets are useful for identifying broad patterns because they hold information about a large number of cases reported over many years. However, because of the limited amount of information about each case, they cannot provide information about contexts, situations and intentions associated with events as different as the killing of a crying infant, the killing of an elderly person during a burglary, a killing during a drunken brawl, or a killing during a rape or domestic assault.

In addition, because it is difficult or impossible to disaggregate data from the Homicide Index by type of homicide, any findings based on the entire dataset are, in fact, likely to reflect the nature and characteristics of the most frequently occurring type of homicide (men killing men) to the detriment of knowledge about other types (e.g. men killing women, men and women killing children, etc.). Despite the limited scope of these datasets, the homicide indexes aided in the development of the specific research questions for this study and the initial identification of types for the purpose of sampling. It provides one side of the triangulation that is a key feature of this research.

Documentary analysis

Casefiles of convicted murderers are held by the Prison Services in England/Wales and Scotland. Because of the gravity of the offence of murder and the indeterminate nature of the life sentence, the respective Prison Services hold extensive information about all individuals convicted of murder. This information is uniquely extensive in the case of men and women convicted of murder (as opposed to manslaughter or other offences). A total of 866 cases were analysed, comprising 786 men and 80 women. As shown in Table 3.1, the sample included about 20 per cent of men and 60 per cent of women serving life sentences for murder in England/Wales and about 35 per cent of men and 100 per cent of women in Scotland. It was obviously necessary to over-sample women in order to have a large enough number for analysis.

Table 3.1 Casefile sample

Country and gender	In prison for murder (no.)*	Casefile sample (no.)	Casefile % of murderers
England and Wales			
Men	3,000	612	20
Women	115	69	60
Scotland			
Men	500	174	35
Women	11	11	100
Total		**866**	

* Approximate number at time of study.

Casefiles typically include about 100 pages containing ten to 50 reports and documents from a range of sources. The contents of casefiles include:

- police reports from the murder investigation, including details of the murder and the context prior to the event; interviews with the offender and others including relatives of the offender and of the victim, neighbours, friends and others;
- coroner's report, including detailed description of injuries and assessment of likely cause of death;
- Trial Judge summary – a one- to two-page summary of key points from the trial, observations and recommended sentence including the tariff;[3]
- pre-sentence and post-sentence reports by a wide range of professionals including psychiatrists, social workers and probation officers, which often contained interviews with the offender and others;
- reports from prison staff throughout the sentence (including reports from psychologists, prison officers, wing governors, chaplains and education staff);
- reports from parole hearings (including reports from prison staff and submissions from the prisoner);
- some files also contained reports from former teachers, employers, probation officers, social workers, etc.

Quantitative and qualitative data were extracted from the sample of casefiles taken from the national archives in England and Scotland and from several institutions. Quantitative and qualitative data about a wide range of topics were extracted:

- *childhood background*, including family circumstances, education, problems as a child (disrupted caretaking, abuse, violence, alcohol and/or drug abuse, mental health problems), contact with the criminal justice system and 'helping' professionals;

- *adult life*, including history of employment, physical and mental health, drug and alcohol problems, social networks and intimate relationships, use of violence, and the nature and number of previous convictions and incarcerations;
- *circumstances prior to the event*, including living arrangements and relationships, alcohol and drug use, the context of the event, prior disputes and problems relating to the murder event;
- *the murder event*, including who was involved, the relationships between victim and offender, the nature of the violence and injuries, the offender's actions immediately after the murder;
- information about the *victim*, including relationship to offender, employment, marital status, etc;
- *the criminal justice process*, including police investigation, arrest and trial, charges, convictions and tariff;
- *life in prison*, including participation in programmes and counselling, offender's behaviour and adjustment, his/her orientation to the offence, problems related to alcohol and drug use and mental health.

Quantitative data were coded for analysis using SPSS and qualitative data were coded for analysis using QSR.NUD-IST. The quantitative dataset included 427 variables and the qualitative dataset contained 26 main nodes.

Combined, these two datasets form the richest dataset on murder in Britain. The casefiles were originally conceived of in a somewhat limited fashion. They were to be used as a source of information about the murder and the circumstances surrounding it and to provide a foundation of knowledge to inform the construction of the structured interview schedule which was originally conceived as the key data source. However, it immediately became clear that the casefile documents were so rich and extensive that they should be given a more central role in the research than originally anticipated. Accordingly, the information from the casefiles afforded the opportunity to create a unique dataset of intensive and extensive information about the risk factors, situational contexts and intentions associated with different types of murder.

Interviews with perpetrators

An important method of studying violence has been interviews with both victims and perpetrators. Interviews with perpetrators of physical and sexual violence have generated valuable information about their actions, perceptions and interpretations (Athens, 1980; Dobash *et al.*, 2000; Gondolf, 1987; Scully, 1990; Toch, 1969; Waterhouse *et al.*, 1994). However, most research about homicide has not used the interview and thus has failed to elicit information directly from perpetrators.[4] One element of the Homicide in Britain study was designed to fill this gap.

The failure to use the interview in the study of murder may be rooted in a belief that the accounts of perpetrators are likely to be so partial as to lose their value.

Indeed, these accounts may be affected by temporal distance from the event; the perpetrator's desire for social acceptability; personal changes since the murder which might affect his/her account of the event; and the interviewee's perception of the interviewer as a potential supporter in challenges concerning perceived maltreatment in the prison system and/or appeal against conviction. However, to see these factors as stripping perpetrators' accounts of their 'truth' is to misunderstand the value of the accounts. The accounts of perpetrators were examined in terms of what they tell us about their experiences in childhood, adulthood and at the time of the murder. They also provide insights into perpetrators' perceptions of the murder, the victim, the circumstances and their own intentions. As we argue below, perpetrators' accounts make an extremely valuable contribution to the understanding of murder and the contexts in which it occurs.

For the Homicide in Britain study, 200 interviews were conducted with 180 men and 20 women serving life in prison for murder (Table 3.2). Access to the interview sample was a complex and protracted process involving three stages: permission from the Home Office and Scottish Office; lengthy negotiations with various prison governors, psychologists and security staff in each prison which participated in the study; and agreement from individual prisoners to participate in the study. The specific approach to the individuals interviewed varied slightly in the different research sites (prisons), depending on the circumstances, regime and requirements of each. In each of the selected sites/prisons, all men and women serving life for murder were informed about the nature of the study, either in person or in writing, and asked if they wished to participate. It was possible to withdraw at any stage.[5]

Interviews were conducted privately on prison wings in interview rooms or other suitable locations, were tape-recorded and were timed around daily routines of work, meals and other activities. We were reliant upon the cooperation of prison staff for whom security was a key concern, but who nonetheless allowed us generous freedom of movement. There were, no doubt, various reasons for agreeing to be interviewed. Some said they appreciated the opportunity to talk in

Table 3.2 Interview sample

Country and gender	Interviews of prisoners (no.)	% of sample
England and Wales		
Men	143	71.5
Women	20	10.0
Scotland		
Men	37	18.5
Women*	0	0
Total	200	100.0

* Because of the small number of women in Scottish prisons, none were interviewed as it would have been impossible to maintain anonymity in the presentation of results.

detail with an independent person not connected with the prison service. A few said they had not spoken in such detail about so many aspects of their life since the start of their sentence. For others, it may have been the break in the prison routine that attracted them to participate in the study.

The interviews were conducted using a structured interview schedule covering the same topics as were covered in the casefiles. The schedule comprised a combination of structured and 'closed' questions in order to ensure that all topics were covered, as well as 'open' questions to enable the men and women to speak at length about any question and to raise additional issues. The interview schedule was over 20 pages in length and contained scores of questions about each of the main topics listed above. Most interviews lasted about one and a half to two hours and were tape recorded and transcribed for analysis using QSR.NUD-IST.

Complementary data from documents and interviews

These three data sources comprise the empirical base of the Homicide in Britain study. Here, we consider the casefiles and the strengths of documentary analysis and reflect on some aspects of its utility relative to those of the in-depth interview. It is not our purpose to elevate one data source over the other but, rather, to consider the relative contributions of each to the overall understanding of lethal violence.

As mentioned above, each casefile contained scores of documents from many different and often independent sources about the event and individuals concerned, particularly the offender(s). In that sense, there were numerous accounts (including that of the offender) that covered the same topics (e.g. childhood, adult circumstances, events prior to the murder, various aspects of the murder, and experiences in prison). Thus, the combined contents of the documents in the casefiles lead us to conclude that the data are both reliable and valid. Regardless of the type of observer (e.g. prison chaplain, medical officer, social worker, etc.), there was considerable continuity in the observations about the offender made by those who had interviewed him/her, sometimes on several occasions, and/or observed the offender on a daily basis. While the architecture of accounts was generally consistent, the content across a single casefile was not always the same, as some observers expressed different ideas or opinions about particular issues, acts or characteristics of the offender. Indeed, these differences reflect the validity of these accounts, which do not simply replicate each other but may reveal differing perspectives, concerns, remits and assessments of the various authors. Nor could the accounts be characterised as always or invariably presenting a negative view of the offender. Indeed, some praised offenders as 'good workers', 'reliable', 'cooperative' and the like. Both positive and negative evaluations of the offender were recorded in the quantitative and qualitative data. These features demonstrate the veracity and robustness of the information in these documents and, in turn, their importance to the findings of this research.

It should be stressed that individual interviews and casefile information were not examined together and that comparisons across the two datasets are made only on aggregate data and at a general level. However, at this general, aggregate level, there appears to be considerable correspondence between the information in the *casefiles* and the first-person accounts from the *interviews*, but there are also differences to be noted. For the purposes of this research, it was important to have a first-person account as we attempted to gain further insight into the motivations and intentions involved in the murder and to increase our insight into rationalisations or justifications that might be used by the offender. While some of this information might already exist in one of the prior interviews contained in the casefile we, nonetheless, wished to probe as deeply as possible into a variety of issues in order to provide a more developed understanding of the murder event. In this sense, it was essential to interview the offenders as well as examine the casefiles in order to have a first-person account from the offender given in interview about *their* perspective, *their* motivations and *their* intentions whatever these may be.

It might be asked, however, whether it was necessary to use the casefile information rather than simply interview the offender and treat this as the only or the most 'authentic' source of information about the person and the event. Here, we consider what, if any, knowledge or information might be available from the casefiles that might not be available from the interview, and *vice versa*, and reflect on the relationship between the two sources.

A key benefit of the casefiles is that they provide a longitudinal account of the offender's life since conviction. Casefiles are regularly updated with documents (which are generated by the parole process) during the time of imprisonment. This means that they contain accounts about the offender over a period of anything from one to 30 years, depending on the length of sentence served. This provides a valuable historical overview of changes in offenders' behaviour and problems; orientations to self, the murder, the victim; attitudes and beliefs. While some interviewees were able to reflect on such aspects of their lives over a period of time, others – typically those who were at an earlier stage of their sentence and/or who were experiencing ongoing problems – were less able to do so. Moreover, in a research interview, when an interviewee reflects on his/her history, s/he does so at one fixed point in time. By contrast, the documents in a casefile are written at different points in time and may thus be used to reflect changes over time. In this sense, interviews generally provide a valuable 'snapshot' while casefiles provide a gradually unfolding, longitudinal account.

As described above, casefile documents provide accounts from a variety of perspectives (e.g. psychiatrists, chaplains, probation officers), based on professional practice observations or interviews with the defendant/prisoner. In this sense, the research interview is one more among the many interviews with the offender. It was stressed that the interviews were independent and confidential. For some, this provided an opportunity to discuss issues (e.g. childhood sex abuse) they may not have discussed before; for others, the interviews with researchers may have differed very little from those with others who had interviewed them before.

An example of the complementary information from casefiles and interviews is revealed by considering information about the stability of caretaking in childhood. Information in the casefiles made it possible to use aggregate data to examine patterns showing the number and type of caretakers during the childhood of offenders from a sample of 866 (Dobash *et al.*, 2002) and similar patterns from the smaller number of interviews (n = 200). In addition, the interviews allowed us to gather more information and detail about the circumstances, perceptions and interpretations of early life from this sample. Here, the casefile data provide a better indicator of the *pattern* of childhood caretaking from a large sample of individuals, while the interview data provide greater *detail* about such circumstances and interpretations from a smaller sample. This is an example of how qualitative and quantitative data support and complement each other, rather than competing for pre-eminence.

For the purposes of obtaining first-person accounts of the offender's motivations, intentions and interpretations, the interview is essential, but it must be stressed that the interview cannot stand alone as the sole source of information for a variety of reasons. For example, a detailed picture of such things as the nature of attacks and injuries or the level of alcohol consumption may be obtained with some accuracy from forensic information in casefiles but may not be known or remembered by the offender and thus it may not always be possible to obtain this information in the interview. Offenders may be unable to give information such as the number of stab wounds in a frenzied attack, or the amount of alcohol consumed before the attack. Here, the offender simply may not be able to provide accurate information no matter how hard s/he tries to do so. On the other hand, there may also be information that offenders may be unwilling to admit such as certain forms of sexual attack or a history of violence towards the victim before the murder.[6]

With respect to issues such as interpretations of the event and the respective roles of offender and victim, first-person accounts given in interviews with offenders sometimes implicate or 'blame' the victim. On the other hand, information in the casefiles provides detail about the context, relationships and behaviours of the victim and offender which may lead to a different interpretation. While this presents a dilemma for the researcher about how to analyse, interpret and present these differing accounts, it is nonetheless important to have such 'alternative' accounts rather than simply relying on the first-person narrative from the interview (for discussion of differing accounts of violent events, see Cavanagh *et al.*, 2001; Dobash *et al.*, 1998).

In addition, having information about both sources of data assisted in the collection of information from each. For example, becoming familiar with the content of casefile reports alerted us to the potential reluctance of some interviewees to admit to certain aspects of the murder. We were thus able to anticipate possible 'gaps' that might occur in the interview and to build into the interview schedule specific 'probes' that might assist us in obtaining information that might otherwise be missed. On the other hand, the interview data complemented the casefile data by providing further insight into issues not always covered at length or not contained in the casefiles. These included interpretations of the murder event, reflections on childhood experiences, and personal insight into the level of dependence on alcohol and the like or, indeed, resistance to the notion of such dependence in spite of a lifestyle that would suggest otherwise. In short, the interview allowed for exploration of information not covered in detail in the casefiles and *vice versa*. Overall, the two types of information could be used in an aggregate form (not by case) to complement one another in terms of obtaining both extensive and intensive information about a large number of relevant issues.

Overall, the aggregate results from the casefile data and the aggregate results from the interviews lead to a more complex understanding of the different types of murder, the risk factors, circumstances and intentions associated with each. As we have discussed, the casefiles may provide valuable information, which may not be available in the interview and *vice versa*. The point here is that the two sources of data strengthen and expand the base of knowledge upon which to build empirically informed explanations of human behaviour. Together, these datasets comprise the most complete collection of data about murder in Britain today. It is our contention that only such an integration of qualitative and quantitative data from a variety of sources can provide such a rich, substantive body of evidence about the event of murder and the situations and circumstances in which it occurs.

Notes

1 This chapter was written when Ruth Lewis was Parsons Visiting Scholar at the School of Law, University of Sydney, Australia.
2 See for example the special edition of *British Journal of Criminology*, 2001; Kirkwood, 1993; Brannen, 1988.
3 The tariff is the recommended period to be served in prison. It is recommended by the Trial Judge and reviewed by the Lord Chief Justice but responsibility for the length of the tariff lies with the Home Secretary. The tariff can be a topic of dispute for prisoners because it is seen as an indicator of the perceived severity of the offence and culpability of the offender. In addition, it has a major influence on the timing of the first parole hearing and the process and timing leading to release. The sentence served by a prisoner is usually longer than the tariff.
4 Australian research on homicide uses both quantitative and qualitative data (e.g. Polk, 1994) that provides a rich picture of the contexts and meanings of lethal violence.
5 A few potential participants were excluded because they were defined by prison staff as a risk to prison security or a risk to female staff/researchers or because they had mental health problems or they did not speak English.
6 For example, men who use violence against their female partners tend to under-report the extent, nature and consequences of their violence (Dobash *et al.*, 1998).

References

Athens, Lonnie, 1980, *Violent Criminal Acts and Actors: A Symbolic Interactionist Study*. London: Routledge.

Becker, H, 1963, *Outsiders: Studies in the Sociology of Deviance*. London: Free Press of Glencoe.

Bosworth, Mary, 2001, 'The Past as a Foreign Country?' in *British Journal of Criminology*, vol. 41, pp. 431–42.

Bourgois, Phillippe, 1995, *In Search of Respect: Selling Crack in El Barrio*. Cambridge: Cambridge University Press.

Bradley, Harriet, 1999, 'The Seductions of the Archive: Voices Lost and Found' in *History of the Human Sciences*, vol. 12, no. 2, pp. 107–22.

Brannen, Julia, 1988, 'Research Note: The Study of Sensitive Subjects' in *Sociological Review* 36/3: 552–63.

British Journal of Criminology, 2001, vol. 41.

Burman, Michele J., Batchelor, Susan A. and Brown, Jane A., 2001, 'Researching Girls and Violence: Facing the Dilemmas of Fieldwork' in *British Journal of Criminology*, vol. 41.

Campbell, Jacquelyn C., 2001, 'Risk Factors for Femicide in Abusive Relationships: Results from a Multi-site Case Control Study', unpublished paper.

Cavanagh, K., Dobash, R. Emerson, Dobash, R. P. and Lewis, R., 2001, ' "Remedial Work": Men's Strategic Responses to Their Violence Against Intimate Female Partners' in *Sociology*, vol. 35, no. 3, pp. 695–714.

Cavanagh, K. and Lewis, R., 1996, 'Interviewing Violent Men: Compromise or Challenge?' in K. Cavanagh and V. Cree (eds) *Working With Men: Feminism and Social Work*. London: Routledge, pp. 87–112.

Dobash, R. E. and Dobash, R. P., 1998, 'Cross-border Encounters: Challenges and Opportunities' in R. E. Dobash and R. P. Dobash (eds) *Rethinking Violence Against Women*. Thousand Oaks, CA: Sage, pp. 1–21.

Dobash, R. E. and Dobash, R. P., 1983, 'The Context Specific Approach to Researching Violence against Wives' in D. Finkelhor, R. J. Gelles, G. T. Hotaling and M. A. Strauss (eds) *The Dark Side of Families*. Thousand Oaks, CA: Sage, pp. 261–76.

Dobash, R. P. and Dobash R. Emerson, 1979, *Violence Against Wives: A Case Against the Patriarchy*. New York: Free Press.

Dobash, R. E., Dobash, R. P., Cavanagh, K. and Lewis, R., 2002, 'Homicide in Britain: Risk Factors, Situational Contexts and Lethal Intentions (Focus on male offenders)', *Research Findings No. 1, Homicide in Britain*, University of Manchester, Dept of Applied Social Science website.

Dobash, R. P., Dobash, R. E., Cavanagh, K. and Lewis, R., 1997, 'Separate and Intersecting Realities: A Comparison of Men's and Women's Accounts of Violence Against Women', in *Violence Against Women*, vol. 4, no. 4, August, pp. 382–414.

Dobash, R. P., Dobash, R. E., Cavanagh, K. and Lewis, R., 2000, *Changing Violent Men*. Thousance Oaks, CA: Sage.

Dobash, R. E., Dobash, R. P., Wilson M. and Daly, M., 1992, 'The Myth of Sexual Symmetry in Marital Violence' in *Social Problems*, 39, 1, pp. 71–91.

Evans, Richard J., 1997, *In Defence of History*. London: Granta.

Featherstone, Mike, 2000, 'Archiving Cultures' in *British Journal of Sociology*, vol. 51, no. 1, pp. 161–84.

Fielding, N., 1981, *The National Front*. London: Routledge and Kegan Paul.

Gondolf, Edward W., 1987, 'The Gender Warrior: Reformed Batterers on Abuse, Treatment and Change' in *Journal of Family Violence*, vol. 2, no. 2, pp. 177–91.

Gresswell, D. M. and Hollin, C. R., 1992, 'Towards a New Methodology for Making Sense of Case Material: An Illustrative Case Involving Attempted Multiple Murder' in *Criminal Behaviour and Mental Health*, 2: pp. 329–41.

Harding, Sandra, 1911, *Whose Science? Whose Knowledge? Thinking From Women's Lives.* New York: Cornell University Press.

Hobbs, Dick and May, Tim, 1993, *Interpreting the Field: Accounts of Ethnography.* Oxford: Clarendon Press.

Johnson, H., 1996, *Dangerous Domains: Violence Against Women in Canada.* Toronto: Nelson Canada.

Johnson, Holly, 1998, 'Rethinking Survey Research on Violence against Women' in R. E. Dobash and R. P. Dobash (eds) *Rethinking Violence Against Women.* Thousand Oaks, CA: Sage, pp. 23–51.

Kelly, Lie, 1999, *Domestic Violence Matters: An Evaluation of a Development Project.* London: Home Office research study, No. 193.

Kelly, Liz, Burton, Sheila and Regan, Linda, 1994, 'Researching Women's Lives or Studying Women's Oppression? Reflections on What Constitutes Feminist Research' in Mary Maynard and June Purvis (eds) *Researching Women's Lives from a Feminist Perspective.* London: Taylor and Francis.

Kennedy Bergen, Raquel, 1993, 'Interviewing Survivors of Marital Rape: Doing Feminist Research on Sensitive Topics' in C. M. Renzetti, and Lee, R. M. (eds) *Researching Sensitive Topics.* Newbury Park, CA: Sage.

Kirkwood, C., 1993, 'Investigating Ourselves: Use of Researcher Personal Response in Feminist Methodology' in J. De Groot and M. Maynards (eds) *Perspectives on Women's Studies for the 1990s: Doing Things Differently?* London: Macmillan.

Lee, Raymond, 2000, *Unobtrusive Methods in Social Research.* Buckingham: Open University Press.

Maher, L., 1995, 'In the Name of Love: Women and Initiation to Illicit Drugs' in R. E. Dobash, R.P. Dobash and L. Noaks, *Gender and Crime.* Cardiff: University of Wales Press, pp. 132–66.

Milner, S. J., 1999, 'Partial Readings: Addressing a Renaissance Archive' in *History of the Human Sciences*, vol. 12, no. 2, pp. 89–105.

Mirrlees-Black, C., 1994, 'Estimating the Extent of Domestic Violence: Findings from the 1992 British Crime Survey (Home Office Research Bulletin, No. 37). London: Home Office Research and Statistics Department.

Nazroo, James, 1995, 'Uncovering Gender Differences in the Use of Marital Violence: The Effect of Methodology' in *Sociology*, vol. 29, no. 3: pp. 475–94.

Plummer, Ken, 1983, *Documents of Life: an Introduction to the Problems and Literature of a Humanistic Method.* London: George Allen & Unwin.

Polk, Kenneth, 1994, *When Men Kill: Scenarios of Masculine Violence.* Melbourne: Cambridge University Press.

Renzetti, C. M. and Lee, R. M. (eds), 1993, *Researching Sensitive Topics.* Newbury Park, CA: Sage.

Reinharz, S., 1992, *Feminist Methods in Social Research.* Oxford: Oxford University Press.

Riedel, Mark, 1999, 'Sources of Homicide Data: A Review and Comparison' in M. D. Smith and M. A. Zahn (eds) *Homicide: A Sourcebook of Social Research.* London: Sage, pp. 75–95.

Scott, John, 1990, *A Matter of Record.* Cambridge: Polity Press.

Scully, D. 1990, *Understanding Sexual Violence: A Study of Convicted Rapists*. Boston: Unwin Hyman.

Smith, M. D. and Zahn, M. A. (eds), 1999, *Homicide: A Sourcebook of Social Research*. London: Sage.

Tseloni, Andromachi, 1995, 'The Modelling of Threat Incidence: Evidence from the British Crime Survey' in R. E. Dobash, R. P. Dobash and L. Noaks (eds) *Gender and Crime*. Cardiff: University of Wales Press, pp. 269–94.

Toch, H. 1969, *Violent Men: An Inquiry into the Psychology of Violence*. Chicago: Aldine Publishing Co.

Waterhouse, L., Dobash, R. P. and Carnie, J., 1994, *Child Sexual Abusers*. The Scottish Office Central Research Unit, New St Andrew's House, Edinburgh, Scotland. Crown Copyright.

Webb, E. J., Campbell, D. T., Schwartz, R. D. and Sechrest, L., 1981, *Nonreactive Measures in the Social Sciences*. Dallas: Houghton Mifflin.

Yllo, Kersti, 1988, 'Feminist Perspectives on Wife Abuse: An Introduction' in Yllo and Bograd (eds) *Feminist Perspectives on Wife Abuse*. Newbury Park, CA: Sage, pp. 11–26.

Part II
Enhancing data on violence

4   Tracking the pathways to violence in prison

*Kimmett Edgar, Ian O'Donnell and
Carol Martin*

'We were unlocked at 4.30. I was on the second landing and he was on the first. I called out and asked him what was in his bowl. He said, "Piss off!" and I said, "Come here". He ran up and we started arguing and then he pushed me against the wall and we started fighting.'

The ways in which sociologists can study prison violence are limited. One way is to measure how often it occurs (the counting approach). A different approach explores the dynamics of interactions that lead to violence. We begin this chapter by describing statistical information about prison violence and how it can be gathered. We then describe a conflict-centred approach by which we analysed prisoners' accounts of the sequences that lead to violence, to set fights and assaults within the context of conflicts between prisoners.

Official statistics give one indication of the rates of fights and assaults, based on the number of times prisoners are charged with an offence against prison discipline by an officer and processed through an adjudication before the governor. However, these figures do not represent the actual rates of violent incidents because prisoners are often reluctant to report incidents to an officer (O'Donnell and Edgar, 1998a: 40–43), and officers sometimes handle incidents informally (Liebling, 2000).

Another counting method, the prisoner survey, relies on the self-reported experience of prisoners, usually gathered through questionnaires. Three examples from the UK are the National Prison Survey (Walmsley *et al.*, 1992), the work of King and McDermott (1995) and the victimisation survey conducted by O'Donnell and Edgar (1998a). Evidence about the extent of prison violence gleaned from these methods is summarised by Anthony Bottoms (1999) in his comprehensive critique of the literature.

A self-report measure of violence

The self-completion questionnaire which O'Donnell and Edgar used to measure victimization in prisons and young offender institutions was predominantly in a tick-box format. The eight-page form was distributed to over 1,700 prisoners and collected by the researchers themselves, thus maintaining the respondents' anonymity. The questions specifically about victimisation were:

How many times over the past one month:

- have you been called hurtful names or have other prisoners made insulting remarks about your family or girlfriend?
- have other prisoners tried to stop you joining in activities, for example not allowed you to play pool or watch TV?
- have you been asked by another prisoner to give him your canteen?
- has anybody stolen your private property from your cell?
- has another prisoner threatened you with violence?
- have you been hit, kicked or in any other way assaulted by another prisoner?

The survey also measured the prisoners' experiences as victimisers, asking them how often they had played the active role in each of the six behaviours listed above.

O'Donnell and Edgar's victimization survey illustrates the kind of information about harmful conduct in prisons that can be gained from a self-report counting approach. Some of their key findings were that 30 per cent of young offenders and 19 per cent of adult males stated that they had been assaulted on at least one occasion in the past one month. Prisoners reported having been threatened with violence at higher rates: 44 per cent of young offenders and 26 per cent of adult males. The self-reported rates of robbery ('demanding one's canteen') were much lower: 10 per cent of young offenders and 4 per cent of adult males. (See further O'Donnell and Edgar, 1998b.)

The data on prisoners victimizing others demonstrated that assaultive behaviour was not limited to a small minority. One in three young offenders and one in six adult males stated that they had assaulted another prisoner in the past one month, while two in five young offenders and one in five adult males reported that they had threatened another prisoner with violence.

Victimization surveys can produce reliable evidence about the prevalence of prison violence. Further, depending on how the questions are constructed and analysed, this method can shed light on risk factors associated with violent victimization, prisoners' attitudes (for example, about personal safety in prison), the gravity of injuries sustained in fights and assaults, and the likelihood that an assaulted prisoner would report any incident of victimization to prison authorities. It also allows statistical tests on the relationships between these variables.

The typical scale of the survey method – often comprising hundreds of self-report questionnaires – means that it is not well-suited to detailed explorations of the circumstances in which interpersonal violence arises. Surveys tend to be silent on what violence and victimization *mean* to the parties directly involved.

A different approach to explaining prison violence requires answers to questions such as:

- Why are some encounters between prisoners more likely than others to result in violence?
- What kinds of relationships between assailants and their victims (or prisoners who fight each other) exist prior to the incident?
- What tensions between the interests of individual prisoners drive them into disputes?
- What tactics do prisoners characteristically use when they are in conflict with other prisoners?
- What do people hope to achieve by using violence?
- What information about interpersonal violence between prisoners would be most useful in attempting to prevent prison violence?

As Bottoms (1999: 212) remarks:

> Researchers speak of 'interactionist' approaches, but they have rarely addressed the minutiae of the average prison day, or considered in detail how violence can arise within this social order.

A focus on interactions between prisoners as a source of explanations for violence in prison requires a method that can gather and analyse the prisoners' interpretations of the situations they face. The approach must also provide a means to build a comprehensive picture of events from as many perspectives as possible. Crucially, violence needs to be explored as a process, rather than an incident caught in a slice of time.

On this last point, Ben Bowling contrasted approaches that focus on individual incidents and those that view social phenomena as part of a *process*. He argued that racist violence was open to distortion when it was described in terms of an isolated incident. Bowling wrote (1998: 158) that conceiving of racist violence as a process

> is dynamic; includes the social relationships between all the actors involved in the process; can capture the continuity between physical violence, threat, and intimidation; can capture the dynamic of repeated or systematic victimization; incorporates historical context; and takes account of the social relationships which inform definitions of appropriate and inappropriate behaviour.

A conflict-centred approach to prison violence

Conflicts and Violence in Prison explored the interactions between prisoners that led to fights, assaults and other violence (see Edgar and Martin, 2001). The primary means of data-gathering were in-depth interviews with those who were associated with violent incidents: the parties directly involved in the fight, assault or other kind of dispute (209); prisoners who witnessed the incident (51); and, where relevant, officers who placed one or both prisoners on a disciplinary charge (58) and governors who conducted the adjudications (32).

The in-depth interviews with the 209 participants, covering 141 fights, assaults and other incidents of interpersonal violence, sought the prisoners' perspectives on the circumstances that led to violence in three ways – via:

- brief descriptions, in their own words, of the incidents;
- responses to over 100 direct questions, exploring, for example, their prior relationships with their counterparts and the interests that divided them, the influence of bystanders, and the role of prison staff;
- the use of an instrument we termed, 'the Escalator', a schema for logging an account of an incident in a step-by-step sequence.

The interactions between prisoners that resulted in violence can be described as conflicts in that the parties pursued competing interests in uncompromising ways. For this reason, we refer to the approach pioneered in this study as a conflict-centred approach to prison violence. The interviews were designed to gather information from the prisoners' perspective to help explain the processes that led one or both parties deliberately to harm the other. To capture the dynamic processes by which conflicts escalated into physical violence, tools were required to record the perspectives of each party; to explore what guided their decision-making, how they understood the other parties' intentions, and how they thought one state of affairs led to the next.

The Escalator

The Escalator was originally developed in the field of conflict resolution (Alternatives to Violence Project (AVP), 1996). We used it as a tool to elicit, from the prisoners interviewed, their version of the sequence of events by which conflicts developed into violence. The Escalator illustrated the conflicts as dynamic interactions between the parties involved. Further, it provided a structure that helped the respondents to explain how they had interpreted the intentions of their counterparts as the disputes evolved.

The participant was shown a blank form indicating a series of steps and asked, 'What was the first thing that happened between you and the other party?' Their response was recorded on the first step of the Escalator. They were asked, 'What happened next?' and the second step was recorded. The participants were then able to complete the process. In some cases, writing down the steps sparked prisoners into recalling further details about the course of events, which were then inserted at the relevant points. The prisoners seemed to benefit from the opportunity to describe a violent incident as a step-by-step sequence in that it reflected to them a satisfying explanation of how their disputes had resulted in violence. A completed Escalator is presented as Figure 4.1.

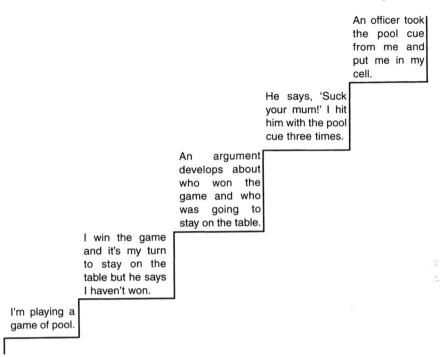

An officer took the pool cue from me and put me in my cell.

He says, 'Suck your mum!' I hit him with the pool cue three times.

An argument develops about who won the game and who was going to stay on the table.

I win the game and it's my turn to stay on the table but he says I haven't won.

I'm playing a game of pool.

Figure 4.1 The Escalator

From each account of the steps leading to a violent incident there emerged a picture of a dynamic interaction through which each party pursued his or her interests. Escalators highlighted the game-like interplay by which one person decided on the next move as a response to their interpretation of the other person's behaviour. Thus, through the Escalator, the route towards violence appeared as partly determined and partly a matter of choice.

When the prisoner was satisfied with the step-by-step account of the escalation of the conflict, the Escalator facilitated other lines of questioning. Examples of supplementary questions and responses are presented in Figure 4.2.

The completed sequence was used to elicit the prisoner's interests in the situation: what he or she wanted to achieve and, in micro-scale, the purpose of any particular action the person had taken. Further, any step could serve as the basis for exploring the person's interpretations of the process and the inferences they drew about the purposes of the other party.

Through questions about the options available to the respondent at points along the way, the Escalator presented the prisoners with the possibility that sometimes the violence could have been averted. In fact, a more complete framework for some of the disputes would show steps going down when a prisoner did something that reduced the tensions or opened up possibilities for a peaceful resolution. It is possible that the ever-ascending staircase and the title, Escalator,

---

Intentions and consequences

Q. What do you think he was trying
  to achieve?

*He was trying to piss me off. He knew it
would wind me up.*

Q. What were you trying to achieve?
Respect.

Q. What did it actually do?
*I got it – in front of somebody else – they
see what happened.*

Q. At what point do you think the
  situation actually became violent?
When he said, 'Suck your mum!'

Prevention

Q. Was there anything you could have
  done to prevent the incident?
I could have just let him play.

Q. Was there anything he could have
  done to prevent violence?
He could have just accepted that he lost.

Figure 4.2 Supplementary questions

modelled for prisoners an image of a mechanical sequence inevitably ending in violence. In one sense this was appropriate, as the basis for interviewing the majority of prisoners in the study was that they had been involved in a fight or assault. In retrospect, it might have been helpful to prisoners to show them a sample which included downward, de-escalating steps.

A particular benefit of using escalators to record personal accounts was the ease with which we were able to juxtapose one version of events against another. Often one person provided information that was lacking in the other's perspective. For example, Box 1 comprises the accounts of Wye and Gregson (fictitious names) about a fight (see Appendix).

Wye was angry because she believed that Gregson had smoked a spliff (cannabis) that was meant for her. Wye's perspective is based on her presupposition that Gregson had smoked Wye's share. Gregson's account suggests that a third inmate was to blame. Their contrasting stories also show how crossed-communication aggravated their dispute. Wye's account stated that she had gone away to calm down by gaining time in the privacy of her own cell. According to Gregson's version, she went to Wye's cell with the intention of resolving the conflict. Gregson had misinterpreted the cue that Wye wanted to be left alone – or she believed that settling the dispute was so urgent that she had antagonised Wye by pursuing her to her cell.

Two-sided escalators generally conveyed a much stronger picture than those from one participant alone, of the dynamic interaction by which disputes deepened and led to physical violence. The different (sometimes contradictory) perspectives of the participants showed clearly how their interpretations of the other's behaviour fuelled the conflict. (Three of the two-sided escalators are appended to this chapter, as Boxes 1, 2, and 3, illustrating the range of situations which this technique opened to investigation and analysis. These transcribe the horizontal chronology of the original staircase into a vertical format so that the two accounts can be seen in parallel.)

The Escalator is not suited to every kind of violence. It works best at the level of interpersonal (as opposed to collective) conflict. Nor is it well-adapted to a focus on the interaction between the prisoner and the social setting. However, the conflict-centred method, through the use of the Escalator, was able to show violence as an outcome of:

- a clear sequence of events;
- an interplay between the behaviour, interpretations and intentions of those involved;
- an interplay between causal chains and personal choices.

Further, the Escalator drew out:

- opposing perspectives – to gain a more balanced and complete understanding of what had happened;
- non-violent options – possibilities for a peaceful resolution of the problems between prisoners that led to violence.

In these ways, the Escalator was a vital tool in systematically analysing the interpersonal dynamics of conflicts between prisoners.

The use of personal accounts in sociology

The use of prisoner narratives is well-established. For example, they have been used to dramatic effect by Sabo *et al.* (2001) in their collection on prison masculinities. However, possible pitfalls arise when people's accounts of events are used to explore social phenomena. For example, Roger Hood and Kate Joyce (1999: 140) who analysed the life histories of three generations of people living in London's East End, highlighted the risks of respondents'

> selective amnesia, telescoping of events, reinterpretation in the light of later experiences and changing self perception, suppression of unpleasant memories or exaggeration of one's own involvement.

The chief benefit of approaches based on personal accounts of events is that these methods honour the person's individual perspective on their experience. Blumer (1969: 2) spelled out the importance of exploring the meanings that people give to their behaviour. He set out three premises on which the theory of Symbolic Interactionism was based:

The first premise is that human beings act towards things on the basis of the meanings that the things have for them. ...

The second premise is that the meaning of such things is derived from, or arises out of, the social interaction that one has with one's fellows.

The third premise is that these meanings are handled in, and modified through, an interpretative process used by the person in dealing with the things he encounters.

We sought to explain violent incidents by analysing the interpretations each person made as their interactions progressed. Our understanding of the geometry of conflicts was made possible by the rich detail we gained from the participants' personal accounts.

Harvey *et al.* (1990) discussed the use of personal accounts in studying the impact of marital breakdown. Their insights about account-making have direct implications for analysing prisoners' narratives of fights and assaults. They suggested that accounts contain an implied causal structure: one event leads to the next in a series of steps. One of the benefits of the Escalator was that the prisoner became engaged in the task of setting out how the exchanges were driven towards a violent outcome through each decision, action or statement.

In many cases, their brief descriptions were limited to records of the physical interaction. In contrast, the escalators uncovered complex patterns of thinking about how one person's responses influenced the other's next move. To take one, particularly stark, example, a prisoner's brief description (in full) stated: 'A *fight with fists – not knives.*' Later in the interview, his escalator account extended to 13 steps:

1   I gave Easton some stuff in trade for five phone cards.
2   He paid me two cards back.
3   He said he would pay me three next week.
4   He didn't come near me.
5   I knew someone he had had some stuff from. I said, 'Has Easton paid you?'
6   He said, 'Yeah.'
7   I went to Easton's cell.
8   I confronted him, 'You've paid other people. You're taking the piss.'
9   Him, 'No, I haven't got any.'
10 I head-butted him.
11 He threw a punch – got me in the eye.
12 I weighed him in [assaulted him].
13 I said, 'Debt done.' I walked out. Finished. Done.

Harvey *et al.* also made the point that, in telling a story, the person declares an identity. The account sets out a representation of the self – in part who they think they are; in part, who they would like to be. In this way, personal accounts can be used to bolster self-esteem. The prisoners' escalators also showed strong evidence of efforts to bolster self-esteem. For example, in one incident, an argument over a game led to physical violence. Each of the participants declared that the problem arose when he won the game. Neither was able to concede, even in the anonymous privacy of a social research interview, that he had lost.

Some prisoners reported that they had inflicted more harm than they really had as a means of making themselves appear more powerful, whereas others under-stated the harm they caused, perhaps because they were afraid of how the interviewer might react to stories of scaldings, stabbings or the use of weapons. The Escalator structure includes few checks on respondent honesty (although when used in conjunction with other, direct questions, we could cross-check responses for consistency.)

The explanation of violence by the person who uses it can be seen as an attempt to claim legitimacy for the use of force. David Riches (1986) argued that moral grounds are used to distinguish force from violence. The need to justify any use of force raises the question: Given that the account-giver was personally involved in a violent incident, how can the account be trusted to be a true reflection of events?

Gresham Sykes and David Matza (1957) listed ways in which respondents could use accounts to justify their behaviour. These techniques of neutralisation link account-making and self-justification. Some of the characteristics Sykes and Matza cited emerged in accounts of violence by the parties involved – the claim that others behaved in the same way, the minimisation of the harm they had inflicted, the evasion of responsibility for consequences and so on. But the possible influence of neutralising techniques can be exaggerated.

Indeed, the opportunity to compare contrasting (and sometimes contradictory) accounts of the same events often produced clear explanations of how a conflict escalated into physical violence. Sometimes the conflicting accounts showed a lack of communication, as each party to a dispute had mis-read the other's intentions. Sometimes the respondents used the Escalator part of the interview to continue their dispute – each vying to give the authoritative version of events. As the escalators comprising Boxes 1, 2 and 3 demonstrate, gathering each party's account enabled us to form a more complete picture of events than would have been accessible through either person's account in isolation. (In particular, compare Shildon's escalator account in Box 2 to the explanation that Leek gave in describing the fight with which we opened this chapter.)

In practice, however, the demands of confidentiality and anonymity sometimes meant that the name of the respondent's opposite number in the conflict was hidden from us. It would have been impossible to ask a prisoner to discuss an incident which he or she had not disclosed personally to us without raising the suspicion that the other party had informed on him or her. The lack of a second perspective was most common in the dispersal (high security) prison. There, we were able to gain both sides to the story in only two of the 14 incidents which had resulted in a fight or assault.

Harvey *et al.* linked explanation to feelings of control. Account-makers use their accounts of events to find a satisfying explanation of what happened, and in those explanations are reassurances of personal control. The aspect of personal control can be claimed in regard to the events the story-teller is relating, when they suggest that they caused something to happen; or, the mere act of retelling a story, by providing a satisfying explanation, can restore the person's sense that they have some control over their lives.

Finally, the structure of an account necessarily implies a plot – a beginning, development and an end. The way in which an account concludes can facilitate closure – both in the emotional sense of feeling that the problem has been resolved and in the more practical sense of providing a picture of events that have fully run their course. The Escalator gave respondents the power to decide when a situation began and when it reached its conclusion. Thus, in the interviews many prisoners presented accounts that ended when physical violence was used. These escalators, unfortunately, lead to the impression that physical violence resolves the problem, or at least brings the conflict to an end.

In terms of narrative structure, violence is often portrayed as the end of a story (see especially René Girard, 1977) – the outcome towards which events were inevitably heading. It is important to recognise and question the myth that locates violence as an end to a train of events. Seeing violence as part of a process rather than an outcome helps to show that an act of violence can lead to a further escalation of the conflict and, equally important, that violence is often undertaken through decisions that could have been different, could have led to non-violent outcomes. These characteristics of account-making imply that methods based on personal accounts have great potential to help explain why violence occurs.

An analytical framework for mapping conflict

The escalators, backed up by data gained through the interviews, official records and field observations, provided a wealth of descriptive material about the circumstances leading to fights, assaults and other violence. The diversity of the accounts created a problem for interpretation – how could these situations be analysed in a coherent and meaningful way?

The origins of the disputes varied greatly, encompassing: disagreements over who had won a game of table tennis, allegations of 'grassing', disputes about material goods (e.g. tobacco or drugs), racial tensions, and other, broader concerns. In their accounts, prisoners placed emphasis on diverse elements of their disputes: some stressed the words each party used; others, the influence of third parties; still others focused on graphic descriptions of physical combat.

The literature of practitioners and theorists in conflict resolution provided hints about how to analyse disputes. Roger Fisher and William Ury (1997) advocated an approach that focused on identifying the interests at stake. John Burton (1990) distinguished material interests that can spark disputes from the underlying basic needs that maintain lasting conflicts. Andrew Acland (1997) identified the importance of relationships, including the attitudes and feelings each party had for the other. Finally, the sociological theory of Symbolic Interactionism provided support for the view that people's interpretations of what was happening would be crucial to understanding why they decided to respond to conflicts as they did (see Herbert Blumer, 1969 and Lonnie Athens, 1997).

From these sources, we began to develop a rough coding frame of the general ingredients of conflict. The key dimensions seemed to be:

- deconstruction: an initial check by the research team of each account for internal consistency, omitted details, implied self images, and discrepancies between the parties' accounts;
- spark: the trigger that immediately preceded the use of injurious force;
- interests: what the conflict was about;
- relationships: the social distance between the parties;
- tactics or catalysts: how the parties conducted themselves throughout the dispute;
- interpretations: how each person understood the other person's conduct;
- motivations: feelings that drove the protagonists to conduct the conflict in specific ways;
- purposes: the reasons why the person decided to use injurious force;
- social context: aspects of the setting in which the conflict arose;
- prevention: what each party did, or thought they could have done, to prevent violence.

Using this template, we examined the full transcript of each of the 209 interviews, recording every response and quotation that shed light on the ten aspects listed above. Gradually, common factors and patterns began to emerge. For example, the tactics of threats and accusations arose frequently, each appearing in almost half of the incidents. Threats and accusations are also well-defined. Tactics that were more vague, or appeared more rarely, took longer to identify. The two researchers independently coded each transcript, then cross-checked the findings of this stage by comparing notes. The two ratings were reassuringly consistent. The process of resolving any differences between the researchers' analyses facilitated a further refinement of the ten concepts.

The next phase involved fine-tuning the coding frame. For example, the 209 entries under interests led, at this stage, to a typology, distinguishing material interests from non-material; and then highlighting the different ways in which any particular material interest could function in a dispute. At this stage, we also narrowed our focus to the six components about which we felt most confident (interests, relationships, catalysts, interpretations, purposes and social context). On this basis, we were ready to explore the ways in which conflicts led to violence on the basis of the prisoners' stories.

Conclusions

Conflicts and Violence in Prison was based on a theoretical model of violence that set fights and assaults within the broader context of conflict. To understand how conflicts led to violence, we drew upon the perspectives of the prisoners who were directly involved, focusing on their interpretations of what was happening. This conflict-centred approach to prison violence could be fruitfully applied in other settings.

The theory, the context and the chosen method led to the use of a particular technique, the Escalator, which made it possible to organise prisoners' accounts in a systematic and chronological framework. Comparing the diverse narratives of many of these situations revealed the reciprocal nature of conflict. The rich detail in the participants' personal accounts opened the geometry of conflicts – the interests, relationships, catalysts, interpretations, purposes and social context – to analytical exploration. The Escalator structure enabled us to identify the patterns of thought and behaviour by which violence was introduced into the process of managing conflict. It uncovered the reasons why someone turned to violence, thus demonstrating, in prisons at least, the dynamic links between conflicts and violence.

Appendix

Box 1: Gregson and Wye Escalators compared

Gregson	Wye
I'd had a share of a spliff, part of which was Wye's. But another girl smoked the rest of it and didn't pass it on.	
Wye must have thought I'd smoked it, she came back on the wing and asked for it. I told her that the other girl had got it but she had smoked it.	Gregson was given a joint for [another inmate], and Gregson smoked it. I found out. I went behind my door.
I heard that and went to Wye's door to say, 'Let's talk about it', and calm her down.	Gregson came to the door.
She told me to fuck off and I said the same to her.	
I turned away and walked down the wing and I heard her running up behind me.	I told her, 'Fuck off!' Gregson replied: 'Why don't you fuck off?' She didn't know the door wasn't locked.
I said, 'Oh, so now I have to watch my back as well' and she swung at me.	I came out of my cell.
	Gregson said, 'Now do I have to watch my back?' Me: 'No. Watch me when I come from the front.' I slapped her on the face, a backhand punch that gave her a black eye.
I threw my hot coffee back over my shoulder and it went all up her arm.	I turned and walked away.
[Another prisoner] came towards us and we stopped.	Gregson threw her coffee on me.
We're mates – no hard feelings.	I carried on walking back to her cell.
	I felt my top was wet, but when I took it off it stuck to my arm.
	They filled out an accident – not a bully – form.

Intentions and consequences

Gregson

Q. What do you think Wye was trying to achieve?

> Don't know. I can't look at life through her eyes.

Q. What did it actually achieve?

> It made me want to walk away – but I'm like a terrier – I wouldn't have left it alone. I'd have been back to sort it out.

Q. What were you trying to achieve?

> Resolution of the conflict.

Q. What did it actually achieve?

> It resolved the conflict but not in the way I intended. Talking would have been enough for me.

Q. At what point do you think the situation actually became violent?

> [Step 7 – when Wye pursued her as she left Wye's cell door.]

Q. What could you have done that might have prevented the violence?

> When I said, 'So now do I have to watch my back?' It might have helped if I hadn't said that.

Q. What could she have done that might have prevented the violence?

> Not run after me; stayed in her room.

Q. At what point do you think violence had to happen?

> At no point did violence have to happen.

Emotional scale

I was calm throughout. I at all times. I never got worked up at all. Afterwards I was a bit shaky and wishing that I hadn't hurt her.

Wye

Q. What did you think when you heard she had smoked the spliff?

> It put a lot of ideas in my head – Is she a friend or not? Should she even be in the posse? You don't give, give, give respect.

Q. Why did you go to your room?

> I went to my room to cool off.

Q. What were you feeling when she came to your door?

> Just fuck off. Go away. Let me deal with this. I wouldn't have hit her if she had left.

Q. What did you hope to achieve by telling her to fuck off?

> To get her away from me so I could cool down.

Q. How did you interpret it when she asked if she now had to watch her back?

> It is putting me down. It's a fucking insult. She is trying to say the worst she can.

Q. What did you intend to do when you struck her?

> Just shut the fuck up. You are not thinking to say that to me.

Prevention

Q. What could you have done to prevent the violence?

> Nothing – talking to me like I'm a twat. I give everyone a chance. I say what I've got to say. She didn't want to listen. She just wanted to throw insults.

Q. What could she have done to prevent the violence?

> She could have walked off.

Q. At what point did you think this had to end up in a fight?

> When she says 'Do I have to watch my back?' But it wasn't a fight. I hit her. She walked off.

Box 2: Leek and Shildon Escalators compared

Leek	*Shildon*
	Since I've been on the wing, he's a tramp, every time he walks past he stinks and every time he walks past my cell and looks in every time whether I'm there or not.
	Over time it winds you up. Particularly on a bad day. Other people didn't like it either. I thought he was a pad thief.
He's on the first landing getting his dinner.	
I call down, 'What's the pudding? What's in your bowl?' He must have thought I said something else. He said something rude to me as he was coming up the stairs.	I got my tea early and came back on the spur and saw him looking out of my cell. 'Oi, what you doing?' He was, 'What you on about?'
I said, 'Piss off.' He started retaliating – it goes to an argument.	I went up to the second landing and went up to him and said the same. I said, 'I'm going to punch you', and he said, 'Alright, come on then.'
He pushed me against the wall and we started fighting.	He threw two punches straight away – I was surprised. I boxed him up to the corner – he was on the floor.
Officers broke it up – we heard the alarm bell and stopped.	The bell went – I got another couple of punches in. I was well fired up – all my aggression was coming out then. An officer came up – I hit him again and he picked the bin lid up.
	That was the end of it.
	The other day – I can't believe it – he came up to my cell door and asked for Rizlas. I kept really calm.

Intentions and consequences

Leek

Q. What were you trying to achieve?
> *I just do whatever goes.*

Q. At what point could you have done something that might have prevented the violence?
> *Nothing – it was going to happen anyway.*

Q. At what point do you think violence had to happen?
> *Six years of crack has left me a mind of concrete. I've done brown but it's not my drug. Crack, it's the devil's drug, but it's nice to take.*

Shildon

Q. What was he trying to achieve?
> *I don't know – he's not all there in the head.*

Q. What were you trying to achieve?
> *I don't know.*

Q. What did it actually do?
> *When he punched me I couldn't just take it.*

Q. At what point do you think the situation actually became violent?
> *As soon as he punched me.*

Q. At what point could you have done something that might have prevented the violence?
> *Right at the beginning.*

Q. What could you have done?
> *I could have said, 'Fuck off, don't come into my cell again.'*

Q. At what point could he have done something that might have prevented the violence?
> *At the beginning.*

Q. What could he have done?
> *He could have walked off and not punched me.*

Q. At what point do you think violence had to happen?
> *After he punched me a second time.*

Box 3: Drayton and Scalby Escalators compared

Drayton	*Scalby*
I went for my dinner with my friend, 'Bob'.	Me and Drayton were in the dinner queue.
We agreed that 'Bob' could have the chocolate cake.	
The cake was ginger so I turned back and said, 'Bob, it is ginger.'	Drayton asked for my ginger cake.
	I said no.
Scalby – his name is also 'Bob' said, 'What did you say?' (Threatening like)	We started arguing.
I said, 'I ain't talking to you. I'm talking to Bob. Are you Bob?'	I said, 'Suck your mum.'
Scalby said, 'Yeah.'	Drayton said, 'Suck your mum.'
I said, 'I ain't talking to you anyway.'	I said: Right. See you on association.
Scalby told me I must mind how I speak to him.	
Scalby told me he will punch out my 32 teeth.	
I said: Go ahead.	
Scalby: Yeah, on association.	
On association, Scalby came up to me.	We both came out on association.
Scalby: Come in the showers.	I said: Let's go in the showers.
I said: I ain't going to the showers.	Drayton walked off.
Scalby swung a punch, grazing my cheek.	Then he turned round and went for me.
I punched him in the mouth.	Staff stopped it.
Other inmates stepped in.	
Officers came.	

Intentions and consequences

Drayton

Q. What did you hope would happen when you told Scalby you weren't speaking to him?
> *Just get him to forget about it.*

Q. What was the effect on him?
> *He take it offensive.*

Q. When he told you mind how you spoke to him, what did you think he meant?
> *Speak to him with more respect – look up to him.*

Q. What was the effect on you?
> *I see him as a little boy.*

Q. What did he mean when he said he would punch out your teeth?
> *He was stepping over the line.*

Q. What was the effect on you?
> *For someone to tell me that – no one ever mentioned those words to me before. I wasn't having it.*

Q. What did you hope to achieve by telling him to go ahead?
> *He is saying the words. Why not do it?*

Q. What was the effect on him?
> *Maybe made him mad.*

Prevention
Q. Was there anything you could have done to prevent the fight?
> [Indicates step 1– going to dinner]
> *I would have just stayed in my cell.*

Q. And after that?
> *No. I think it was just made to happen.*

Q. Was there anything he could have done?
> [Indicates step 8]
> *He could say, "Oh, I thought you was talking to me." And that is it. That could end the whole thing.*

Scalby

Q. What did you mean when you said 'See you on association?'
> *To tell him on association I was going to move to him.*

Q. What do you think he meant to achieve by turning on you after he started to walk off?
> *Scared to go in the showers. Wanted to do it in front of the govs.*

Prevention
Q. Was there a time you could have prevented the fight by doing something different?
> *No. He told me to suck my mum.*

References

Acland, Andrew F. (1997) 'Dealing with Disputes in the Voluntary Sector'. National Council for Voluntary Organisations.

Alternatives to Violence Project (1996) *Supplement to the Basic and Second Level Manuals.* New York: Alternatives to Violence Education Committee.

Athens, Lonnie (1997) *Violent Criminal Acts and Actors Revisited.* Chicago: University of Illinois Press.

Blumer, Herbert (1969) *Symbolic Interactionism.* New Jersey: Prentice-Hall.

Bottoms, Anthony (1999) 'Interpersonal Violence and Social Order in Prisons', in *Crime and Justice*, vol. 26, Tonry, Michael, ed. Chicago: University of Chicago Press.

Bowling, Benjamin (1998) *Violent Racism: Victimization, Policing and Social Context.* Oxford: Clarendon Studies in Criminology.

Burton, John (1990) *Conflict: Resolution and Prevention.* London: Macmillan.

Edgar, Kimmett and Carol Martin (2001) *Conflicts and Violence in Prison.* Violence Research Programme Research Findings: Economic and Social Research Council.

Edgar, Kimmett and Ian O'Donnell (1998) 'The Reluctant Informer', *Prison Service Journal*, 117: 44–6.

Fisher, Roger and William Ury (1997) *Getting to Yes: Negotiating an Agreement without Giving In.* London: Arrow Books Limited.

Girard, René (1977) *Violence and the Sacred.* Baltimore: Johns Hopkins University Press.

Harvey, J. H., A. L. Weber, and T. L. Orbuch (1990) *Interpersonal Accounts: A Social Psychological Perspective.* Oxford: Basil Blackwell.

Hood, Roger and Kate Joyce (1999) 'Three Generations: Oral Testimonies on Crime and Social Change in London's East End', *British Journal of Criminology*, 39: 136–57.

King, Roy and Kathleen McDermott (1995) *The State of Our Prisons.* Oxford: Clarendon.

Liebling, Alison (2000) 'Prison Officers, Policing and the Use of Discretion', *Theoretical Criminology*, 4: 333–57.

O'Donnell, Ian and Kimmett Edgar (1998a) *Bullying in Prisons.* Oxford: University of Oxford Centre for Criminological Research, Occasional Paper No. 18.

O'Donnell, Ian and Kimmett Edgar (1998b) 'Routine Victimization in Prisons', *The Howard Journal of Criminal Justice*, 37: 266–79.

Riches, David (ed.) (1986) *The Anthropology of Violence.* Oxford: Basil Blackwell.

Sabo, Don, Terry Kupers, and Willie London (eds) (2001) *Prison Masculinities.* Philadelphia: Temple University Press.

Sykes, Gresham and David Matza (1957) 'Techniques of Neutralization: A Theory of Delinquency,' *American Sociological Review*, 22: 664–70.

Walmsley, Roy, L. Howard, and Sheila White (1992) *The National Prison Survey.* London: HMSO.

5 Dilemmas of control

Methodological implications and reflections of foregrounding children's perspectives on violence

Christine Barter and Emma Renold

Introduction

Residential care for children and young people[1] arouses much controversy. There have been several UK scandals involving the physical and sexual abuse of residents, leading to public inquiries and reports (Utting 1997, Waterhouse 2000). Although scandals have almost all concerned abuse by staff, research has indicated that children are likely to be at risk from other residents (Sinclair and Gibbs 1998, Farmer and Pollock 1998, Morris *et al.* 1994, Lunn 1990). Yet violence within children's homes has long been an area of concern, if not of research (Berridge and Brodie 1998, Millham *et al.* 1981, Tutt 1976). Residential children's homes exist primarily for adolescents whose behaviour is regarded as too challenging for foster care. Often, both victims of abuse and those exhibiting harmful behaviours are placed together (Pollock and Farmer 1998). Official guidance on the management and control of violent behaviour within residential settings (Department of Health 1997) has emphasised management and staff competence, rather than the context in which children interact. These measures have not resolved the problems (Barter 1997). For example, Sinclair and Gibbs (1998) found that 40 per cent of children had been bullied in their children's home and a quarter of girls had experienced unwelcome sexual behaviour from other residents.

Little research attention has been paid to children's perspectives on violence in homes or other contexts, although youth violence is known to be common. Between 30 and 40 per cent of school pupils experience bullying in some form, and sexual assault in childhood and adolescence is more likely to be experienced from other young people than from adults (Cawson *et al.* 2000). Significant gender differences exist (Stanko 2000), thus older teenage boys form the single largest group of offenders in statistics of violent crime (Home Office 2000), while the use by girls of physical violence is still relatively uncommon (Batchelor *et al.* 2001). Children are known to assess and manage potential safety and danger in school and community environments and to develop strategies to deal with risks (Smith and Sharpe 1994, Hood *et al.* 1996, Harden *et al.* 2000). While levels of reported violence found in research on children's homes seem comparable to those found in studies of schools and community settings, Millham *et al.* (1976)

caution against uncritically transferring what is known about violence in one context to a completely different setting.

Research objectives

The central aim of our research was to develop understanding of children's experiences of peer violence within residential settings by exploring both children's and staff's understanding of the meaning and effects of violence, children's protective strategies, and the extent to which children and staff had shared reference systems for dealing with violence. Consequently, children's perspectives were viewed as being important in their own right and not just in relation to their social construction by adults (Brannen and O'Brien 1996, James and Prout 1998). Children are seen as being actively involved in the construction of their social lives, of the lives of those around them and of the societies in which they live. They are, therefore, viewed both as constrained by structure and as agents acting within and upon it (James *et al.* 1998). By exploring the relationship between these two levels, we can then begin to elucidate the link between given, and largely adult-defined, social institutions and the activities which children construct for and between themselves. Ultimately, the aim of the project is to contribute to the development of effective residential safeguards surrounding peer violence by enabling children's own interpretations, definitions and evaluations to inform policy and practice, rather than simply reflecting adult interpretations, realities and solutions.

Sample

Fourteen residential children's homes took part in the research; 12 were for adolescents (aged 12–17) and two for younger children (under 12). Reflecting the national balance in England, the majority were managed through local authorities (nine), three were under private ownership and two were run by voluntary organisations. The homes were situated in urban and rural areas. Seven homes had fewer than six placements and eight had more than six; the largest home in the sample had 12. The majority of homes were designated as medium term, but two were designated as short term and three had long-term provisions. All homes were mixed, except three which were male only.

Seventy-one children participated in the study, 44 boys and 27 girls. Twenty-one per cent of the sample were from minority ethnic groups (representing the wider balance in national provision generally). Ages ranged from 6 years to 17 years, but the majority were teenagers, with 14 children aged 12 or less. A selection of 71 residential staff also took part, and these were chosen to represent different grades, gender, age, ethnicity and length of service.

Research ethics

Following the British Sociological Association's *Statement of Ethical Practice* 'special care' was taken with young research participants who are vulnerable by factors of 'age, social status and powerlessness' (Morrow and Richards 1996). Introductory meetings were held in each home with both staff and children. All children and staff were sent leaflets before we visited, explaining the aims of the research, the voluntary nature of participation, confidentiality, and giving researchers' phone contact numbers alongside their photograph. The younger children, who might have had limited reading ability, were given audiotapes explaining the research. A form detailing participants' rights within the research (for example, their right to end the discussion whenever they wished, or to revoke their consent for their discussion to be used upon completion of the interview) was provided, and children signed this to indicate their understanding. Leaflets detailing the research project were also produced for parents and external social workers. Participants were assured that information would be confidential to the research team, unless researchers were told of circumstances in which children were in 'immediate serious danger'.[2] In these situations the formation was reported to an appropriate senior person (hopefully with the child's consent), and a suitable management contact was negotiated in each managing agency. Throughout the fieldwork we reminded children of these rights and especially the limitations of confidentiality, to ensure that children did not disclose information which they might later regret. This process is described by Thorne (1980) as 'renewed consent'.

Developing appropriate methodology

In addition to our general theoretical framework, we also needed to develop a methodology that could: engage children to participate in 'sensitive research'; enable a discussion both of personal experiences of violence and types of violence that participants may not have directly encountered; explore the interpretations and meanings different actors ascribed to different situations and courses of action; and, additionally, provide children with a greater level of control over the research interaction. Two complementary techniques were employed to fulfil these diverse aims. First, semi-structured interviews were used in which children could identify, define and contextualise their own personal experiences of violence.[3] Second, vignettes were employed to depict different forms of violence to which children could respond and within which they could locate themselves. Alongside these formal data collection techniques, researchers spent a considerable amount of time in each setting informally observing and interacting with participants. This aspect of the study was extended after feedback from the pilot stage of the project which indicated that children needed more opportunity to get to know the researchers before they felt comfortable discussing their experiences of violence with them.

Much methodological literature exists concerning the use of qualitative semi-structured interview techniques, which we shall not rehearse here. Portraying 'active listening' and a 'non-directive stance' (Whyte 1984), and making efforts to convey a non-judgemental attitude (Hill 1997), avoiding asking 'leading questions' (Lofland and Lofland 1995) and instead asking 'contrasting', 'descriptive' and sometimes 'structural' questions (Spradley 1979) were all central components in our interview techniques. In contrast, although vignettes have been used by researchers to explore diverse social issues, few methodological papers exist which examine the use of this technique within social research (but see Barter and Renold 1999, Schoenberg and Ravdal 2000), and, particularly, its application within qualitative research with children (see Barter and Renold 2000). Within qualitative research, vignettes have been increasingly employed to elicit cultural norms derived from participants' attitudes to and beliefs about a specific situation and to highlight ethical frameworks and moral codes. Hughes (1998: 384) states that 'vignettes highlight selected parts of the real world that can help unpack individuals' perceptions, beliefs, and attitudes to a wide range of social issues'.

Within our study, four written vignettes were used. Each depicted a different aspect of behaviour including sexual, emotional, physical and verbal forms of violence and was based on children's 'real' experiences derived from earlier pilot interviews and on data from previous research (Barter 1996). Each vignette was adapted to use with younger children (aged 6–12) and adolescents. Questions following each vignette included how they thought characters in the story would feel and behave and how they themselves might feel and respond if presented with a similar scenario and why. The reasons surrounding each response were then freely explored with each participant, thus allowing them the space to re-define contexts and behaviours by drawing on their own and others' experiences. We found a number of advantages to using vignettes within a multi-method study on violence.

Engagement with sensitive topics and participation

Vignettes were useful in engaging with children in many ways. For example, the shift away from face-to-face discussions that can involve intrusive direct eye contact, to focusing on the reading of a vignette, can help to facilitate a non-threatening environment by creating a comfortable distance between the researcher and the participants. Vignettes also provided variety within the research interaction itself, allowing discussions of personal experiences to be dispersed with more abstract debates surrounding children's beliefs and attitudes. Feedback from children on using vignettes was generally positive: 'Yeah, I like these stories, they're good, cos they're realistic'; 'they're top'; and 'wicked ... better than just talking all the time cause that's boring'. That they were based on children's own experiences was seen as particularly important by young participants in these assessments (Neff 1979).

Control over the research process

Feminist researchers insist that issues of power be placed as central components within the research process. Fundamental to this is the need to attend to the unequal power relations between the researcher and the researched by engaging with participants as active subjects (Stanley and Wise 1993). Vignettes provided a useful tool enabling participants to determine for themselves when, *and whether*, to introduce their own personal experiences to illuminate their abstract responses. Thus children were controlling actors within the process, shaping both the content and the format of the research interaction. Indeed, as we shall see in the next section, children were rarely passive recipients. However, for the more reticent and for those who did not wish to discuss personal experiences, commenting on stories about other people's experiences was viewed as less threatening and also encouraged participation.

Comparing disparate groups

Our research also sought to explore residential workers' experiences and attitudes towards violence between residents and to compare these to children's accounts and beliefs. The application of vignettes offered the opportunity to compare and contrast different groups' interpretations of a 'uniform' situation while at the same time providing the opportunity to identify and isolate certain structural factors such as gender, age and ethnicity. This enabled the wider context surrounding different groups' judgement around violence to be explored, and ultimately permitted the development of benchmarks for understanding differences in interpretation, which may be unavailable through using other methods.

Compensating for a lack of personal experience

Sampling from a general residential population meant that we had no prior knowledge of children's experience of violent behaviours within the residential homes. Not knowing the extent or even existence of children's experience of violence, the vignettes became an invaluable part of the methodology by providing a focus for participants who had no personal experience of violence. Thus their attitudes and responses to a range of violent situations were not lost and could be explored regardless of whether they had any personal experience on which to draw. However, children's ability to engage with the story may be enhanced if they have personal experience of the situation described.

Having explored some of the major benefits to using vignettes in studying violence, some methodological dilemmas also need to be addressed before moving on to look at the impact of researching violence in residential contexts.

Methodological dilemmas

The most frequently cited theoretical limitation of employing this technique surrounds the distance between the vignette and social reality; what people believe they would do in a given situation is not necessarily how they would behave in actuality (Faia 1979). However, some writers have argued for a different theoretical perspective in relation to belief and action (Douglas 1971). Finch (1989) suggests that it is not always necessary to be concerned about the inconsistency between principles (beliefs) and practice (actions) as it is perfectly possible to agree in principle to a general norm, but believe that it is not relevant in particular circumstances or that it does not apply for particular reasons. Therefore it is not the outcome (or action) that is of research interest, for this will always be situationally specific, but the process of meanings and interpretations used in reaching the outcome that is of central concern to social scientists. Vignettes can thus provide a very useful tool to illuminate and tap into this complex process.

Another major criticism, related to the above, centres upon the artificiality of the technique. Integral to social life are the continual interactions between individuals and their environment; as vignettes are unable to duplicate this complexity, it is maintained that findings derived from this method cannot be generalised to any aspect of people's social lives. A counter argument to this criticism is that, as processes in the social world are complex and multiple, vignettes offer researchers the opportunity to manage this complexity by isolating certain aspects of a given social issue or problem. Ultimately, no research tool can completely capture the complexity of social existence; however, by adopting a multi-method approach, researchers can build on the individual strengths of different techniques.

In this section we have documented the formal development of our methodology which aimed both to foreground children's own views and meanings about violence, and simultaneously to address some of the unequal power relations between researchers and the researched. However, unequal power relationships also manifested themselves in other ways throughout the fieldwork process. These are considered below, alongside other 'process' factors which not only impacted on the management of the fieldwork process, but also had significant repercussions on understanding both the impact and the nature of violence within the 14 settings we visited.

IMPACT OF RESEARCHING VIOLENCE IN RESIDENTIAL CONTEXTS

Implications of peer group dynamics for the fieldwork process

Each of the residential homes exhibited very different peer group dynamics. Most were based on some form of hierarchical power relationships between children, sometimes supported by, and indeed perpetuated through, staff recognition. These hierarchical dynamics surrounded a wide range of factors. Upon closer examination these separated into two distinct categories: relations based on what we have termed 'perceived authority' or 'violent reputations'. 'Perceived authority' characteristics included intelligence, length of stay, age and maturity while violence, threats of violence, intimidation or verbal attacks underpinned 'violent reputations'. Often these peer group hierarchies, including those based on violent reputations, were normalised by workers through 'pecking order' narratives. In some homes, not only were these power relations viewed as an inevitable characteristic of peer group relations, but they were additionally seen by some workers as beneficial.

Worker: 'It's the pecking order, so that once a new resident comes in, they get
              to know who to respect and who you don't respect, who's more
              vulnerable, let's put it like that.'
Researcher: 'How do they do that?'
Worker: 'Don't ask me … but a new resident in a month or so, they just slot
              into their little places, it's incredible … it's absolutely amazing and
              they do benefit from knowing where their place is, suppose it makes
              them feel secure.'

In contrast, many children, and especially those occupying lower status positions in violent reputation hierarchies, viewed their experiences as victimisation. This is vividly illustrated by the young person below, whose experiences had been previously described by the above worker[4] (from the same residential home) as beneficial.

Researcher: 'Could you tell me a little about what happened?'
14-year-old boy: 'Locking us in his room, whipping us with belts and tying us up
                  against the radiator so you got burnt on your back and
                  stuff … really bad stuff.'

Consequently, it quickly became apparent when researching violence that it was imperative that we both recognised the peer group dynamics present within each of the settings and considered the possible implications of these dynamics before implementing the fieldwork. In each children's home, we spent time informally observing and interacting with children and staff. Through these interactions we became aware of the peer group dynamics present within each of the settings. Often, a clear consensus emerged between children and staff regarding children's positioning within the peer hierarchies. Staff often spoke in terms of 'top dog', 'deputy dog', 'worker' or 'lap dogs', the first two denoting positions of superiority, while the latter two refer to lower status positions. Children rarely used such descriptions, although one young man publicly affirmed his position by declaring to his counterparts 'Who's daddy? I'm the daddy'. Alongside these evaluations, our observations of peer interactions enabled us to develop independently our own understanding of how the peer group dynamics were mobilised and structured within each setting.

One-third of homes (four) exhibited dynamics based around 'perceived authority'. In many of these homes, the high-status children took it upon themselves to initiate interest in the research. Often they positioned themselves as being opposed to intimidation and violence. Frequently, these key children volunteered to be interviewed first, and subsequently reassured their lower-status counterparts that the process had been a positive experience. Thus, many were instrumental in gaining participation for the research as other children respected their opinions and trusted their judgements.

Dynamics based on violent reputations were generally more covert and complex, resulting in a more problematic, and sometimes distressing, atmosphere in which to undertake the fieldwork. As children and staff became progressively used to our presence within their establishments, these peer dynamics became more visible and sometimes quite overpowering for the researchers. In common with their high-status counterparts in the previous homes, those wielding power in these settings were also very controlling, although in fundamentally different ways. These children were often highly domineering in our interactions with their lower- status counterparts. Strategies included purposely disrupting our attempts at general conversation, publicly negating our research as worthless and us as 'do-gooders' and, most difficult of all, humiliating other children who showed an interest in participating.

Some of these children also confronted us directly with their own use of violence, through verbal and non-contact forms of intimidation, such as spitting at us, making jokes at our expense and through the use of verbal insults. Often these tactics were aimed at our humiliation. In one residential home, we were purposely locked in an unused bedroom for about half an hour while our 'incarcerators' ran around outside shouting insults at us and publicly gloating about their superiority over the gullible researchers. In a few instances, physical violence was used, for example 'accidentally' throwing a chair in our general direction. Generally, such 'attacks' were only initiated against us when the children concerned had an audience; often individually they acted very differently with us. The above strategies seemed to serve two main functions. First, to signal to us their control over other children and by implication their power over us through their capacity to act as gatekeepers in relation to participation. Second, to demonstrate to other children their ability to exert power over the 'adult' researchers and therefore to reaffirm, and indeed enhance, their own standing within the peer dynamics. We found this a difficult position to be in, not only because of the effect such behaviour had on us personally, but also because our presence was being manipulated directly to reinforce and perpetuate violent reputations.

Such direct confrontation was mostly undertaken by girls, but boys were also active in this process, although they used slightly different strategies. The central component of the verbal abuse directed at us from both girls and boys concerned sexuality, although the exact use of this construction was highly gendered. Girls' main mechanism of 'humiliation' was through challenges to our (hetero)sexuality. For many of these young women, their heterosexual status may be the only axis of privilege to which they have access (Haney 1996), and therefore the only one which could 'legitimately' be wielded against their perceptions of us as 'white, female, middle-class' researchers. Boys' challenges mostly positioned us as being sexually available to them, or indeed, sexually predatory. We generally received fewer verbal attacks from boys that were not posed as humour. Boys more often sought simply to distance themselves physically from us, whereas girls were more likely to engage directly, to the extent of following us around the building which further prohibited our attempts at interacting with other members of their peer group.

Generally, it often felt as if we were being put through some form of initiation rite. Children in one of the most violent homes we visited overtly confirmed this, stating that all new admissions (whether children or staff) were put through this 'trial'. Two of the main instigators in this home proudly stated that they had to date 'got rid' of two new members of staff in this manner, although so far no researchers. This was evidently their way of testing our suitability for the job. Later in the fieldwork, these same children spoke to us honestly and in great depth about their use of power and intimidation, and the contradictions this raised for them. In relation to our 'trial period', children often stated that they respected our ability to endure and the fact that we had stood up to their tests (reflecting their wider hatred of weaker peers who, in their eyes, could not defend themselves in the face of their intimidation).

In reality, we often felt that we were simply trying to get through these initiation periods as best we could. We tried numerous strategies in our attempts to deal with these confrontations including: ignoring the behaviour (generally unsuccessful), humour, challenging the insults, diversions (for example, making a meal for everyone or becoming involved in some form of group task). On a few occasions we decided that the best strategy was to abandon the fieldwork for that day. In some settings we found the initial 'test period' to be both emotionally exhausting and, in a minority of cases, daunting, especially as we were required constantly to evaluate how to respond to such challenges and to consider the possible implications of our responses (both for children and for our position as 'observers'). In addition to this, our responses were keenly watched by residential workers. However, although the above challenges sometimes became very uncomfortable, we were aware that we could simply leave, an option not available to the children, and perhaps not always to the staff, who were also exposed to such intimidatory tactics.

Fundamental to the aims of our research was the positioning of ourselves as less 'adult-centric' (Mandell 1988; Mayall 2000). This involved us in being non-judgemental and stopping ourselves from intervening, even when comments were deliberately aimed to harm others. In such situations, Fine and Sandstrom (1988) advise researchers to listen but not to intervene. We found that this was immensely difficult at times, particularly when children were being physically violent, or verbally attacking or humiliating another young person in our presence. Often in these instances we felt distinctly uneasy in our passivity, as a swift intervention from us could have halted the abusive interactions. We knew that by witnessing and not intervening, these interactions would continue to be performed in front of us. There was always the danger that, if we did intervene, these interactions would occur privately, away from sight. Yet, as Connolly (1996) notes, not intervening can reinforce and almost condone attitudes and behaviours. We decided that we would thus neither encourage nor condone such insults but would 'offer the space through which their ideas could be drawn out and critically explored' (Connolly 1996: 33). Sometimes, simply repeating what they had said and asking what they had meant by that allowed us to question their beliefs without condoning them. Thus, when our least adult-centric position became too uncomfortable we sought to project ourselves into the abusive encounter and thereby remove or at least divert attention away from the 'victim'.

In some instances, direct intervention was necessitated for the protection of children from physical injury. Many of the physical fights we observed directly were for 'display' only, generally performed for our benefit. When we questioned these instances, both participants would quickly state that they were only 'messing around'. To overreact in these situations gave us the impression that we had in some way failed the test set, especially if we informed staff. The most productive response was to leave the immediate environment, depriving them of their target audience (although we remained close enough to ensure the 'fight' was discontinued). However, making these judgements was sometimes problematic, especially if we had only been in the setting for a short period and were still unravelling the peer dynamics. Often it was the reaction of other children, alongside our own 'common-sense' feelings, that guided our assessments. In some situations, it was impossible for us to remain passive observers and we felt compelled to protect children by informing staff if our own attempts at de-escalating the situation were not heeded.

The main method employed to counteract the hierarchical peer group dynamics consisted of engaging with children in isolated groups. Generally this meant interacting outside the residential context, for example through accompanying children on trips to the shops, school runs, outings, etc. This enabled us to spend time with 'lower-status' children away from their dominating counterparts. In addition, as most of the fieldwork was undertaken in pairs (at least at the beginning of research in each home), we were able to separate and therefore engage with different children. Although this separation allowed us to interact with 'lower-status' peers more easily, it also meant that one of us was generally left to deal with confrontational tactics in isolation.

The above dynamics also impacted on the ordering of the fieldwork process, although sometimes we had little control over how we implemented this in practice. Overall, we found that, if possible, it was best to interview first the dominant-status participants, although this priority again risked enhancing hard reputations. However, the fear of the unknown was greatest for these children, who had a lot invested in their power positions. Although they portrayed themselves as secure, their anxiety about our presence showed how precarious they viewed their power position as being. Often, when these interviews had taken place, their interest in challenging us waned, and we were able to undertake the fieldwork with much more ease.

Other researchers have raised similar concerns regarding undertaking research in situations of ongoing power relations. Hey's (1997) ethnographic study of girls' friendship groups explores the impact of undertaking research with young women who occupy different status positions within a single peer group hierarchy. Some commentators have directly explored the methodological implications that these social relations may have. Mitchell (1999) explores in her work the distinctions between using focus groups and individual interviews and suggests that the former may be particularly constraining for 'low-status' participants, especially when children are in positions of continuing social contact outside the research context.

Feminisation of the research process

As well as the above hierarchical dynamics, gender also played an important role in relation to the research process. Most of the fieldwork, as already stated, was undertaken by the two female authors. Early in the fieldwork we found that, especially among adolescents, perceptions of the research processes were highly gendered. Girls were often much more vocal in their support of the aims of the research, volunteered more readily and were more overtly interested in our own motivations and personal lives. Girls generally provided altruistic reasons for participation including their desire to assist others in similar situations; in some instances they described themselves as taking pity on the researchers and wanting to 'help us out'. In contrast boys exhibited great public reluctance to take part or even to be seen to engage with us in any meaningful way, thus distancing themselves from the research process. When boys did contribute, they often portrayed to their male counterparts a grudging reluctance to their participation. Subsequently, this often meant that girls were interviewed early on in the fieldwork, leaving only the boys to take part.

Other commentators have proposed that 'talking about things', and especially feelings, is perceived as a feminine trait while physical activity denotes masculinity (Connell 1995, Frosh *et al.* 2002). Often the masculinities on show in the residential homes concerned the portrayal of 'hard' exteriors, so that any allusions to 'feminine' characteristics would have been detrimental to this performance. The role of researching violence should not be underestimated in this process. When we introduced our research we did not overtly state that we were looking at violence, as we wanted to guard against imposing our own agenda on children. Instead, we stated that we were interested in finding out what were the good and bad aspects of living with other children in residential settings. Nevertheless, most children assumed that violence was our central concern, even before we talked with them in depth, thus indicating the central role that violence played in many of their peer group interactions. This inevitably led to a heightened recognition of power inequalities, and, especially, of victimisation, within the residential settings, leaving many young men feeling vulnerable to challenges to their 'hard' masculine exteriors.

All these factors accumulated in the reaffirmation of the feminisation of the research process. For these reasons, it was often impossible to pre-arrange interview times with boys, and instead we were often forced simply to wait around in the hope of spontaneously interviewing young men once the coast was clear (of other boys). This feminisation of the fieldwork had major practical as well as ethical implications for the research process as a whole. Often, to ensure that boys took part, researchers had to stay in the settings for significantly longer than expected, even though the original time frame for each setting had already been extended from the initial proposal. In addition, we were aware that our continuing presence in some settings disrupted normal living arrangements, impacting negatively on those whose home we were visiting. Indeed, the more ingrained boys' public displays of reluctance became, the more difficult it was to try to encourage participation without appearing to them, and indeed to ourselves, as if we were harassing them. However, we knew from our discussions with boys who did participate that, generally, wider social relations rather than any misgivings about our research accounted for their reluctance.

Taking all these factors into account, we decided about one-third of the way through our study that we needed to provide children with some form of public 'excuse' to participate. We decided that we would offer children a £10 gift voucher to compensate them for their time.[5] Paying children for participating in research, especially research on 'sensitive' topics, has been a contentious issue in the past. The main area of dispute concerns the disproportionate influence that monetary gain may have on a young person's decision to participate, thus overpowering concerns about the personal impact that discussing potentially upsetting issues may have.

In practice, we found not only that vouchers provided an excuse for young men and 'lower-status' children to take part but that generally young participants appreciated our recognition of their input in this way. We did encounter some detrimental effects; for example, some young men timed the length of interviews stating they didn't 'work' for less than £10 per hour (well above the minimum wage!). However, given the contentious nature of the subject, alongside the hierarchical peer dynamics and the hard masculinities on show in many of the settings, vouchers seemed to provide more of an 'excuse' to participate rather than a disproportionate incentive to those genuinely unwilling to become involved. Even with the vouchers we encountered refusals and it appeared to us that the offer of payment did not sway any children to participate who had previously declined. Indeed, as we have already seen, children rarely acted as passive subjects in the fieldwork, but were often controlling actors within the process.

Role of staff

We experienced overwhelming support from children's homes' staff for our research and most made every effort to make us feel welcome. Many took part, even though it was often very difficult for them to spare the time. We tried as much as possible not to inconvenience staff by our presence and attempted to compensate by undertaking some of the more mundane residential tasks such as preparing meals, washing up, etc. Staff were also active in talking with children about the research and encouraging participation. However, we did encounter a few instances where staff seemed purposely to be undermining our attempts at interactions with children. In one residential home, one of us experienced sexual harassment from a male worker, which was not only a difficult situation to deal with at the time, but also raised worries regarding the appropriateness of this worker for the job. Some lower-grade staff declined to answer questions regarding sexual violence between children, reflecting their wider insecurities about working in this area generally. In addition, some were worried that we were concerned only with children's experiences and rights and would not understand the pressures and difficulties which the staff encountered in their everyday working practices. In addition to our obvious interest in their perspectives, the fact that one of the authors had previously worked in residential children's homes also went some way to alleviate these fears.

The emotional impact of researching violence

Feminist researchers have placed considerable emphasis on the integral role that reflexivity plays within the research process (Maynard 1994, Holland and Ramazanoglu 1994). Among other things, this entails a consideration of the emotional impact of doing research and it is to this aspect that we turn now. There are serious theoretical and epistemological consequences in ignoring the many roles that 'emotionality' plays in research (Pickering 2001), but emotion is often deemed epistemologically irrelevant (Code 1993). Thus, the image of the disinterested 'expert gaze', bereft of emotionality, has by and large characterised scientific inquiry. Small (1997) and Ellis and Flaherty (1992) argue that scientific investigation is underpinned by a 'set of feeling rules' concerning both the conduct and reporting of research, where introspection has little part. Within our study, the emotional impact of researching violence manifested itself in a number of significant ways. These not only impacted on us personally, in ways that were sometimes difficult to acknowledge, but also had implications for the research process itself and, ultimately, for the way in which we conceptualised violence within the study.

Although a central concern in the design of our methodology was to minimise the potential distress for children that talking about violence may bring, ultimately our role as researchers was to 'discover' and explore these violent incidents. Inevitably, some of these experiences were very painful for children to talk about and for us to listen to. Throughout the process, we tried to ensure that the young person remained in control over what was discussed and over the extent of the detail, but in practice this was not always so clear-cut. We are both experienced researchers, but the need to continue to probe what is obviously a distressing experience, no matter how sensitively this is undertaken, is difficult and brings up contradictory feelings. We both have recollections of undertaking very demanding interviews, most often concerning experiences of sexual violence, which we found to be traumatic and upsetting. In these interactions, we had to make rapid judgements about whether or not to stop the interview, take a break, change the direction of the interview and return to the 'distressing' bit later. We were also acutely aware of the possibility of making an inappropriate comment or remark, or that our body language may have contradicted our (verbal) efforts to be 'non-judgemental' or 'comfortable' with what participants were saying, especially when they were discussing their own use of violence. Ultimately, we can both recollect saying things that we wished, with hindsight, we could have rephrased or responded to differently. In addition, the reading and re-reading of interview transcriptions served to re-ignite memories of difficult interviews including remorse about insensitive responses. Often these omissions seemed very stark in black and white.

Linked to this was the need to maintain some sort of emotional distance and avoid being perceived by the children as counsellors. This was an especially problematic stance to maintain when children were using the interview as a space in which to unburden themselves. Although we practised 'active listening' where we acknowledged the children's experiences and pain, our role was not to provide counselling. We did, however, offer participants information regarding services that would be able to provide this specialist support if they wished. We also asked the young person if they would like a worker or a friend to stay with them after the interview, or if there was anyone we could contact on their behalf. However, despite all our efforts, and even though many children stated that they valued the opportunity to talk and to have their views taken seriously, we were both acutely aware that ultimately some of these children would have to deal with the impact of revisiting these painful experiences.

We also had to contend with issues of personal safety caused by physical violence. For example, in one home a physical fight broke out between two young men in a narrow corridor, which trapped one of us in the middle. Feelings for personal physical safety were heightened in this case after we found out that one of the boys had a knife on his person. However, another team member present at the time viewed the incident as minor, underpinning the importance of recognising that different researchers will apply differential interpretations of risk and danger depending on their past personal and professional experiences. In some instances we also questioned our professional ability. For example, in one home a young man with a history of severe mental health problems and violence wanted to take part. This raised dilemmas for us not only regarding his ability to provide informed consent but also for our own personal safety. In the interview, the young man would only talk about his use of violence when he was wearing a 'Scream mask'.[6] This was both unnerving and unsettling, especially as staff seemed to minimise both his mental health problems and his use of violence. Eventually, we chose not to include this interview in the final analysis, as we were not clear whether his use of violence was real or imagined.

However, possibly the most troubling impact that undertaking research on violence had on us personally concerned our anxiety around its absence. Both at the time of the fieldwork, and even now nearly two years after concluding the data collection process, this still generates complex and ambivalent emotions. After completing fieldwork in five of our 14 residential homes, we had found comparatively little 'violence'. We were feeling dispirited yet, at the same time, recognised that this was obviously a good thing. However, in the sixth residential home we encountered the worst physical and emotional violence we were to see. This produced feelings of relief, in that we had 'at last found some data', and at the same time feelings of despair at what we were hearing from both the children and the staff involved. That we felt any form of 'release' in the face of such truly dreadful acts, described by one participant as constituting 'physical, emotional and psychological torture', provoked feelings of revulsion and made us question whether we had become desensitised, 'cold-blooded' researchers. Though we tried to rationalise these feelings, they were a powerful reminder to us of how our 'job' of collecting data on violence, if not guarded against, could overpower our personal feelings of empathy and dismay in the face of other people's suffering.

Throughout the project, discussions on the impact of researching violence took place between the main researchers. Often in the fieldwork phase these took the form of informal debriefing sessions, generally after the completion of each day's fieldwork. Sometimes because of travel, limitations of time (one researcher was only employed part-time) and prior commitments this was not always possible. However, we tried always to prioritise time to explore how we felt, and the impact of this on our role as researchers, and also to reflect on how these experiences were impacting on the data-collecting process. Thus, through sharing our experiences of the research process and also our own personal lived experiences that surfaced regarding the topic, we were able to work reflectively. This method was also transferred into the analysis phase of the project. Unfortunately, this level of reflexivity was less evident in our more formal meetings where all team members met to discuss progress, and in these the structural aspects of the research often took precedence. Although time was given to discussing particularly difficult encounters, in retrospect the emotional impact of researching violence should have been more prominent.

Conclusion

Our study of peer violence in children's homes was located within the wider debate of challenging the traditional conceptualisation of children as passive objects of adult-defined knowledge and understanding. Consequently, the need to resituate children both theoretically and methodologically as active controlling agents has shaped our conceptualisations of the research question. Thus, we sought to prioritise children's own definitions, perceptions, and evaluations of violence, including its nature and extent; to compare these with professional understandings; and, at the same time, to develop a methodology that allowed young participants greater control and input over the research process. Two complementary techniques were employed to fulfil these diverse aims. Semi-structured interviews offered a platform for participants to draw on their own experiences of violence, and vignettes provided an opportunity to explore children's abstract evaluations, while at the same time providing them with the freedom to determine when, and if, to interject personal experiences in their exploration of the scenarios presented. These methodologies were implemented within a context of continuing contact with homes, which allowed researchers the opportunity to develop relationships with children essential for tapping into the hidden nature of the violence experienced.

However, children, like adults, are constrained by structure as well as being agents acting within and upon it. By exploring the relationship between these two levels we have been able to elucidate the link between adult-defined situations and the overt and covert behaviours, including violence, which children construct for and between themselves. Consequently, our findings do not present any simplistic, homogenous reconstruction of violence as a single unified concept. Instead our methodology enabled a much more complex understanding to emerge, allowing both commonalties as well as fractures to be made visible in interpretations both of impact and of the nature of peer violence. The use of a methodology that prioritises children's own meanings and interpretations as primary not only served both to contextualise and to delineate the impact of different forms of violence within the lives of children, but ultimately provided a powerful critique of how violence has traditionally been defined and conceptualised and of the complex interrelationship between the verbal, physical and the sexual components of this contentious construction (see Renold and Barter 2002).

Too many debates surrounding methodology and ethics in social research occur in theoretical isolation from more 'concrete' practical issues. As we have shown, the dynamic process of undertaking fieldwork in situations of ongoing violence not only influenced the management of the data collection process but also had significant repercussions on our understandings of both the impact and the nature of violence. In addition, we have explored the central role of reflexivity within the research process, and especially the impact of 'emotionality', a subject often considered peripheral to the substance of investigation (Pickering 2001).

Ultimately, the lack of attention to 'process' factors not only serves to restrict our ability to predict methodological and ethical problems and share solutions but also conceals how the active process of research itself serves to mediate our understanding of violence. Thus, although this study centres upon a specific group of children and professionals, the multidimensional methodology used and the implications of this for generating insights into the concealed and contested nature of violence are wide-ranging.

Notes

1 To aid brevity the term children will be used throughout to denote both children and young people.
2 Serious danger was explained as physical or sexual violence which they, or another young person, were currently experiencing.
3 Staff were similarly asked about their experiences and management of violence between children in their care.
4 Although the worker stated later in the interview that she had been unaware of the extent of the physical violence used.
5 We also retrospectively sent vouchers to all previous young participants and contacted all young people who had initially refused, offering them the opportunity to take part.
6 The scream mask comes from a popular US horror film.

References

Barter, C. (1996) *Nowhere to Hide: Giving young runaways a voice*. London: Centrepoint.
Barter, C. (1997) 'Who's to blame: conceptualising institutional abuse by children'. *Early Child Development and Care*, 133, 101–4.
Barter, C. and Renold, E. (1999) 'The use of vignettes in qualitative research'. *Social Research Update*, issue 25, University of Surrey.
Barter, C. and Renold, E. (2000) 'I wanna tell you a story: the application of vignettes in qualitative research with young people'. *Social Research Methodology, Theory and Practice*, 3 (4), 307–23.
Batchelor, S., Burman, M. and Brown, J. (2001) 'Discussing violence: Let's hear it from the girls'. *Probation Journal*, 48 (2), 125–34.
Berridge, D. and Brodie, I. (1998) *Children's Homes Revisited*. London: Jessica Kingsley.
Brannen, J. and O'Brien, M. (1986) *Children in Families: Research and policy*. Brighton: Falmer Press.
Cawson, P., Wattam, C., Brooker, S. and Kelly, G. (2000) *Child Maltreatment in the United Kingdom: A study of the prevalence of abuse and neglect*. London: NSPCC.
Code, L. (1993) 'Taking subjectivity into account', in L. Alcoff and E. Potter (eds) *Feminist Epistemologies*. London: Routledge.
Connell, R. (1995) *Masculinities*. Cambridge: Polity.
Connolly, P. (1996) 'Racisms, gendered identities and young children'. Unpublished thesis, University of Leicester.
Department of Health (1997) *The Control of Children in Public Care: Interpretation of the Children Act 1989*. London: Department of Health.
Douglas, J. (1971) *American Social Order*. New York: Free Press.
Ellis, C. and Flaherty, M.G. (eds) (1992) *Investigating Subjectivity: Research on lived experience*. Newbury Park, CA: Sage.
Faia, M.A. (1979) 'The vagaries of the vignette world: a document on Alves and Ross', *American Journal of Sociology*, 85, 951–54.
Farmer, E. and Pollock, S. (1998) *Sexually Abused and Abusing Children in Substitute Care*. Chichester: Wiley.
Finch, J. (1989) *Family Obligations and Social Change*. Cambridge: Polity.
Fine, G. and Sandstrom, K.L. (1988) *Knowing Children: Participant Observation with Minors*. London: Sage.
Frosh, S., Phoenix, A. and Pattman, R. (2002) *Young Masculinities*. Basingstoke: Palgrave.

Haney, L. (1996) 'Homeboys, babies, men in suits: The state and the reproduction of male dominance'. *Amercian Sociological Review*, 61 (5), 759–78.

Harden, J., Beckett-Milburn, K., Scott, S. and Jackson, S. (2000) 'Scary faces, scary places: children's perspectives on risk and safety'. *Health Education Journal*, 9, 12–22.

Hey, V. (1997) *The Company She Keeps: An ethnography of girls' friendship groups*. Milton Keynes: Open University Press.

Hill, M. (1997) 'Ethical issues in qualitative methodology with children', in D. Hogan and R. Gilligan (eds) *Researching Children's Experiences: Qualitative approaches*. Trinity College Dublin: The Children's Research Centre.

Holland, J. and Ramazanoglu, C. (1994) 'Coming to conclusions: Power and interpretation in researching young women's sexuality', in M. Maynard and J. Purvis (eds) *Researching Women's Lives from a Feminist Perspective*. London: Taylor and Francis.

Home Office (2000) *Criminal Statistics England and Wales 1999*. London: Home Office.

Hood, S., Kelly, P., Mayall, B. and Oakley, A. (1996) *Children, Parents and Risk*. London: Social Science Research Unit, Institute of Education.

Hughes, R. (1998) 'Considering the vignette technique and its application to a study of drug injecting and HIV risk and safer behaviour'. *Sociology of Health and Illness*, 20, pp. 381–400.

James, A., Jenks, C. and Prout, A. (1998) *Theorizing Childhood*. Cambridge: Polity.

James, A. and Prout, A. (eds) (1998) *Constructing and Reconstructing Childhood*. Basingstoke: Falmer.

Kelly, L. (1987) 'The continuum of sexual violence', in J. Hammer and M. Maynard (eds) *Women, Violence and Social Control*. London: Macmillan.

Lofland, J. and Lofland, L.H. (1995) (3rd edn) *Analysing Social Settings: A guide to qualitative observation and analysis*. Belmont, CA: Wadsworth Publishing Company.

Lunn, T. (1990) 'Solution or stigma'. *Social Work Today*, 22 (9), 20–1.

Mandell, N. (1988) 'The least-adult role in studying children'. *Journal of Contemporary Ethnography*, 16 (4), 433–67.

Mayall, B. (2000) 'Conversations with children: Working with generational issues, in P. Christensen and A. James (eds) *Research with Children: Perspectives and practices*. London: Falmer.

Maynard, M. (1994) 'Methods, practice and epistemology: The debate about feminism and research', in M. Maynard and J. Purvis (eds) *Researching Women's Lives from a Feminist Perspective*. London: Taylor and Francis.

Millham, S., Bullock, R. and Hosie, K. (1976) 'On violence in community homes', in N. Tutt (ed.) *Violence*. London: HMSO.

Millham, S., Bullock, R., Hosie, K. and Haak, M. (1981) *Issues of Control in Child Care*. London: HMSO.

Mitchell, L. (1999) 'Combining focus groups and interviews: telling how it is; telling how it feels', in R.S. Barbour and J. Kitzinger *Developing Focus Group Research: Politics, theory and practice*. London: Sage.

Morris, S., Wheatley, H. and Lees, B. (1994) *Time to Listen: The experience of children in residential and foster care*. London: ChildLine.

Morrow, V. and Richards, M. (1996) 'The ethics of social research with children: An overview'. *Children and Society*, 10, 39–49.

Neff, J.A. (1979) 'Interaction versus hypothetical others: the use of vignettes in attitude research'. *Sociology and Social Research*, 64, 105–25.

Pickering, S. (2001) 'Undermining the sanitized account: Violence and emotionality in the field in Northern Ireland'. *British Journal of Criminology*, 41, 485–501.

Renold, E. and Barter, C. (2002) 'Shifting ground: challenging traditional conceptualisations of violence from young people's own experience', in E. Stanko (ed.) *The Meaning of Violence*. London: Routledge.

Schoenberg, N.E. and Ravdal, H. (2000) 'Using vignettes in awareness and attitudinal research'. *International Journal of Social Research Methodology, Theory and Practice*, 3 (1), 63–75.

Sinclair, I. and Gibbs, I. (1998) *Children's Homes: A study in diversity*. Chichester: Wiley.

Small, W. (1997) 'Keeping emotion out of it? The problem (and promise) of the investigator's feelings in social research'. *Australian Journal of Social Research*, 4/1: 97–118.

Smith, P. and Sharpe, S. (eds) (1994) *School Bullying: Insights and perspectives*. London: Routledge.

Spradley, J.S. (1979) *The Ethnographic Interview*. Boston, MA: Holt, Rinehart and Winston.

Stanko, E. (2000) 'Rethinking violence, rethinking social policy', in G. Lewis, S. Gerwirtz and J. Clark (eds) *Rethinking Social Policy*. London: Sage.

Stanley, L. and Wise, S. (1993) *Breaking out Again: Feminist ontology and epistemology*. London: Routledge.

Thorne, B. (1980) 'You still takin' notes?: Fieldwork and problems of informed consent'. *Social Problems*, 27 (3), 284–97.

Tutt, N. (ed.) (1976) *Violence*. London: HMSO.

Utting, W. (1997) *People Like Us: The report of the safeguards for children living away from home*. London: The Stationery Office.

Waterhouse, R. (2000) *Lost in Care: The report of the Tribunal of Inquiry into the abuse of children in care of the former county council areas of Gwynedd and Clwyd since 1974*. London: The Stationery Office.

Whyte, W.F. (1984) *Learning from the Field: A guide from experience*. London: Sage.

6 Safety talk, violence and laughter

Methodological reflections on focus groups in violence research

Leslie J. Moran, Beverley Skeggs, Paul Tyrer and Karen Corteen

Introduction

Laughter is a mode of human expression that is rarely associated with those who are the objects of targeted violence. Likewise, laughter is not an object of study commonly found within scholarship that seeks to examine the experiences of those who live with danger from that violence and who work to produce security in both public and private spaces. However, data generated by way of a series of focus groups exploring the experiences of violence and safety of three different groups previously identified as 'high risk' by victim surveys (lesbians, gay men and straight women) undertaken as part of the Violence, Sexuality, Space research project,[1] challenge this state of affairs. In total we conducted 35 focus group meetings. We ran groups for gay men, lesbians and straight women in each research location: Lancaster, a small city with a relatively large student population, and Manchester's gay Village, both in the north west of England. Each group (with one exception) met on six occasions. Laughter is recorded in the transcripts of all the group meetings and is a pervasive feature of the data generated through the focus groups.

We begin this chapter with a brief description of the wider methodological landscape of the project and set out some of the key reasons that informed our use of focus groups. After exploring some of the general challenges related to the use of focus groups we turn to consider a particular aspect of the data, laughter. We offer a preliminary analysis of the uses and meanings of laughter in this context. We conclude with some reflections upon the methodological and epistemological challenges raised by this laughter.

Focus groups in a multi-method project

The Violence, Sexuality, Space research project used a multi-method approach in each research location to produce data over a 30-month period. We undertook structured interviews with key informants selected on the basis of their commercial, institutional (local government, police) and community expertise, connections and involvement (21 in Lancaster and 34 in Manchester). Questions focused upon the historical development and contemporary use of space by lesbians and gay men, current safety issues and practices, and safety policy development. A survey produced the richest quantitative data set to date on lesbian and gay perceptions of safety. The Manchester survey was conducted on a Friday (lunchtime and evening) in February 1999 after key informants identified Friday as the 'most dangerous and heterosexual' time in the Village. It sampled people in 13 venues selected from over 30 on the basis of sexual constituency, popularity and location. The Lancaster survey was carried out on two evenings (Wednesday and Friday when gay events were held) in May 1999. The surveys generated over 900 responses (703 in Manchester and 213 in Lancaster). Completion rates were exceptional: 95 per cent in Lancaster and 97 per cent in Manchester. The content and design of the questionnaires drew upon key informant interview data, prior research and knowledge, research group discussions and a pilot study. Throughout data were gathered by way of local knowledge, participant observation at each site, informal contacts, national networking (e.g. Against Homophobia, 'Keep the Streets Safe Campaign'), prior research on local sites, and representational analysis. Data were also generated from magazine and Tourist Information Centre listings, GIS (Geographical Information Systems) and through literary, biographical and internet searches. Focus groups are the final piece of the multi-method picture.

The use of focus groups in work on violence and safety is rare. As others have noted, focus groups have largely been used in commercial contexts (particularly market research). More recently they have been used by governmental and voluntary agencies to explore the success or otherwise of service provision and service needs (Fern 2001; Kruger 1994; Morgan 1998; Stewart and Shamdasani 1990). The use of focus groups in the Violence, Sexuality, Space research project represents something of a departure from this.

Previous research on homophobic violence has taken the form of victim surveys that seek to establish the existence and levels of previously unrecorded and unreported violence, but our research had a different focus. It took homophobic violence as its point of departure and had the objective of generating new information about how lesbians, gay men and straight women, as groups, vulnerable to social conflict, social instability and social exclusion, produce sustainable security in public spaces.

Various factors influenced the decision to use focus groups. Commentators have drawn attention to their use in the context of new and exploratory research (Fern 2001; Stewart and Shamdasani 1990: 15). We were particularly interested in the method's capacity to generate a rich body of data by way of both individual contributions and group interactions. More specifically it is a method through which novel data about how research participants talk about the phenomenon of safety and its relationship to danger might be generated (Fern 2001: 7–8).[2] Another important factor was the production of data related not only to individual but also to shared beliefs and common everyday practices of safety and danger. We used focus groups in a multi-method context (cf. Morgan 1997) to promote triangulation. The focus groups began after the completion of the structured interviews and continued while we undertook the two surveys. They were used to explore reactions to and generate reflections upon this data. Groups also responded to data generated in other parallel focus groups. Finally, they were used to provide feedback upon and evaluation of current policies and practices relating to safety and security, issues more traditionally associated with focus groups.

Prior experience made us aware that research in the area of violence and safety would need to be handled with care. While the focus on safety might provide a less threatening and stressful context in which to raise these matters, our previous experiences suggested that we needed to proceed with caution.[3] Undertaking research in this area would call for management of emotional consequences of dealing with a subject matter evoking strong sentiments both from those being researched and from the researchers. Group discussions to address difficult topics such as experiences of danger and violence pose particular problems. We were also aware that the group setting might provide a more supportive environment in which to raise issues of safety and danger. Our seed corn research groups had pointed to the importance of the group's ability to generate an environment of trust and confidence.

Various strategies are available to promote cohesion to enable and support participation (Fern 2001: Ch. 5). Homogeneity, Fern suggests, is particularly appropriate for 'phenomenological groups' where the focus is everyday experience (*ibid*: 8). Kruger draws attention to its importance as a device for ensuring high levels of trust and comfort within the group, an issue pertinent to research on violence and safety (1994: 11). We established and ran three parallel groups (lesbian, gay and straight women) in the two locations. This provided a degree of group homogeneity by reference to gender and sexuality. However, homogeneity also posed problems. We were concerned that homogeneity reproduces illusions of the singularity of sexualised identities, gay, lesbian and heterosexual women. In response we planned for a degree of heterogeneity. However, difficulties encountered in recruiting the groups imposed some limits on our ability to realise our original plans.[4] Ultimately we achieved a degree of diversity within our groups by reference to age, work status, living arrangements, and location. In Manchester the groups also had a racial mix (23 per cent were Black or Asian).

The plan, design and conduct of the groups was also informed by the specific challenges of the research topic. We paid due attention to the organisation of the space, and formulated rules of engagement to avoid the creation of hierarchies of truth within the group and to promote participation. At the beginning of the first session, we introduced the ground rules. We asked participants to show respect to other group members (disagreements are great for the richness of the research and one of the strengths of focus groups; personal attacks are not) and got their agreement to the rules. We also reminded people that we were not counsellors – so unable to deal with any personal difficulties that the session brings up. We had contact lists for helplines and other support mechanisms should the need arise. As group facilitators we also reflected upon strategies we might use to facilitate participation in response to the emergence of dominant members of the group.

Focus groups: violence and laughter

While laughter is not unique to the focus group data, it is particularly prominent in that context.[5] Laughter occurs in the context of the general themes of the discussions and in the detailed discussion of experiences, perceptions, ideas and policies relating to violence and safety.[6] It appears in the context of reflections on issues arising out of key informant interviews, during the course of reflections on survey data generated by the research team and in reflections on data generated from the other focus groups. References to violence, threats of violence and harassment are a regular feature of these discussions about safety. Our transcripts record violence on the street, in bars (both gay and straight), in the work place, educational institutions, near to and in the home. Perpetrators of violence and harassment range from school teachers to neighbours, from colleagues and family members to strangers. At the same time, these discussions of danger and safety are regularly punctuated by laughter.

The juxtaposition of danger, safety and laughter appeared early in the focus groups. For example, during the course of the first lesbian focus group in Lancaster, one of the first focus group meetings of the research project, participants were asked to talk about their knowledge and experience of local places considered to be safe from the threat of homophobic violence and harassment. Karen, the facilitator, asked participants to explain how they became aware of these locations. One lesbian, a student, explained that the University Lesbian Gay Bisexual (LGB) group had been a good source of information about safer places in Lancaster. Karen asked, 'Did they say anywhere specific where not to go?' The response, by another member of the group, recorded in the transcript, reads, 'The Nag's Head. [laughter]'. Elsewhere in the same transcript another group member offered information about 'The Nag's Head'. She explained:

> I went to the Nag's Head [laughter] ... I was there like in a pin stripe suit and a tie because I mean we'd all been for dinner and all the men were like camp ... We just got literally chased out and like my friend got touched up and stuff. So I just wouldn't go there if you just look gay. So that wasn't a very nice experience.

The 'Nag's Head' appears here as a location associated with the threat of homophobic violence and an experience of social exclusion connected with a perception of sexual orientation. The juxtaposition of 'Nag's Head' and '[laughter]' seems to offer a rather odd proximity. A review of the focus group transcripts shows that the juxtaposition and proximity of danger, safety and laughter is far from exceptional.

The challenge of laughter: to perpetuate or question a prejudice

Laughter offered us various challenges. Perhaps the first challenge is the perception that laughter is not only unexpected but, more specifically, out of place in the context of discussions about the experiences of danger and safety. What are we to do with 'laughter'? Is it hard evidence to be subject to rigorous analysis or the accidental mark of an over-zealous transcriber? Is it serious data or idiosyncratic trivia? If data, how is laughter to be understood?

These responses to laughter echo sentiments found in Nietzsche's *Gay Science*:

> In the great majority, the intellect is a clumsy, gloomy, creaking machine that is difficult to start. They call it 'taking the matter seriously' when they want to work with this machine and think well ... And 'where laughter and gaiety are found, thinking does not amount to anything': that is the prejudice of this serious beast ... Well then, let us prove that this is a prejudice.
>
> (Nietzsche 1974: 257, para. 327)

In general, laughter, he suggests, is taken to be antithetical to serious thinking. Transposed into the context of violence, reflections on laughter might be thought of as being outside and beyond the realm of thinking seriously about violence and safety. We were then faced with a methodological dilemma. If laughter is antithetical to serious thinking then serious thinking about violence should have little time for laughter. But Nietzsche's reflections suggest that this would be to perpetuate a prejudice. This is not something to be embarked upon lightly in the context of work that seeks to explore and challenge a pervasive form of prejudice in the form of homophobic violence. More specifically, to exclude laughter might threaten to be insensitive to the data generated by way of particular methodologies that work to report and record how marginal and vulnerable groups produce sustainable security in public spaces. In the main the laughter comes from our research participants and is generated by them. To ignore or trivialise that threatens to silence a particular dimension of their experiences, perceptions, ideas and responses to danger and safety.

In our attempt to take laughter seriously we want to engage briefly with Freud's work, 'Jokes and their relation to the unconscious' (Freud 1976). In exploring jokes by way of a series of contrasts with (for example) the comic, satire, smut, irony, cynicism, puns, laconic remarks, absurdity or repartee, Freud offers an analysis of a wide range of social practices associated with laughter.[7] Two aspects of his study are of particular significance. The first focuses upon Freud's consideration of the techniques of laughter. The second is concerned with what is achieved by way of these techniques. Their interconnection is also important.

Laughter work, Freud suggests, deploys a wide range of techniques. His study offers a rich catalogue of terms that describe these techniques. They include abbreviation, comparison, condensation, connection/unification, displacement, exaggeration, inference, nonsense, overstatement, repetition/double meaning, startling juxtaposition, substitution and transformation. Freud connects these techniques to the production of meaning. They work to reveal that which is otherwise covered and hidden. This might take the form of a rediscovery or be the production of something that has escaped the notice of others. The techniques are characterised by Freud as a set of practices that overcome repression and censorship. They provide a means of 'undoing the renunciation and retrieving what was lost' (Freud 1976: 145). A study of the laughter techniques provides an opportunity to examine the cultural practices through which meaning and the absence of meaning are produced.

Uses of laughter

We now want to consider some examples of 'laughter' from our focus group data. It is not possible in the limited space available here to explore the many examples found in our transcripts. What follows is a selection that offers a preliminary exploration of the diverse settings, different forms and uses of laughter techniques and the rich complexity of 'laughter' in our data. Various factors have influenced the selection. To represent the pervasive presence of laughter, examples are taken from the gay, lesbian and straight groups in both locations. They have been chosen in order to illustrate the complexity of 'laughter' and the problems that laughter generates for any analysis. They are organised into two general sections. The first focuses upon laughter as a technique in conducting focus groups. The second explores laughter by group participants. Neither use of laughter is mutually exclusive. They are frequently connected.

Laughter as focus group technique

While, as group facilitators, we planned and reflected upon strategies to facilitate participation we did not plan to use humour or seek to evoke laughter as a technique. Nor, would it seem, is this an exceptional state of affairs. References to laughter as a technique in methodological guides and critical reflections on focus groups are rare. Stewart and Shamdasani (1990: Ch. 2) note that focus groups are generally considered by participants to be 'fun'. Reflecting upon techniques that might be used to conduct the focus group, they suggest that a 'joke may serve to break the ice and let everyone know that it's OK to have a little fun. ... A skillful moderator will use humour to the best advantage in such conditions.' (*ibid*: 100) Here laughter, in the form of jokes, is offered as a positive technique associated with the generation of group 'intimacy' and 'comfort'. They also warn of the dangers of laughter highlighting 'unfair attempts at humour' that signal humour as a potentially hostile practice more akin to producing discomfort and distrust than intimacy and trust. It is with these thoughts in mind that we want to turn to some examples within the transcripts of uses of humour by members of the research team.

We open with an example from the first Lancaster straight women's group.[8] Bev facilitated. 'Laughter' occurred in the context of a discussion of stereotypes:

Vannessa: But most gay people are very camp.
Bev: Gay men or lesbians?
Vannessa: Gay ... it's very hard to put camp to a lesbian. I don't know, I always identify a lesbian to be very butch, not camp ... But camp for somebody who's gay ...

Bev: Juliet, were you going to say something or were you just yawning?
          (*Laughter*)
Juliet: I think, sometimes you have to generalise but sweeping generalisations
          like that just don't really … there are so many differences from that,
          that its not entirely helpful generalising in that way. You can sort of say
          'if she's a butch woman and she looks like she's a dyke' …
          I would think that most of the time that they are. Like if men look
          camp, I would think that most of the time they usually are [gay],
          you know.

This exchange is interesting in various ways. First, how are we to define the
technique used here? Freud's work on jokes (1976) is useful here. First, the
humour in the facilitator's comment uses comparison. It also seems to generate a
particular set of relations within the group. Freud suggests that a joke has specific
characteristics. It is both self-conscious (rather than unintended) and requires a
third party; the one who tells the joke, the subject of the joke and the third party
(the audience for the joke). The third party is of particular significance here.
Laughter, Freud suggests, is more evident in the third party rather than in the
person who tells the joke or in the person who appears in the joke. It is useful to
reflect on these relations in the context of Stewart and Shamdasani's (1990)
concerns about the use of jokes and humour. The structure of a joke, in particular
when the subject of a joke is within the group, may make jokes a particularly
problematic device, separating the subject of the joke from the 'third party' who
laughs at the joke. It is in this structure that there is the potential for jokes to
produce group hierarchy and participant exclusion. Different recording methods,
in particular the use of video, might have enabled us to examine the distribution
of laughter within the group in more detail. At the same time this example
problematises the crude distinction that separates the subject of a joke from the
'third party'. Here the 'joke' has a certain ambivalence. The context is also
important. One feature of focus groups is the requirement of participation. While
the facilitator's comment might point to the non/slow participation of a member
of the group, it is also an invitation to participate. Laughter has particular
significance here. Katz has noted that laughter is always a relationship; of being
with another (1999: 94). Laughter may also be a device to summon another to
participate; an invitation to co-presence (*ibid*: 93, 126). It is perhaps in this
context that laughter facilitates rather than excludes.

Laughter has another significance here. A problematic feature of focus groups,
commentators have noted, is the limited opportunity for individual participation.
Much time is spent listening to others, preparing to speak and waiting to speak.
Laughter not only offers opportunities to participate but opportunities to
participate as a collective experience. Laughter provides a means of multiple
simultaneous participation. Furthermore, by way of a distinction between the
initial laugh and the 'second phase' of laughter that may go 'well beyond' the first
phase, Katz points to the potential of laughter to provide not only a collective but

also an individual mode of participation and expression (Katz 1999: 127). In this instance humour generates participation, both individual and collective.

The collective aspects of laughter also have another significance. This is a group of heterosexual women with lesbian and gay friends who use lesbian and gay space. Our seed corn research drew attention to the likelihood that these women would not have experienced these relations as part of an identity in common. This is in sharp contrast to the lesbian and gay groups where sexual identity offered (albeit problematically) a certain immediate experience of commonality. Thus the laughter that occurs in this group's first meeting may be different from that in the other groups. Here we particularly need to consider the place of laughter as a Mode of interaction used by strangers (cf. Mahony *et al.* 2001).

Another example of laughter used by the research team comes from the first Manchester gay men's focus group: Paul, the facilitator, began the ice-breaker exercise. The two men who followed introduced themselves by reference to the fact that they had moved to Manchester from Yorkshire. Paul responded, 'All these Yorkshire boys coming over to Lancashire. What will people say…'. Another member of the group added, 'As another Yorkshire-man, [laughter] I moved to Manchester about fourteen years ago…'. The humour of the facilitator's comment is produced by the 'startling' juxtaposition of a historic opposition between the houses of York and Lancaster: gay Yorkshiremen ('outsiders') in Manchester's (Lancastrian) gay Village. The laughter in response has various meanings. It might suggest a degree of comfort and intimacy in the group. 'I think laughter can be an important thing. You know if you are in a bar and there is laughing … then you feel more relaxed in yourself,' commented one of the group. But this begs the questions: whose comfort? which group? At least two possibilities exist here. One is a group within the larger group; the three Yorkshire men who also turned out to be pre-existing friends. Here laughter is indicative/constitutive of particular interpersonal bonds that might be over against the facilitator and over against the rest of the group. The laughter may also be that of the rest of the group, over against the sub-group and with the facilitator. The laughter might warn here of the dangers of pre-existing friendships upon intra-group dynamics (Morgan 1997: 35–9). Here the laughter is neither singular nor unambiguous. It is also an instance of the use of laughter as a technique and a resource by participants. It is to the use of laughter by members of the group that we now turn.

Laughter as data

Before examining laughter as a mode of communication by members of the group, some preliminary points need to be addressed. In many ways laughter as focus group data occupies a problematic position. It straddles the divide between the non-verbal and the verbal. As a physical reaction (cf. Boston 1974; Freud 1976; Katz 1999: Ch. 2), it is a form of communication that is often overlooked as a part of the data generated by focus groups (Kruger 1994: Ch. 8). In turn, depending on the mode of recording adopted, the physicality of laughter (a belly laugh in contrast to a titter or uncontrollable laughter) may also be a complex mode of communication that is unrecorded.[9] Furthermore, even when recorded as verbal communication, as we noted earlier, laughter continues to have marginal significance as 'serious' data. With these insights in mind we now want to move on to consider some examples of 'laughter' from our focus group participants.

Laughter as blockage

The following example of laughter as blockage or resistance comes from the Lancaster straight women's group. Bev, the facilitator, asked, 'What makes it feel comfortable?' The reply unfolded as follows:

Juliet: You don't get any knob heads [*laughter*]. Throwing their weight around.
Vannessa: You would never get anybody like that in there. I mean I didn't go there for quite a few sort of ... I've never known a fight or anything ...
Bev: Can I have a definition of knob head for the tape please [laughter].
Juliet: No [laughter].
Bev: We need to know what would make a place dangerous.
Jackie: The presence of knob heads [laughter].
           (*Talking at once*)

Here laughter first emerges in the context of a colloquialism: 'knob head'. It names attributes associated with safety and danger. Bev's request for further elaboration is met with a formal refusal followed by laughter. Further requests produce an unruly situation, laughter and 'talking at once', bringing the exchange to a close. Freud noted that laughter often occurs in the context of censorship and repression. Here laughter seems to produce a silence. But there is a need to be cautious here. The laughter is part of a collective exchange between members of the group and with the facilitator, which suggests the possibility of a range of shared experience. Far from denoting an absence of meaning, laughter appears to be a particular mode of production of meaning that in this instance is marked (expressed) by way of laughter; a common knowledge. Laughter keeps the facilitator outside that community of meaning. Laughter highlights the potential unruliness of focus groups and the difficulties of control associated with group participation (Kruger 1994: 36–7).

Making connections

We now want to turn to some examples that allow us to examine some of those shared meanings. Our first example comes from the opening exercise of the Manchester gay men's group, drawing and describing their personal maps of safety and danger in the Village. One of the members of the group explained:

I come in [to the Village] at the [eastern] end of Canal Street because I live in the Northern Quarter so I walk through Piccadilly and through that dodgy car park that you were just telling us about! [laughter] … the Velvet end because I usually go to Velvet … I don't really tend to use that other car park near Cruz because I never go to Cruz.

Here the laughter occurs in the context of the remark, 'that dodgy car park'. It is a phrase that refers back to a comment made earlier by another member of the group.

Because it is dark and there are never any cars there because they are not allowed to park after six or something and it is just like full of trees, there's no lights on so you look at it and you think, 'Oh, this is a bit dodgy'. I mean it used to be the other way round. You know the one at the top of, I think it is the top of Bloom Street or something, it is where the Magistrates Court is. Now that used to be quite notorious there. I would never walk there. If I used to get off the bus, the 219, I used to walk across there very reluctantly and there always used to be somebody walking past asking you for something. I didn't realise it at the time but it was a bloody […], selling their sex and I am thinking, why are they asking me this? I was very naïve then!

The laughter emerges by way of repetition of the term 'dodgy'. 'Dodgy' functions as an ellipsis producing an abbreviation. It produces a syntax, connecting a later comment back to something that was said earlier and said more elaborately. Through the ellipsis the connection is made as an absence of the earlier detailed remark about the different experiences of danger associated with different aesthetics of two car parks that are experienced as dangerous. Laughter marks the moment when the group members are connected back to the earlier observations. The earlier reference to 'dodgy' not only articulates an experience of danger associated with the absence of people (the first car park) but also names an experience of danger associated with the presence of particular people, sex workers, pimps (the second car park). But why should the repetition that brings these reflections back into the frame generate laughter?

One answer is to be found in the reference to 'naïve' that is used by the speaker to characterise the encounter with danger in the second car park. Freud explains the connection between the naïve and 'the comic' in the following terms. The naïve relates to an 'inhibition' that is 'completely disregarded', the inhibition not being 'present' to the one who disregards it (Freud 1976: 240). In this example the naïve marks a moment of self-reflection by a group member. He notes his own complete disregard of a prohibition, not to cross a 'dodgy' car park, in this instance associated with dangers that might range from unwelcome propositions by sex workers to perhaps the threat of robbery and assault. But it is important to note that the 'laughter' does not arise in the context of the self-declaration of naïveté. The laughter arises only in the context of the repetition.

Another important feature of this humour is its appearance by way of another member of the group. This raises further questions not only about the technique of laughter but also about the inter- and intra-personal dimensions of the technique. In this example the comic naïve is produced in an inter-relational context that is more akin to a joke: the one who makes the joke, the third party and the subject of the joke. Various intra- and inter-personal factors may be significant here. The joke may work as an expression of the heroism and bravado of the joke teller, providing the means and opportunity to represent his capacity to manage safety in the face of danger. Doing this by way of naïveté may suggest that this position is achieved at the expense of another person. This draws our attention to the possibility that the joke may be at the expense of, in this instance, someone in the group. More specifically, the joke may have the effect of differentiating those who are skilled at safety from those who are less skilled, producing a hierarchy within the group. The inter-personal dynamic may be to produce an outsider within the group. This may also have significance in the constitution of an experience of membership of the wider community of gay men in which competence to manage safety and danger might have significance separating out the good gay from the bad gay, the deserving victim from the undeserving victim (Stanko 1999: 99). The laughter of the other members of the group may also indicate their recognition of such a marginal position, if not within the focus group or the wider gay community, then at least in terms of the dominant heteronormative social order of things. Here the laughter draws attention to the intra-personal dimension of the inter-personal, as an expression of self-effacement, and an acceptance of oppression, self-oppression.

How are we to understand the intra- and inter-personal dimensions of laughter that emerge in this context? One problem we face is the limits of our techniques of data generation. Our transcripts and tape recordings may impose some limits on our ability to plot the distribution of laughter; who laughs and how they laugh. Another problem is in a will to reduce the complexity of the interaction. It is important not to lose sight of laughter as a way of retrieving and restoring the complexity of the interaction. In that spirit we would add a further reading of the laughter event.

Is it necessary to conclude that the joke is told *against* the member of the group who self-identifies as naïve or the group that recognises itself in that position? In this instance we would suggest that this is not the inevitable interpretation (cf. Juni and Katz 2001). A return to Freud's reflections on the nature of the joke is useful here. He emphasises the capacity of the joke to bring forward something that is concealed. What is concealed/revealed in the joke in this instance? First, the revelation (and thereby the laughter) may be the exposure of the cultural connection between the comic and the naïve that does not appear in the initial description. Second, the laughter might relate to the repetition of a taboo; the public dimension of sex work. By way of repetition, that which ought not to be spoken of is given a public airing. Third, it might be generated by way of the absurdity (the nonsense) of heterosexual sex workers offering sex for money to a gay man. Here a gay man on the fringes of the gay Village is confronted with an experience of being both in place and out of place. This offers a comparison, again a laughter technique noted by Freud. Finally, the laughter may relate to the heroics of safety management. In particular the absurdity of the encounter that assumes heteronormativity offers a moment of laughter that is not so much a reference to a hierarchical differentiation within the group that positions gay men as the excluded and vulnerable other, but a moment of consolidation. Here the intra- and inter-personal is made over against the heterosexual outsider. In the final instance we would stress the need to assume the possible simultaneity of these (and other) possible meanings.

Our second example comes from a series of exchanges that took place in the Lancaster gay men's group. It arises again in the context of a series of reflections about perceptions and experiences of danger and safety focusing upon particular types of behaviour in particular locations, for example 'kissing another man'. Paul asked the following: 'What about camping it up or butching it up? Do you camp it up or butch it up in different places?' The immediate responses distanced respondents from camp by emphasising 'butching it up'. One of the members of the group, having explained that he mainly 'butched it up' in the company of straight people whom he didn't know, went on to talk more generally about 'butching it up':

> My friends have recently been trying to get me to walk straight because they're saying that my walk's put on. They're trying to get me to walk straight. So we're walking home and they're saying, 'right put your hands in your pockets and walk with your legs apart'. So I was doing that for them and then they were laughing because it looked odd. [laughter]

He then proceeded to put this experience into the context of another incident that drew attention to the place of these techniques of the male body in the control of safety and management of danger:

> we were walking to the bus stop and I was with this friend ... and there was this argument going on in front of us with these two really rough lads. [One lad was] just like shouting at this other lad ... 'oh you fucking puff'. So I put my hands in my pockets and started walking straight past them. [I thought] 'Yes, this could come in handy, definitely' ... I just use butching it up when I'm like that. But I'll camp it up quite a bit at the university occasionally when I'm just walking down the spine, my hands will start to go out when I'm walking, I'll do whatever it takes and I'll just attract attention, but that's because I'm a drama studies student.

Paul replied, 'And is that really how you felt when you were walking past those lads. You took it as a joke?' In response the group member said, 'Yes, quite handy.'

Laughter appears in three contexts in this exchange. First, the laughter of others is reported: that of the speaker's straight friends in the context of his attempts to walk 'butch'. It appears a second time as a response of focus group participants to the speaker's anecdote about the problematic (failed?) attempt to perform particular gendered, 'butch', practices of walking. Third, laughter appears in a reflection on the use of particular performances of walking as a safety strategy for gay men, both in the performance of the safety story and in Paul's final probing question. These three moments offer very different but contiguous contexts and manifestations of laughter. Analysis should seek to examine the specifics of each instance as well as their interconnection.

The first laugh arises in the context of a particular danger, stranger straights, a particular set of practices and aesthetics of masculinity and a particular audience, friends. It is a laughter that seems to appear by way of the technique of comparison; the walking practices of a gay man with 'butch' walking. The laughter appears in the context of the 'visible labour' (cf. Kirkham and Skeggs 1998: 296) of masculinity that normally remains hidden, and the failure to 'get it right'. The laughter of the straight friends might also relate to a comparison between their own failed performances of gender and those of the person who is performing them. In close proximity to the laughter of the straight friends is the laugh of the focus group participants. Again comparison might have some significance here, but this time the comparison is between gay men. What is revealed in and through this laughter? One possible answer is that it repeats their own experiences of the labour demands of 'butch' masculinity as safety. It might also reveal their experiences of failure to achieve these demands. While this second laugh might be read in terms of a recognition of inevitable oppression, the speaker does not end on this pessimistic note. He counterpoints an instance of the 'successful' performance of 'butch' in the face of a threatening homophobic situation.

This brings us to the last laugh in this example. Paul's question, 'You took it as a joke?', sought to probe the 'jokey' manner in which the story of successfully 'butching it up' had been told. The response, 'Yes, quite handy', could be taken as an avoidance of the issue or at best an equivocal response. Is the jokey presentation a practice of a self-effacement that perpetuates the negative associations connected to other masculinities and links them to the loss of self-esteem and self-oppression? Maybe. But in addition it may be a response that points to the masquerade of safer (hetero) masculinity as an albeit fleeting moment of victory and of self-esteem (cf. Juni and Katz 2001). The jokiness also connects experiences of danger and safety to pleasure; here maybe the pleasure of retelling. Rather than reducing the performance of safer hetero masculinity to practices of domination and erasure, it is important to recognise their relation to pleasure. Furthermore, in the context of a fleeting moment of self-esteem, this pleasure need not be reduced to a form of delusion or self-oppression. It may offer an instance of the pleasure of self-assertion and of self-confidence.

These issues also surfaced in an exchange taken from a Lancaster lesbian group discussion. They arise in the context of a discussion of the danger attendant upon kissing in public, the labour involved, and the possibility of a failure to achieve safety through these practices of self-reflection. One of the group members explored these issues in the context of a reflection on kissing her partner in the street. She explained that in that context she is only willing to give her partner a 'peck'. She continued:

that is when the whole cookie is crumbling really because you have to make a decision and you find the more you think about it the more likely someone is going to spot you because if you just went (kiss) 'goodbye' and you are off you know. I do feel self conscious, I must admit. You just don't know who is going to walk past and I feel sort of annoyed that I am worried about it and then walking away. Like tonight, we sort of split our various ways and a guy was walking up the road and I kind of looked at him. He looked at me first and I looked at him as if to say 'yes' sort of thing. I had to kind of do that consciously. I felt to say 'Yes, I am still here. I am a real person.' Then I crossed the road. I don't feel comfortable with the whole, I feel that I have to mentally prepare myself for that and yet it is just a kiss.

Amanda: It is about practice though isn't it. It's about the more you do it the more confident you become with it.
          (*Laughter, all talking at once*)
Natalie: (*laughing*) I don't need to practice it's just my ....
Alexi: Great chat up line.
          (*Laughter, everyone talking at once*)
Amanda: I find myself saying to myself 'fuck them, get on with it', the more you don't the more you have to sit there with the thoughts that go with it, ... and the more you practice something the more you get used to it and you become more confident with it. It is about getting out and doing it.

Here the laughter, the laughter technique of opposites, highlights contradictions of safety and danger. The opposition is between the demands of safety techniques that seek to limit kissing and the generation of new kissing opportunities occasioned by the need to be competent in the practices of safer kissing. What oppresses and undermines also strengthens and creates new opportunities to perform that which is forbidden. The pleasure invoked and licensed by the safety techniques also takes the form of self-assertion against the oppressive and limiting aspects of these techniques, as evidenced in 'fuck them, get on with it'. Here the practices of safety are linked to the production of confidence and a particular visibility. In this instance laughter brings out an aspect of the experiences of safety and danger that may not have been thought of previously; it has a certain serendipitous quality (cf. Kruger 1994: Ch. 4).

Laughter and serendipity

An instance of laughter and serendipity is found in the following extract. It comes from a discussion about safety strategies by Lancastrian gay men adopted in the context of the perceived threat of 'kids of about 14 to 16 hanging around because they haven't got spaces to go to' encountered in the journey to and from the centre of town. Phil explained:

I do [think about safety], I catch myself doing it. If I see them out of the corner of my eye, I'll sort of push myself to make myself look bigger than I actually am. You hear about things, like people who go on holiday giving advice, 'look as if you know where you're going', but I've no sense of direction at all. I get lost going anywhere. Even if I'm going the totally wrong way I will continue to go down that way until they can't see me and then turn round and come back the other way. Because, as I said, I'm paranoid, I will try to push my shoulders out and look bigger than I am so I get less trouble.

Daniel:	I put my mittens into my pockets. [*laughter*]
Paul:	Well what is it about mittens then Daniel?
Tony:	Take off your telly tubby badge …
Daniel:	I don't know, it's something about having nice warm gloves that makes you a soft target. So I hide them. Because all the potential hecklers and attackers will not be wearing gloves.
Paul:	Is that something about hardness? In Sheffield, where I lived for a long time, you'd go out on a Friday night and people had basically no clothes on, almost. They were walking down the street and there was three inches of snow; T-shirt and shorts to make themselves look tough.
Christopher:	You can always do that, try to look tough.
Tony:	To avoid the cloakroom charge. [*laughter*]
Paul:	I thought of that but it was too cold to be worrying about 50p.

Paul, facilitating, probes the 'unsaid' marked by the laughter. The immediate context of the reference to 'mittens', a type of fingerless glove, is the prior elaboration of a catalogue of masculine corporeal techniques of safety (looking bigger). The response in the wake of laughter makes a connection by way of a sharp contrast. 'Mittens' as a sharp contrast depends upon the attribution of particular characteristics. The first is produced by way of metaphor: telly tubby. 'Telly tubby' is a reference to a British television show designed for children under 2 years of age. This connotes 'mittens' as infantile and infantalising. But 'telly tubby' has other meanings here. It also refers to the TV show's cult status within a celebratory gay politics. The character 'Tinky Winky' with a triangle on his head and a handbag has become something of a gay icon. This iconic status is also in part a response to some Christian fundamentalists, particularly in the US, who have promoted (in order that it be condemned) the character as a negative association between gay and femininity. 'Telly tubby' conjoined to 'mittens' condenses a multiplicity of meanings that may also be contradictory.

Thereafter the exchange makes associations between 'mittens' and softness, which also has connotations of femininity. Putting the mittens in 'my pockets' refers us back to the earlier reference to the practice of 'pockets' in the performance of 'butch' hetero-masculinity. But, in this instance Daniel raises a note of caution. The use of pockets may itself be less than the required masculinity. This leads to a reflection by Paul about sartorial practices of masculinities that are given a particular geographical location, Sheffield. The banter ends with another outbreak of laughter. This exchange brings another frame of reference into play in making sense of the performance of masculinity as safety: class. Daniel's comments give the practices of 'butch' a class aspect. More specifically, they are made to signify the working class. In this instance and in the reflection that follows, class is produced by way of a series of metonyms where a part stands for the whole. Thus the absence of gloves, the wearing of inappropriate clothing, the desire to avoid the payment of the cloakroom charge are all signs of working class. Sheffield, with its industrial, blue-collar associations and its labour traditions, is a spatial reference to working class. In and through this chain of associations a link is forged between the working class, gendered violence and particular gendered strategies of safety in response to that violence (cf. Moran 1999; Skeggs 1999). In this instance it is in the class dimension of violence and safety that the failure and success of the safety practices is located.

Conclusions: taking laughter seriously

The use of focus groups in the Violence, Sexuality, Space research project produced many challenges. Some we were prepared for. Others, such as the challenge of laughter, we were not. Having found laughter as a pervasive presence in our data, our attempt to take laughter seriously brought us up against a well-established set of assumptions that position laughter as antithetical to 'serious thinking'. Laughter brought us up against the limits of our epistemological assumptions.

This is a set of assumptions that not only separates laughter from other data but marginalises it and relegates it to a place beyond knowledge and understanding: a form of data denied the status of truth. It is by way of these assumptions that laughter is associated with the trivial, the private, the individual and the corrupt (Bakhtin 1984: 101). Its low status is also marked in its place within social institutions. It continues to be predominantly associated with 'lower canonical genres' (*ibid.*) and specific cultural locations, the novel, burlesque, the popular stage. This is reflected in academic scholarship. Work on humour and laughter appears predominantly in humanities scholarship and rarely within the social sciences. The editors of a recent collection of papers on humour in the discipline of psychology suggested that within social science scholarship the study of humour and laughter is at a relatively 'early stage of development, still gaining legitimacy and recognition' (Mahony and Lippman 2001: 117). One of the challenges we faced was to think against the grain of this dominant order within the social sciences.

In many ways both our initial reaction to the laughter found in the focus groups and the absence of reference to laughter in the methodological literature on focus groups, either as method or as important data, mirror the values that separate laughter from 'serious thought'. In this chapter we offer a challenge to that traditional picture of laughter: an analysis that explores laughter as 'serious data'. This allows us to break away from the either/or that separates out laughter from knowledge and truth, making possible the production of a more nuanced perspective. This has particular significance in the context of work on violence, social exclusion and social marginality. Taking laughter seriously, Bakhtin suggests, promotes 'open seriousness'. 'Open seriousness', he argues, is a response to an approach to data and truth that promotes the singularity of meaning which is produced by way of exclusions. It promotes an awareness 'of being part of an uncompleted whole' (Bakhtin 1984: 122). These insights warn that the marginalisation and denigration of 'laughter' as significant data threaten to (re)produce silences and absences that perpetuate hierarchies of knowledge (cf. Foucault 1980). More specifically, 'open seriousness' offers to promote a style and form of knowledge that works against a process of truth formation which appears to share many of the attributes of the violence; of exclusion using fear, intimidation, intolerance and fanaticism, to name but a few. Thus to perpetuate the marginalisation and the denigration of laughter as research data threatens to (re)produce those social hierarchies that critical research on violence and safety seeks to challenge. Taking laughter seriously restores 'ambivalent wholeness' (Bakhtin 1984: 123).[10]

The analysis offered in this chapter suggests that there is much to be gained within the social sciences from an engagement with humour and laughter. Laughter elevates and gives emphasis to values, ideas and associations that might otherwise be less than apparent. As such it offers opportunities to gain insight into the generation of social and cultural orders. It is a complex mode of communication that offers many methodological challenges. Its multiplicity of meanings and the contradictory meanings of laughter raise formidable challenges for those who seek to understand the meaning of laughter. Our preliminary analysis suggests that laughter is an important source of data through which we can gain an understanding of the everyday practices of safety and the management of danger by those who are subjected to targeted violence. The prejudice against laughter in social science research in general and in the specific context of work on violence and safety needs to be challenged.

Notes

1 ESRC award reference number L133251031.
2 For examples drawn from the focus group data see Moran *et al.* 2001 and Moran 2002.
3 These had arisen in the context of undertaking focus groups in a seed corn research project on sexuality and space funded by a grant from the Institute of Women's Studies at Lancaster University. The findings from that project provided the basis for our ESRC project.
4 For more information see Tyrer, P. *et al.* 'Researching Sexuality: A methodological outline of a research project' available on the Violence, Sexuality, Space website, http://les1.man.ac.uk/sociology/vssrp
5 There are some instances of laughter recorded in the structured interviews but these are exceptional. The surveys conducted in entertainment spaces also generated instances of laughter. Sometimes these occurred in the context of distributing, completing and returning the survey form. Other instances are to be found in the responses to the

survey questions. Jokey responses to survey questions were sometimes indicated by the respondents' use of exclamation marks. Laughter was also a part of the research team's response to undertaking the survey.

6 Citizens' Inquiries were a unique part of the project's methodology. In each locality they facilitated interaction between our focus group participants and individuals nominated as key local individuals. The events took place in March (Lancaster) and April (Manchester) 2000. Each meeting lasted just over two hours. We drafted a statement of policy issues synthesised from the focus group discussions to be circulated in advance. The invited speakers were asked to address these issues in a short opening presentation. Following questions and discussion, participants reviewed the policy papers. (See website above, note 4.)

7 In Freud's study laughter itself is reduced to a physiology of 'mental excitation' and 'psychical energy', its flows and its discharge, its economy (Freud 1976: 192–202).

8 All participants in the focus groups were given the option of anonymity. Where participants took that option we asked them to select a name. Not all participants chose that option. They expressed concern that anonymity denied them a voice and a right to be heard. All the names used in this article are the result of that process of consultation and decision.

9 Our data were collected by means of audio tapes, contemporaneous note taking and subsequently recorded moderator reflections.

10 On the theme of ambivalence, see Moran 2002.

References

Bakhtin, M. (1984) *Rabelais and his world* (trans.) Helen Iswolsky. Bloomington: Indiana University Press.

Boston, R. (1974) *An anatomy of laughter*. London: Collins.

Fern, E.A. (2001) *Advanced focus group research*. Thousand Oaks, CA: Sage.

Foucault, M. (1980) *PowerKnowledge*. Brighton: Harvester.

Freud, S. (1976) *Jokes and their relation to the unconscious*, Pelican Freud Library, vol. 6. London: Penguin.

Juni, S. and B. Katz (2001) 'Self effacing wit as a response to oppression: Dynamics in ethnic humor', *Journal of General Psychology*, 128(2), 119–43.

Katz, J. (1999) *How emotions work*. Chicago: Chicago University Press.

Kirkham, P. and B. Skeggs (1998) 'Absolutely fabulous: Absolutely feminist?', in C. Geraghty and D. Lusted (eds) *The television studies book*. London: Arnold, 287–98.

Kruger, R.A. (1994) *Focus groups: a practical guide for applied research*. Newbury Park: Sage.

Mahony, D.L., W.J. Burroughs and A.C. Hieatt (2001) 'The effects of laughter on discomfort thresholds: Does expectation become reality?', *Journal of General Psychology*, 128(2), 217–27.

Mahony, D.L. and L.G. Lippman (2001) 'Theme issue on humour and laughter: Guest editors' introduction', *Journal of General Psychology*, 128(2), 117–19.

Moran, L.J. (1999) 'Homophobic violence: the hidden injuries of class', in S. Munt (ed.) *Cultural studies and the working class*, London: Cassell, 206–18.

Moran, L.J. (2002) 'The poetics of safety: lesbians, gay men and home', in A. Crawford (ed.) *Crime, insecurity, safety in the new governance*. Cullompton: Wilans, 274–99.

Moran, L.J., B. Skeggs, P. Tyrer and K. Corteen (2001) 'Property, boundary, exclusion: Making sense of hetero-violence in safer spaces', *Social and Cultural Geography*, 2(4), 407–20.

Morgan, D.L. (1997) *Focus groups as qualitative research* (2nd edn). Thousand Oaks, CA: Sage.

Morgan, D.L. (1998) *The focus group guide: Focus group kit* vol. 1. Thousand Oaks, CA: Sage.

Nietzsche, F. (1974) *The gay science* (trans.) Walter Kaufmann. New York: Vintage Books.

Skeggs, B. (1999) 'The appearance of class', in S. Munt (ed.) *Cultural studies and the working class*. London: Cassell, 129–51.

Stanko, E. (1999) 'Identities and criminal violence: Observations on law's recognition of vulnerable victims in England and Wales', *Studies in Law, Politics and Society*, 16, 99–119.

Stewart, D.W. and P. Shamdasani (1990) *Focus groups: Theory and practice*. Newbury Park, CA: Sage.

7 Researching violence

Power, social relations and the virtues of the experimental method

Mark Levine

Introduction

The aim of this chapter is to reclaim and rehabilitate the experimental method as a useful tool for those engaged in violence research. This is no easy task, not least because it will be extremely difficult to persuade violence researchers from across the social sciences to read beyond the opening sentence. Most social scientists see 'the experiment' as embracing both an outdated positivism and a naïve realism – stripping away what is important about social relations under the guise of experimental 'control'. Of course, there is a level at which they are absolutely right. Some experimentalists are clearly unreflexive about their practice. They impose their own categories or assumptions upon data and assume that these are shared by research participants. They control the context in which information is generated and then imagine that their findings are universal rather than context specific. Finally, they treat research participants in a manner which fails to respect their experience or contribution to the research process. However, these are not charges which apply only to those who use the experimental method. Social scientists who employ questionnaire or survey methods, or those who conduct interviews or ethnographic studies, or even those whose data comprise official or historical records, are not immune from such criticism. They are all open to accusations of decontextualisation, reification or 'imperialism'. In other words, all methods (including the experimental method) are theory in disguise. They contain assumptions (both implicit and explicit) and practices which are instrumental in creating the object of enquiry. There is nothing intrinsically evil about the experimental method. Researchers (including experimentalists) can be more or less reflexive about the degree to which their methods play a role in 'producing' knowledge. Just as good social science research is predicated on the reflexive examination of the researcher's own practice (see the other chapters in this collection), so good experimental work (shorn of the non-reflexive tendencies of some experimentalists) can contribute to knowledge in the violence research tradition.

That is not to say that experiments do not have their limitations. Like any method, the experiment can help in answering some questions and not others. However, this chapter will suggest that the experimental method has particular advantages for the study of violence. In particular, the chapter will suggest that the experiment is an excellent arena for the study of inequality, oppression and power, and that a concern with these dimensions is central to research on violence. For example, almost all violence research begins with the question of definition. In order to be able to study violence, researchers need to make decisions about what constitutes violence and how a violent act can be identified. While the specifics of this debate are complex, there is general agreement that violence involves the operation of power. Violence can appear in iniquitous social relations as well as in acts of physical force. The experiment, properly understood, is a domain which allows for the exploration of power in such social relations. It has a structure which allows some people (the experimenters) the power to constrain, coerce and observe, while others (the 'subjects') are constrained, coerced and observed. In an experiment (as in life) there is always space for resistance to power – but more usually (as in life), the 'subjects' work within the constraints imposed upon them by powerful others. It is by making the social relations of the experiment explicit – rather than treating the experiment as some kind of value free or neutral context – that the relevance of the experimental method to violence research becomes apparent.

Experimental methods and violence research – the 'bystander' paradigm

In the hope of demonstrating some of the virtues of the experimental method for violence research, the remainder of the chapter will focus on some examples of our work in the Violence Research Project (VRP). Our project was concerned with the role of the bystander in respect of violent crime. We began with the insight that most research on violence ignores the role of bystanders. It concentrates instead on exploring the characteristics of the perpetrator or the characteristics of the victim, or more dynamically, the relationship between perpetrator and victim. While there is clearly much to be learned from such approaches, we argue that the neglect of the role of the bystander is a crucial omission. Nearly all violence has an audience who either witness the violence directly, or who know about it indirectly. How such bystanders behave will affect, in large measure, whether violence is stopped, is allowed to continue, or is even escalated. For example, a number of theorists have pointed to the role played by bystanders during the Holocaust. There are accounts of individual rescuers of Jewish men, women and children (Oliner and Oliner 1988). There are carefully documented descriptions of the failure of entire societies to intervene against the systematic persecution of the Jews (Staub 1989, Hilberg 1992). Equally importantly, there are stories of collective resistance of societies against the Nazi attempts at genocide (see Toderov (2001) on the way in which Bulgarian polity and society prevented the elimination of Bulgarian Jews).

Despite the crucial role played by bystanders in the trajectory of violence, the bystander is largely absent from traditional social science research on violence. However, in social psychology, there is a body of literature which attempts to explain the behaviour of bystanders in emergencies. This literature traces its origins to the brutal rape and murder of a woman called Kitty Genovese, in New York in 1964. Genovese was attacked on her way home from work and, over a period of 30 minutes, was raped and then murdered. Horrifying as this was, what shocked people even more was the fact that 38 witnesses (all located in the surrounding buildings) failed to intervene. It was the inaction of the bystanders that prompted two social psychologists, John Darley and Bibb Latané (1968, Latané and Darley 1970) to explore the behaviour of bystanders in emergency settings. They conducted a number of elegant and carefully choreographed field experiments which placed people in emergency settings. This included hearing someone apparently having an epileptic seizure, or someone falling off a ladder, or sitting in a room which begins to fill with smoke. The finding of experiments such as these (and a whole raft of similar studies reviewed in Latané and Nida 1981) was that the greater the number of people who witness an emergency event, the less likely each individual is to help. This became known as 'the bystander effect'.

The experimental work in support of traditional bystander theory has much to commend it. Its strength lies primarily in the fact that it deals with real intervention behaviour, as opposed to professed intention to act or post-hoc rationalisations of (in)action. If you ask people about the likelihood of intervention, they usually say that they will help – however, when actually confronted by an emergency situation, people tend to help much less than they think. For this reason alone, experimental work can add value to the violence research paradigm. However, there are also important limitations in traditional bystander experimental work. Despite the volume of evidence for the 'bystander effect', the whole research tradition appears to lack utility. It has never been used successfully to increase the likelihood of intervention in violent attacks. As Latané and Nida (1982) so eloquently put it, 'none of us has been able to mobilise the increasing store of social psychological understanding accumulated over the last decade to ensure that future Kitty Genoveses will receive help' (p. 322). Part of the reason for this can be traced, Cherry (1994) argues, to the way in which the original experiments were devised. Cherry points out that, in trying to create experimental analogues of the Genovese murder, Darley and Latané stripped out the two most important components of the original act. They neglected the social relations which were central to the event (this was an attack by a man on a woman) and removed the focus on violence. Instead, the experiments focused on emergency helping situations which contained neither a perpetrator nor violence. Cherry suggests that this was a result of what she calls 'culturally embedded theorising' – a kind of theoretical myopia (when it came to male violence towards women) in pre-feminist 1960s America. Add to this the difficulties of simulating violence experimentally, and it becomes easier to explain why the experiments focus on helping rather than intervention in violence.

Our research work (see Levine *et al.* in press) revisits this paradigm, but attempts to reintroduce the concern both with social relations and with violence. The former is much easier than the latter. Where Darley and Latané focus only on the presence or absence of bystanders, we have explored the meanings of social relationships between bystanders and fellow bystanders, between bystanders and victims and between bystanders and perpetrators of violence. However, putting violence back into the experimental method is a much more difficult task. For a variety of ethical, logistic and pragmatic reasons, simulating violence in laboratory conditions has become extremely problematic. Social psychologists have not felt able to attempt such work since the seminal obedience to authority experiments of Stanley Milgram (1974).[1] This inability to deal with violence at first hand, however, is not something which is confined to experimental work alone. Researchers who carry out non-experimental work are seldom in a position to deal with violence directly. Their data usually consist of 'second-hand' accounts of violent events (interviews, questionnaires, media reports, legal papers, official records, etc.). This 'distance' from the original violent act can have consequences for violence research. We have already seen the slip between words and deeds in the study of bystander behaviour. Similar concerns can be raised whenever research relies on texts (of all kinds) which by definition (re)present violence. The violent act is not accessed directly but read through the filter of intervening 'stakes'. For both experimental and non-experimental work on violence, there is always the question of how this gap between violence and its representation should be negotiated and understood.

Social relations and bystander behaviour: some experimental work

Our experimental work began with an attempt to explore the social relationships between all those present at a violent incident. This included the perpetrator and the victim as well as the bystander. Our aim was to examine both the differential and the combined effects of these (inter)relationships on the behaviour of bystanders in the context of violence. In order to be able to do so, we utilised the structure of the experimental format to shape how people viewed themselves and their relations to others. By availing ourselves of the power of the experimenter to define and prescribe social relations, respondents were sometimes directed to pay attention to their relationships to other bystanders, sometimes directed to their relationship to victims, and at other times directed to their relationship to perpetrators.

While we could not present our respondents with 'real-life' violence, we attempted to create conditions which approximated to the kinds of violent incidents in which intervention decisions would need to be made. Thus, the focal point of the experiments consisted of a three-minute video of a violent incident in a car park. The video appeared to be footage captured on a CCTV camera (although in reality it was a simulation made by the research team as data protection legislation prevents the use of genuine CCTV footage). The footage, which showed an attack by two men on a third man, was deliberately grainy and indistinct. This provided a degree of ambiguity in the action and a lack of distinguishing features on the individuals in the footage, which allowed us to tell different stories about what might be seen in the video. It also fitted with respondents' stereotypes of how CCTV footage looks (an important consideration in the face validity of the experiment), although in fact, current technology means that real CCTV footage is clear and distinct.[2]

All our experiments used students as respondents. While this is sometimes seen as a weakness of experimental work (some experimentalists have a tendency to make universal claims based on specific student populations), in violence research, using a student population can be a strength. Students belong to the stratum of young people most at risk from violent assault, spend much time and money in the 'night-time' economy where they are likely to witness violence, and share a social group membership which can be meaningful at particular times and/or places. In other words, students have experience of, and exposure to, the kinds of phenomena which are of interest to violence researchers.

We carried out three sets of experiments using the video. In the first we explored the importance of relationships between bystanders and fellow bystanders. Students watched the video in groups of four. However, two of the four were confederates of the experimenters. In different experimental conditions, the confederates were asked to present themselves as ingroup members (students from the same university as the naïve subjects) or as outgroup members (students from a local college). They were also asked to indicate that they felt the violence was serious and worthy of intervention, or that the violence was not serious and unworthy of intervention. In our experiment, it was only when the confederates presented as ingroup members that their opinion and willingness to intervene (or not to intervene) influenced the naïve subjects. In this way we were able to demonstrate that it is only when people think that fellow bystanders are ingroup members that what they say or do will be influential.

In the second experiment we explored the relationship between bystanders and victims of violence. In this experiment students watched the video in large groups. Some of the groups were told that the video captured an attack on a student, other groups were told that the video captured an attack on a local youth. This experiment allowed us to argue that people are more likely to (express the intention to) intervene when they believe the victim is an ingroup rather than an outgroup member.

In the third experiment we explored the relationship between bystanders and perpetrators. Once again, students watched the video in groups. Some groups were told that this was an attack carried out by students, others that it was an attack carried out by local youths. The findings of this study were more ambiguous. Sharing group membership with a perpetrator of violence could just as easily result in intervention on the side of the perpetrator as it could in intervention to stop the perpetrator carrying out the violence. What seemed most likely to persuade bystanders to stop violence from ingroup perpetrators was when that violence might damage the reputation of the group as a whole.

Taken together, these experimental studies paint a complex picture of some of the factors which are important in bystander behaviour. They provide a challenge to traditional social psychological theories which are more concerned with the presence or absence of others in an emergency situation, rather than the meaning of social relations between them. They point to the importance of group membership for explaining the behaviour of all those present during a violent episode. Finally, they challenge the pessimism which surrounds previous public policy interventions designed to increase a sense of responsibility for the welfare of others. However, despite their strengths, they are still experiments which demonstrate intention to act rather than actual intervention behaviour itself. As we have already seen, intention and action in emergency situations are not always the same. The importance of social group memberships for intervention behaviour in 'real life' remains to be demonstrated. Thus, the final phase of our experimental work on bystander behaviour moved from laboratory-based experiments to field experiments which measured actual intervention, rather than intention to act.

Exploring intervention in 'real life' settings: some field experiments

In designing field experiments to explore bystander behaviour, the difficulties presented by the simulation of violence are particularly apparent. It is extremely difficult to create a simulation of a violent event which has the kind of face validity required to make it believable. It is almost impossible to reproduce the simulated 'real life' violent event from trial to trial in order to ensure reliability. Finally, the intention to expose people to a violent event (even in simulation) raises ethical problems which are extremely difficult (although not impossible) to address. Our field experiments therefore stepped back from attempting violence simulations and addressed instead the general issue of the importance of perceived social relations for helping in emergencies. We felt that it was a necessary first step to demonstrate the role played by social group memberships in 'real life' bystander intervention and that the issues raised by the inclusion of violence could be addressed at a later stage.

Our field experiments therefore concentrated on creating an environment in which we would examine the actual behaviour of those exposed to a potential emergency – and yet be able to control experimentally the nature of the social relations that bystanders believed existed between them and the 'victim'. To do so we took advantage of the current British fashion for wearing football (soccer) team shirts as casual wear (as opposed to wearing team colours to the stadium only). These shirts signify potential group membership and are a clear demonstration of potential relations to others. The fact that people are used to seeing these shirts in a variety of different (and non-football related) contexts, and can easily 'read' the group affiliation of the wearer, was turned to experimental advantage.

Before the experiment is described in detail, it is important to know more about the place of football (soccer) in an English social context and about the importance of different kinds of football related social categories (and the nature of their intergroup relationship). In terms of popularity and appeal, Manchester United are currently the most famous and high-profile team in England. In addition to their widespread popularity they have, in the past ten years, been the dominant team in English football. At the same time, and perhaps as a result of this success, fans of all other football clubs treat Manchester United fans as potentially inauthentic (not 'real') fans who are just attracted by glamour and success. Moreover, fans of Manchester United have a long-standing rivalry with supporters of Liverpool Football Club. Liverpool and Manchester are competing regional cities in the north west of England. Although they are only 30 miles apart, people born in the respective cities have different accents, different self images, and draw on different historical and industrial traditions. Moreover, where Manchester United currently dominate English football, Liverpool FC were the dominant team of the 1980s. The history of animosity between some of the fans of the teams is played out in communal chants which are directed at opposition fans inside football grounds as well as in occasional violent skirmishes outside football grounds. Attachment to group identities and the intergroup rivalry between Manchester United and Liverpool fans is therefore deeply held and extremely meaningful.

The field experiment began with the recruitment of people to take part. For several weeks prior to the experiment, recruitment posters inviting people to take part in a study of football fans were posted around the university. Those interested in signing up were asked for their names, a contact number, and the team they supported. Only those who indicated that they supported Manchester United were then recruited to take part in the study (the others were contacted, thanked for volunteering and told that we had sufficient people for the study). The Manchester United fans were thus unaware that they had been chosen for their particular group affiliation. Each volunteer was asked to come to the psychology department at an appointed time, and upon arrival, taken to a small research cubicle. There he was asked to write a short essay about his team, and to fill in a short questionnaire about his team. This was designed to make him feel strongly identified with his Manchester United group membership. When he had completed this task, he was told that he needed to go to another building to watch a video about football (the cubicle was too small for this purpose) and then answer some more questions. He was escorted out of the building and to the start of a car park which separated the psychology department from the building housing the screening room. At this point, the experimenter made an excuse about meeting the next participant, and asked the volunteer to go to the screening room (where he was told he would be met by another experimenter) on his own. As the volunteer began to cross the car park, an accident was staged in front of him. A person came into view running towards the car park. When he reached the top of a grass bank on the edge of the car park, he slipped and fell, grabbing hold of his ankle and shouting out in pain. The only difference was, in some trials the 'victim' of the accident was wearing a Manchester United football shirt, in other trials he was wearing a Liverpool Football Club shirt (Manchester United and Liverpool are arch rivals), and yet in other trials he was wearing an ordinary (not football related) sweatshirt.

The results from this field experiment were clear. In almost 75 per cent of the trials when the 'victim' was wearing the Manchester United shirt, the bystander stopped to help. However, when the 'victim' was wearing the Liverpool or the 'ordinary' sportshirt, help was only offered on about 35 per cent of occasions. It seems from this that recognising signs of common group membership in a stranger in distress will lead to an increase in the likelihood of bystander intervention.

A second field experiment further reinforced the importance of perceived group membership for bystander intervention. We ran the study in the same way as before – participants were recruited in the same way, were all Manchester United fans, and came to the psychology department as before. However, this time participants were asked to write essays about being a football fan (as opposed to a Manchester United fan) and to fill in a questionnaire about being a football fan. The aim of this procedure was to make them feel strongly identified with a group membership which included all other football fans (not simply their team identity). It was hoped that this more inclusive, or higher order categorisation, would mean that they would identify with all other fans (including Liverpool fans) and therefore be more prepared to offer them help in an emergency. The experiment then proceeded in the same way as the first study, with participants exposed to the injured victim who was wearing either a Manchester United, Liverpool, or 'ordinary' sweatshirt. This time, however, participants were equally likely to help the victim in the Manchester United or Liverpool shirt, but not if he was wearing the ordinary sweatshirt. This field experiment therefore provides strong support (given the antipathy that exists between supporters of Manchester United and those of Liverpool at a club level) for the importance of making social categories as inclusive as possible in order to promote more widespread feelings of responsibility for the welfare of others.

The strength of field experiments such as this is their graphic demonstration of the importance of social group membership for bystander behaviour. Moreover, the field studies provide evidence of actual behaviour rather than of intention to act. They also identify the importance of the boundaries of social categories for increasing the likelihood of bystander intervention. The more inclusive the social category, the more likely we are to feel the kind of social solidarity which is important for ensuring the welfare of others (especially when those others are 'strangers'). These are the kinds of themes which are important for tackling societies in which feelings of communal responsibility seem to have been eroded and where so-called fear-of-crime runs rampant.

From experiments to qualitative work – and back again

Although the aim of this chapter has been to argue for the rehabilitation of experimental methods in violence research, it has not been our intention to claim some kind of superiority for experimental work over other methodological approaches. On the contrary, we are arguing against the kind of fetishisation of methods which can sometimes be read in the work of those who advocate qualitative or quantitative methods exclusively. Our research in the VRP was concerned more with the kinds of questions that needed to be asked, and only then with the kinds of methods which were most suited to answering those questions. The field experiments outlined in this chapter allowed us to look at the consequences of imposing certain kinds of social relations on others and to examine the behavioural consequences which flowed from these different relationships. However, they tell us very little about why people are behaving in the way they are, or how they account for their behaviour. The experiments allow us to argue that social group memberships are important, but we can only speculate about whether people act because of feelings of responsibility, notions of common fate, ideas about obligation, diffusion of responsibility, analysis of costs and benefits and so on. Moreover, while experiments are useful for looking at what happens when particular social group relationships are held constant, in real life, group relationships are much more fluid, dynamic, and subject to moment-by-moment change. People constantly negotiate, justify and contest not only the nature of their social relationships, but also the meaning of their behaviour. In order to know more about the experience of intervention (or non-intervention), and to know about these in the context of violence, we needed a different set of methodological tools.

To that end, and alongside our experimental work, we carried out a number of non-experimental research projects. The first was a series of 38 face-to-face interviews with a cross section of people in Lancaster, a small city in the north west of England. In this study, the aim was to sample as heterogeneously as possible to include men and women from a variety of age ranges, social class memberships and employment conditions. Interviews were carried out in the homes of respondents and focused on eliciting personal experiences of intervention (or lack of intervention) as a bystander to violent episodes. The interviews were structured around a scrapbook which contained four newspaper stories of violent incidents (two local stories, two national stories; two which described bystander intervention, two which described bystander inaction). The interviews were used to explore the norms which surround bystander behaviour in the context of violence, to elicit information about social group relations which either inhibited or facilitated intervention, and to weigh the assumptions of theories of bystander behaviour against the experiences of the bystanders themselves.

These individual interviews were then complemented by a group interview phase in which different factions of the same community were brought together to discuss community relations, violence, and bystander behaviour. In this research, seven groups (12/13-year-old youths; 18-year-old men; women from a community centre; members of a residents' association; members of the chamber of commerce; homeless men; the elderly) ranging in size from four to eight members, were recruited. The group interviews were focused around a map of the locality in which all participants lived. Each group was asked to indicate areas on the map that they felt were safe or dangerous; places where they had witnessed violence and intervened (or not); and places where they had been helped by others. The group interviews were then used to collect experiences of inter-group relations, accounts of intervention and feelings of community responsibility (self for others and others for self).

The strength of the face-to-face interview data lay in eliciting not only a set of normative beliefs about intervention, but also a wide variety of (non)intervention stories. These stories were useful not only for providing corroborating evidence for the picture which emerged from the experiments, but also in allowing us to understand more clearly the nature of behaviour in the experimental context. More importantly, the wide range of (non)intervention stories provided a rich source of material for later experimental work. The group interviews allowed us to combine our theoretical interest in inter-group relations with collective experience of violence and bystander behaviour. By allowing different factions of a community to talk through their relationship not only to each other but also to where they lived, we were able to deepen our understanding of bystander behaviour. These group interviews also served the function of allowing us to reflect back on the experimental work, and to look forward beyond the limits of experimentation.

While there is not space in this chapter to describe analysis of the face-to-face or the group interviews in detail, what is worth emphasising is the effort to integrate these different methodological approaches in order to broaden and deepen our understanding of bystander behaviour. The experimental work, the face-to-face interviews and the group interviews each play a significant part in the overall story which emerged from the research. None claims priority nor is any reduced to a purely supporting role. Rather we have attempted to 'triangulate' these different methods in a way that allows us to build a more sustained and persuasive argument.

Conclusion

The aim of this chapter has been to argue for a rehabilitation of experimental methods in violence research. The experiments described here are offered as an illustration of the kinds of questions which can be addressed in an experimental frame. Of course, the story which has been told about bystander behaviour is by no means complete – but this is not the time or the place to work through all those remaining loose ends. Instead, the chapter will conclude by revisiting its central argument – that violence researchers, be they experimentalists or non-experimentalists, face a common set of problems. They all have to deal with questions of definition in respect of violence. They also have to think about social relations and the dynamics of power which inhabit them. Finally, they are confronted with the problem of (re)representation – the fact that most violence data is 'second hand'. This chapter has argued that it is how these kinds of questions are dealt with – rather than the *faux* distinction between experimental and non-experimental methods – that makes for good violence research. In other words, what counts is what Bruno Latour (1988) might describe as an infra-reflexivity in approach to violence research. Latour describes an infra-reflex approach as one in which an account given of an object is applied to the account also. If we take Latour's injunction seriously we can see that the experimental method can be an exemplary method for violence research. The experimental method, with its instantiation of iniquitous relations of power between experimenter and 'subject', provides an analogue of the social relations of power which enshrine violence in society. By making these explicit in the context of the experiment it becomes possible actively to explore (rather than simply to reflect) not just the behaviour of bystanders, but also the relationship between power and violence as a whole.

Notes

1 In a series of experiments, Milgram asked people to give (what they thought were) electric shocks to a 'learner' in a memory experiment. The shocks increased in severity from 15 volts to 450 volts (labelled XXX and described as lethal). In the baseline experiment, 60 per cent of subjects gave the maximum voltage.
2 We made several pilot videos for the experiment. When we shot the videos with clarity and detail people tended to be more suspicious of their provenance. For the CCTV footage to be convincing, we had to shoot it not as it is, but as our respondents believed it to be!

References

Cherry, F. (1994) *The Stubborn Particulars of Social Psychology*. London: Routledge.
Darley, J. and Latané, B. (1968) 'Group inhibition of bystander intervention in emergencies'. *Journal of Personality and Social Psychology*, 10, 215–21.
Hilberg, R. (1992) *Perpetrators, Victims, Bystanders: The Jewish Catastrophe 1933–1945*. New York: HarperCollins.
Latané, B. and Darley, J. M. (1970). *The Unresponsive Bystander: Why Doesn't He Help?* New York: Meredith Corporation.
Latané, B. and Nida, S. (1981) 'Ten years of research on group size and helping'. *Psychological Bulletin*, 89, 2, 308–24.
Latour, B. (1988) *Laboratory Life: The Social Construction of Scientific Facts* (2nd edn). Princeton: Princeton University Press.
Levine, M., Cassidy, C., Brazier, G. and Reicher, S. (in press) 'Self-categorisation and bystander non-intervention: two experimental studies'. *Journal of Applied Social Psychology*.
Milgram, S. (1974) *Obedience to Authority: An Experimental View*. New York: Harper & Row.
Oliner, S. and Oliner, P. (1988) *The Altruistic Personality*. New York: Free Press.
Staub, E. (1989) *The Roots of Evil: The Origins of Genocide and Other Group Violence*. New York: Cambridge University Press.
Toderov, T. (2001) *The Fragility of Goodness: Why Bulgaria's Jews Survived the Holocaust*. London: Weidenfeld and Nicholson.

8 The rising tide of female violence?

Researching girls' own understandings and experiences of violent behaviour

E. Kay M. Tisdall

'Gangs put boot into old ideas of femininity.'
The Guardian, 22 July 1998

'Scottish girls leave out the sugar and spice as violent crimes rise.'
The Express, 30 March 1999

'Deadly as the males. Experts probe explosion of violence by girl gangs.'
Daily Record, 30 September 2000

'Girls lead the pack in new gangland violence.'
The Observer, 15 April 2001

Introduction

For the past several years, the media have frequently printed sensationalistic stories on 'violent girls'. The stories have typically hypothesised about the growth of girl gangs, the 'rising tide of female violence' and the convergence of girls' violence with that of boys. Yet in the UK these stories had no systematic evidence on which to base such views, with literature available primarily on men's violence and the most substantial research on girls being based on North American data (e.g. see Artz 1998; Baskin and Sommers 1993, 1998; Campbell 1984, 1990; Chesney-Lind 1997; Miller 2001).

The research study 'A View from the Girls: exploring violence and violent behaviour' sought to address such a knowledge gap.[1] The study used three main methods, with girls aged 13 to 16 across Scotland: a self-report questionnaire (671 girls), focus group discussions (18 groups, 89 girls) and individual interviews (12 girls). Fundamentally, the study proposed to examine 'ordinary' girls' own understandings of, attitudes to and experiences of violence and violent behaviour.[2] As outlined within current ideas of the sociology of childhood/childhood studies (e.g. see Christensen and James 2000; Hill and Tisdall 1997), girls' own views were considered essential to inform policies and practices that affect them. Such an aim, however, raises both ethical and methodological dilemmas, caused by the interweaving of research undertaken with children/young people, on a sensitive issue such as violence, with the goal of understanding its 'meaning' to them and their lives.

Two methodological literatures helpfully reflect on such dilemmas: the first on 'sensitive research' and the second on ethical research with children.[3] The 'sensitive research' literature has a slightly older history, with seminal articles and books published in the early 1990s (e.g. Lee 1993; Lee and Renzetti 1993). The literature takes a holistic view of the research process, beginning with how to gain funding and research access. Much discussion is given to the external controls put on methodology and subject matter at these initial stages. Advice is given on methods and data collection, such as accessing alternative sources and how to gather valid information. Problems and strategies are discussed in the production of research findings, from control of these by communities, gatekeepers and/or the researcher, to dealing with press interest.

A particular contribution from the literature is the recognition that research may not only pose problems for the participants but may also impact on the researcher's own career and safety. Lee's definition of 'sensitive research' is much-quoted: 'Research which potentially poses a substantial threat to those who are or have been involved in it' (1993: 4). Research may be threatening:

> (a) where research intrudes into the private sphere or delves into some deeply personal experience, (b) where the study is concerned with deviance and social control, (c) where it impinges on the vested interests of powerful persons or the exercise of coercion or domination, and (d) where it deals with things sacred to those being studied that they do not wish profaned.
>
> (Lee and Renzetti 1993: 5)

All four reasons can apply to research with children and, particularly, our research on girls and violent behaviour. The fundamental concern of the childhood literature (and thus the reason why it is sensitive), however, is not fully captured by this list: i.e. the greater power adults have than children in society, in general, and in research, in particular (Harden *et al.* 2000). This flows into concerns about the exploitation of children for researchers' own benefit, about how children understand research and can truly give 'informed consent' to participate, how the research will be used and presented, and children's own access to the research findings. Such concerns have particular salience for research on 'violence', which can be equally accused of an adult-centred and adult-dominated tradition in its definitions and methods.

The childhood literature has grown immensely over the past decade, with much-quoted works produced by such researchers as Alderson (1995), Christensen and James (2000), and journal articles within *Children and Society* Vols. 10–12. This literature strongly critiques past research for treating children as passive subjects rather than active agents in their lives — as 'human becomings' rather than 'human beings' (Qvortrup 1994) — and for unhelpfully focusing on a 'normal' childhood based on set child development stages. According to this critique, such research then risked having serious ethical and methodological flaws. By not recognising children as having rights themselves, consent for research participation was requested through parents rather than children. No concern was given to a child who might want to participate but whose parents refused on the child's behalf. Children might be participating in research without knowing what it entailed, what it was for and what would happen to the information collected. Discussions of confidentiality and anonymity were not necessarily held with children. Methodologically, past studies might have asked adults to describe children's experiences without considering that children (even at a very young age) may be well able to express their own views. Rather than presuming that a child is incompetent, the critique would challenge the researchers to consider how competent they and their methodologies are in gathering the desired information.

Reflecting on this critique, a large literature now exists describing the dilemmas of research with children and recommending methods to solve these. Strong commonalities exist. The need for informed consent is a pervasive theme, with a focus on ensuring that children receive accessible and relevant information so they can decide on their participation, on themselves giving consent and not (only) their parents, and seeing consent as an ongoing negotiation rather than one-off. Consent, though, is only one part of the ethical literature, which stresses the need to take a holistic approach to the research process from design to dissemination (see Alderson 1995). The power dynamics between adult researchers and child participants is much discussed in the literature, in the ethics of consent and in terms of methodology. Methodological recommendations are made – and debates held — on how the adult researchers might present themselves and on methods such as focus groups or paired interviews that provide children with more collective 'power' and control over the process. Methods beyond the more traditional written survey or oral interviews/focus groups are recommended, justified both to engage children in the research process and to gain improved data that recognise the extent of their knowledge and competencies. So, for example, the use of drawing, sentence completion exercises, role play and vignettes are explored in the literature and frequently recommended for consideration (Greig and Taylor 1999; Harden *et al.* 2000; Mauthner 1997).

What insight do these two literatures provide to the dilemmas faced in our research on girls and violence? Dilemmas are explored here at three stages of research (access, fieldwork and dissemination): first, accessing girls through adult/institutional 'gatekeepers'; second, research participants themselves having control of the research process and findings; and lastly the presentation of the 'sensitive research' itself.

Gatekeepers and consent

In discussing research ethics, Dingwall (1980: 878) describes a 'hierarchy of consent'. Senior personnel in the institution to be studied may be able to withhold consent. Once these personnel have agreed to participate, however, Dingwall doubts that subordinates would feel similarly able to withhold consent. Dingwall gives two reasons. First, subordinates who refuse to participate are at risk of 'official disfavour' (*ibid.*). Second, consent-seeking can be manipulated. The example provided is that of Dingwall attending group meetings to do a 'pitch' for the project and requesting co-operation. Subordinates can find it difficult to disagree, partly because their supervisor is present and partly out of politeness.

We were similarly concerned in undertaking 'A View from the Girls' within schools.[4] We had decided to recruit girls through schools, as a time- and cost-effective means to gain our required range and number of girls for the self-report questionnaire. We, too, were concerned about girls fearing 'official disfavour', once their school had agreed to take part. Like Dingwall, we made a 'pitch' to girls to participate (with preliminary visits to schools wherever practical), before schools handed out the consent leaflets for them and their parents.

Two further issues also seem to fit aptly under Dingwall's phrase 'hierarchy of consent'. First, schools are in many ways controlling institutions over children (Wyness 2000), tending to see children as 'human becomings' (Hill and Tisdall 1997), and are thus problematic as research sites (Morrow 1999). While numerous exceptions have been documented and schools are changing (Alderson 2000; Maguire and Marshall 1998, 2001), children's participation and the negotiation of consent are not traditional features of (Scottish) schools. Schools may require teachers to be present during fieldwork, which can significantly constrain what children say. Children are often acutely aware that teachers do not keep what children say confidential (Maguire and Marshall 1998). Asking children to fill in a form or undertake a task can feel like a school 'test', that they must do and to which there is a right and wrong answer.

We took certain steps to ameliorate these problems, with varying success. We sought to stress to girls that we were not teachers and there were no right nor wrong answers. Nonetheless, girls often would not speak unless spoken to and put up their hands before contributing to the discussion. Most schools presented no difficulty in our meeting with the girls in private during fieldwork, although this was not always the case. In one school, for example, the link teacher remained present during the completion of the questionnaire. Despite our requests to the contrary, s/he attempted to answer pupils' questions about the research and flicked through the girls' completed questionnaires. In another school, the only place available for us to conduct our focus group was the staff common room, where teachers were within earshot.

Our second issue could be described as the 'hierarchy of refusal'. This research needed to seek permission first from local authority education departments, then from schools and then from parents, before we ever spoke to or contacted girls. Local authorities, schools and parents could say 'no' to girls' involvement in the research and girls had limited opportunities to know about the research otherwise and to opt-in independently. The research was reported in the media and a web site was created but active recruitment through advertising and girls' magazines was not used. More positively, schools that agreed to participate were very willing for us then to have girls themselves actively consent to participate. Even if consent from all parties were given, risks of exclusion continue. For example, children may be held back from participating because they have not finished their work or are being disciplined (Morrow 1999). The flip-side may also be true: more academic girls may be excluded because of teachers' concern about their examination results. Not only does this limit the range of children involved in the research but children who may have wanted to participate are prevented from doing so.

We also made an explicit decision from the research design stage to access girls through informal institutional sites – i.e. youth groups and recreational opportunities in the study's age range – and not just through the formal institutional site of girls. This alternative approach would not provide us with sufficient numbers for quantitative analysis but, we hoped, would supply an important complement. Youth groups tend to support explicitly young people's participation and control of how the groups work. Youth groups typically are funded in more disadvantaged areas and thus may include more girls who do not attend school, who may be perceived as having behavioural problems or who do less well in school. Access through youth groups did seem to deliver on both of these ethical and methodological aspects. Unlike many of the girls accessed in schools, girls in youth groups regularly quizzed us throughout the research, wanting to know about our lives and our experiences of violence, what would happen with the research, and why we were interested in girls and violence in the first place. Participation at these youth groups was voluntary and, while a disappointment at times to us, if a girl did not attend at the designated research time, this could be seen as 'voting with her feet'. Girls did seem to have increased 'power' within these more informal research sites. Methodologically, girls were accessed through youth groups, who had particular circumstances not found in schools. For example, young mothers were accessed through one youth group and no young mothers (that we were aware of) were accessed through schools.

Certain of the girls accessed through youth groups did describe extensive experiences of violence that girls accessed through (mainstream) schools did not. In turn, the data gathered via schools supported the belief that girls generally, whatever their backgrounds or personal histories, experience a high level of 'everyday' violence. Some patterns were also observed about the type of violence being discussed, depending on setting. For example, girls in schools would mention violence in school corridors or when travelling to and from school, while girls in youth groups were more likely to talk about violence in their local communities.

Community control

The sensitive research literature describes the dilemmas of being, and being perceived as, an insider/outsider, in terms of first gaining access and then gathering meaningful data. Some communities are reported as being increasingly reluctant to be involved in research unless the research meets their own interests and they have considerable control over the origins, process and dissemination (Lee 1993, drawing on feminist research; disability studies has also experienced and discussed this (*Disability, Handicap and Society* 1992 Vol. 7 No. 2)). Only very recently have children been integral to the whole research process and been researchers themselves, in externally and relatively well-funded research (for example, see Hazekamp 2000; The Young Researchers 1998). Barriers still exist: from the need to develop research proposals within a highly jargonised and dense literature and theoretical context for more academic funders; to considering employment of children as researchers (potentially illegal under recent European and domestic legislation, with some exceptions); to being able to budget for the support and training costs of involving children on what are often tight tenders and funds.

This research did not undertake the most intense involvement of children but it did attempt to engage girls at various research stages as 'experts'. The research is based on an issue that very much concerns girls, as indicated in our pilot research (funded by the Gulbenkian Foundation) and consultations more generally with children (Scottish Executive 2001). A group of girls we first met in the pilot research were willing to act as a 'youth advisory group' (note the girls chose this title) for us in the full research.[5] We met this group five times during the project, and had other contact. The group advised us on how they wanted to participate, on the survey design and other methods and on ideas about the findings. The girls' contribution influenced such features as the graphical presentation of the questionnaire, certain wording and questions asked, and a range of questions to raise at analysis. We did not pay the girls for their time although we did invite them to the University (because they wished to come and see it), paid any expenses and frequently took them for meals out at a local fast-food restaurant, and gave vouchers to thank them for their participation at the end of the project.

The girls' involvement was not unproblematic. Cuts in community education funding during the second year meant that the youth group's continuation was insecure. Because the research (from pilot to completion) took place over four years, the membership of the youth group changed as girls grew up and out of the youth group and new members joined. It took considerable commitment from the girls, the youth group leader and ourselves to maintain contact. These girls had not (knowingly) been involved in any research before. Thus, we faced the challenge of trying to describe to them what, to our minds, research was for and what it could do.

This was exemplified by a feedback session we had with the group after the pilot research. We had intended to let the girls know what we had found, ask them what they thought of the findings and canvass their ideas on how we should disseminate the findings. The girls were very interested in what we had found – as a stepping stone to continuing our discussion about their lives and their experiences. They did not seem interested in our agenda of engaging them in decisions about what should be done with the findings. They were 'just happy to have helped us out', to paraphrase one girl's comment. This example can be seen in different ways. One, the research team may simply have failed to explain the possibilities for engagement and dissemination. Two, Hogan's comment may apply: 'If they [children] are not being treated as a partner or as an equal in their everyday life, in whatever context they live, is it appropriate and ethical for researchers to force that model of adult–child interaction upon them?' (1998: 9). The girls had not had experience in influencing policy at local or national levels and many had negative experiences of powerful adults (e.g. teachers, police) ignoring their views. Three, the girls may not have been interested in dissemination. The fight to gain recognition of children's right to be heard has been so hard-fought that only recently, as the principle is more accepted, has the literature begun to recognise that children may not necessarily want to be involved at the most inclusive end of decision-making but may indeed want to have lower levels of involvement (Green 1999). The research team does not know which of the three reasons provides the best explanation. The experience does, however, point out the need to go beyond promoting children's participation in principle to working out its practicalities. This includes recognising the diversity of children and how they would like to participate.

Presentation of 'violence'

As described above, the sensitive research literature extensively explores the difficulties of gaining access from gatekeepers, of finding available data sources (whether participants or other) and of gaining 'valid' data or indeed any data at all from people who do participate (e.g. Lee 1993; James and Platzer 1999). This research found particular difficulties and dilemmas on the presentation of violence in three ways: in the research itself; in how the researchers and how the girls presented themselves; and in dissemination.

Identity management – the research

Lee (1993) explores the possibilities of undertaking covert research, recognising that it may be unethical. The research team never seriously considered this option. The research aim and questions of exploring girls' own views and attitudes suggested a methodology weighted towards directly asking girls. The childhood literature considers informed consent to be a cornerstone of its ethical requirements; the childhood literature would thus appear to go beyond the sensitive research literature. The childhood literature emphasises extensively the need to maintain ongoing consent with children (e.g. see Alderson 1995). This difference could be understood by the 'gap' mentioned at the beginning of this chapter on what makes research sensitive, i.e. the greater power of adults over children. Covert research may seem more justified if the 'powerful' are being studied by those less powerful.

The research team – with the help of both adult and youth advisory groups – debated how to present the research in gaining access and then consent to participants. The funding had been given under the ESRC Violence Research Programme and, thus, the application had been directed around girls' experiences of violence. It was decided that it would be dishonest to rename the research or to not state its focus. In this research, girls would not have informed consent if such fundamental changes were made.

The research was introduced to gatekeepers and girls, though, in its fuller context. It had been conceptualised as seeing violence as part of girls' everyday lives: 'Violence, and the threat of violence, form part of the range of social behaviours that govern and structure social interaction. Importantly violence, as a social phenomenon involving action and interaction, is not automatically an exceptional or extreme behaviour but can be negotiated or used in everyday life.' (original proposal). Influenced by research on bullying and feminist criminology, we had begun with a focus not solely on 'violent girls' but on girls potentially having different roles in violence as bystanders, victims and/or perpetrators. Thus we described the project as: 'looking at girls' lives, what they think about various things, and what experiences they have had including violence' (consent information). We were careful to point out that we were eager to hear the views and experiences of all girls and not only of those who considered themselves violent.

While we had anticipated great problems in gaining access through schools, we did not experience such problems. It took considerable time and much effort to negotiate access but most local authorities and schools were receptive to participation. Equally, we were unaware of any significant proportions of parents who refused permission for us to ask their child to participate (although it is very possible that some girls who had very significant experiences of violence did not participate).

What we became very aware of during fieldwork was the impact on our data collection of being up-front about the topic. We had practical issues, such as girls genuinely wanting to demonstrate violent activities that concerned us in terms of safety (see Burman *et al.* 2001 for discussion). We had the well-rehearsed methodological issues with our self-report questionnaire, in how to encourage girls' honest reporting and we attempted some of the common solutions (see Lee 1993). We also had methodological and analytical dilemmas – which in turn created some opportunities – in the qualitative research, which are described below.

Identity management – the researchers

Mandell (1991: 40) advocates that researchers take on the 'least adult role'; even physical differences can be minimised to the extent that they become inconsequential in working with children. Recent discussions, however, question whether this is possible or desirable (e.g. Harden *et al.* 2000; James *et al.* 1998). The research team did not seek to present themselves to girls as 'insiders' but followed advice frequently expressed in the sensitive research literature: we were interested adults who very much wished to hear girls' perceptions, views and experiences. We were all women but we have limited evidence that girls considered that 'insider' status. Girls did ask us whether we were friends and wanted to know if we were married, parallels to two very important issues in their lives. What remains untested is whether, if one of our research team had been male, differences would have been found in both access and data.

In a potentially significant way, the research team denied themselves 'insider' status by not offering complete confidentiality to girls. Hey (1997: 48), who undertook extensive ethnographic research on girls' friendships, reports 'the trial of my acceptability as a researcher' as replicating the social tests of girls' friendships: i.e. whether Hey would tell the teachers what girls had said. The research team would have failed this test.[6] After discussion with the advisory groups, the research team decided that it would need to be up-front in the qualitative fieldwork and that confidentiality would not be maintained if we knew that a girl or someone else was at risk of significant harm.

This protocol is common in much of childhood research, particularly in areas touching on child protection. Schools in the UK frequently have this exception to confidentiality as a condition of access (and, indeed, sometimes require a teacher to be present during data collection). The exception may well have curtailed what girls told us in qualitative fieldwork, particularly of present or planned experiences of violence. There may have been merit in trying not to have this exception, given that our very exception was directly related to our topic. In practice, we did gather detailed descriptions of violent behaviour both performed and experienced by girls. We thus did not lack for descriptions of violence but these may be an underestimate of girls' experiences, given the possible self-censoring of girls.

Most girls seemed very accepting of the limits of confidentiality, as explained to them as part of consent procedures, with few questions asked and indications of acceptance (nods, comments). Girls in one residential school, however, did not and one girl in particular commented sharply that full confidentiality was not being offered. The implication from the off-the-record discussion was that they would have preferred us to promise full confidentiality. These girls would have accessed the school through legal systems and as a result may have already experienced the limits of confidentiality – perhaps after they had told someone of violence perpetrated against them.

This reaction suggests that researchers should be clear on how they are addressing 'confidentiality'. While internally a research team may be clear that there are limits in confidentiality, this is not always and consistently put on research information and consent forms. In this research, we ensured that it was. We were less clear on our terminology. We used the term 'confidentiality' when we meant that we would seek to protect anonymity in data reporting. The issue of confidentiality has particular salience for girls, both in keeping secrets among friends (Hey 1997) and in their interactions with adults. Researchers would benefit from using the term sensitively themselves, when working with girls.

Identity management – the girls

Exploring girls' own conceptualisations of violence was an explicit research objective. 'Violence' as a term has strong negative moral associations, with its implications of intentional harm in virtually every academic and criminal definition (Bradby 1996). The negative associations with the term 'violence' may have precluded girls telling us about certain experiences.

There were certain 'silences' within our data. For example, certain types of violence, such as physical assaults between siblings, were seen by girls as 'normal' and 'within the rules'. Both the quantitative and qualitative data show that girls were very fearful of sexual assault but they did not commonly associate sexual assault with the term 'violence'. Discussion of sexual assault was typically elicited at the instigation of a researcher, although when prompted girls tended to agree that this was a form of violence. In contrast, girls appeared to draw on a well-rehearsed discourse around bullying. Girls from black and minority ethnic groups were eloquent in discussing the racism they experience in their daily lives.

The negative associations with 'violence' can also be observed within the strategies used by girls in their presentation of self, their peers and their neighbourhoods when speaking to us. Girls tended to be reluctant either in groups or in individual interviews to identify themselves as 'violent girls' and actively sought to avoid or distance themselves from this label. This compares with 10 per cent of girls who described themselves as 'violent' and 10 per cent who reported having committed seven or more different types of physically violent acts (e.g. punching, kicking and hitting with object) in the self-report questionnaire. There was a 5 per cent overlap between these two groups in the questionnaire results. These different findings demonstrate the potential benefit of a self-report questionnaire, which may elicit information on sensitive subjects that participants may not report in face-to-face qualitative methods.

This reluctance to be identified as a 'violent girl' was particularly evident when girls did describe their own physical violent behaviour. Several strategies were used. First, older girls would describe any physical violence as in the past, with an explanation that girls 'grow out of' or 'mature out of' violence. The exchange between two girls in a focus group exemplifies this:

A: But I dinna [don't] really fight about things like that any more.
V: I used tae.
A: I've had to grow up a lot.

Second, physical violence would be set within a wider context that provided some justification. For example, girls living in a range of different areas described the need to be perceived as 'tough' in order not to be the constant victim of violence. Thus they might need to be violent following a direct or indirect verbal or a physical assault, in order to maintain this reputation. The following quotation demonstrates this:

Jane [researcher]: Do you think violence is always a bad thing?
M: No.
G: Not always. Only when you are not defending yourself.
Kay [researcher]: So it is OK if you are defending yourself?
G: Yes. I feel that yes. If you are sticking up for yourself to make sure

you are not getting hurt and you are saving your own self that is fine, or saving someone else.

Examples were also given of girls being physically violent because of insults to their family (particularly mothers). While certain girls said they would not tend to react physically if they had been personally assaulted, they felt they needed to do so when their mother was insulted.

Third, girls tended to deny or worry about having the label of being violent. Groups of various different background characteristics (from more disadvantaged neighbourhoods as well as more advantaged) were concerned that the research team would go away thinking they or their neighbourhoods were particularly violent.[7] In several instances, a focus group ended with the girls concerned about the impression they had made. For example:

Jane [*researcher*]: You know when we go away from here tonight, what sort of impression do you want me and Susan [researcher] to take away of you, as girls?

M: That we are nice wee girls.

Jane: Right.

E: No. I dae [don't] want yous to think we've made yous look as if we are bad people for sayin' all this and a'hin.

Girls seemed to want to make a distinction between their potential to use violence, their actual use of violence and being a 'violent' person.

The group interaction over girls who described experiences of being victims was also illuminating. In one instance, a girl described her experience of bullying for what appeared to be the first time to her present friendship group:

L: I got bullied quite bad in first, no, second year, this year and everyone was saying stuff and I was, every night I just didn't want to go into school the next day. And we all ... we tried to get a ... we tried to move [from X] and stuff, but then I decided that I had to sort of stay and try and stick it out.

Jane [*researcher*]: When was this?

L: Second year.

S: Why? Who bullied you?

L: Well, everyone was just like calling me names and stuff, and I just couldn't take it anymore.

S: ....That is how I felt not that long ago.

This example illuminates many of the general findings of the research. First, friendships are central to girls' lives – positively to support or negatively to harm their self-esteem, peer status and happiness. One can observe the 'emotion work' (see Frith and Kitzinger 1998) happening in the group, beginning in this example and subsequently in the discussion not quoted here. By sharing the victim's experience, in telling this narrative, the group seemed to become closer and the past victim bonded even more to this particular friendship group. Second, it demonstrates the importance of friendship *talk* in girls' lives (see Griffiths 1995). Verbal assaults were very hurtful to the girl in the past. The example demonstrates the potential value of focus groups and ongoing contact with girls' friendship groups in researching violence, which may be even more true for girls than for boys. Such methods allow for observation of the 'emotion work' and friendship talk in action. (For further discussion of the key research findings, see Batchelor *et al.* 2001.)

Dissemination

If policy, academic and common-sense conceptualisations of violence tend to have negative moral associations, nowhere is this more strongly represented than in the media. At this point, the objectives and guiding principles of researchers in data presentation will very likely differ from those of journalists. Tewksbury and Gagne discuss their approach to analysis and presentation of 'sensitive research' data:

> Although researchers may personally condemn or approve of the behaviors, lifestyles and worldviews of communities under investigation, interpretive theory demands that descriptions of the group be written from the perspectives of community members. Analyses that help readers understand the community and the unusual behaviors or worldviews of its members are likely to be accepted by the community under study.
>
> (1997: 147)

In contrast, journalists want information that is newsworthy, is likely to interest their audience and runs counter to everyday expectations (Sieber 1993: 23). Journalists are said to prefer quantitative research findings over qualitative, to oversimplify content and exaggerate the certainty and conclusiveness of the research (Channels 1993: 269). Fenton and colleagues (1998) summarise journalists' four main criteria for 'newsworthiness', from their British research:

- topicality (issues currently in vogue);
- generality ('intrinsically interesting', 'entertaining', and/or about social control and integration (p. 105));
- distillation (favouring 'facts');
- illustration (stories that create empathy in the readership/viewership and/or can be personalised).

All four criteria can be applied to this study.

The research team easily anticipated that considerable media attention would arise at the first launch of its findings. Thus, the research team sought help to develop a press strategy in advance of its national conference. How could it represent its findings without feeding into negative cultural stereotypes (James and Platzer 1999: 78)? The media were likely to use the findings in particular ways and these did not match the findings or conclusions of the research:

- Growth in girl gangs? The research did not find a single group of girls who fit any of the accepted definitions of gangs (e.g. Klein and Maxson 1989), even when we spoke to girls because they had been perceived by others as having that reputation.
- Rising tide of female violence? The research did not find a large number of 'violent girls' nor did it find evidence that girls were being violent because they were becoming 'more like boys'.
- Convergence of girls' violence with that of boys? This study could not answer whether girls were becoming more violent because it had no historical data for comparison. Criminal statistics, while available over time, are poor indicators of violent behaviour because of the problems of under-reporting, classification of behaviours and so on that are well documented in the criminology literature (e.g. Anderson 1999).

The research strategy sought to use many of the recommended techniques to ensure that the research was well presented: from an exclusive with a well-briefed journalist in advance of the general press release, to live coverage so that messages cannot be cut in editing, to warning participants (and, in particular, schools) in advance that there might be press coverage. Still, it was frustrating to the research team to see the manipulation of and false attributions to the research in certain newspapers (see Batchelor 2001 for further discussion). More positively, some journalists themselves admitted that they had come with one story in mind and realised that this was not the story to be had. A proportion of stories, then, used this as their peg and the research findings were presented more accurately. The press continue to be interested in the research and perhaps there will be longer-term shifts in media presentation. Indeed, Fenton and colleagues (1998) suggest that social scientists can have more influence at a 'meta-level', in the stories covered over time, rather than the individual reporting of a particular research study. Such media experiences are common to 'sensitive research' and were thus not unexpected.

Girls' participation in the national conference itself, however, raised a dilemma less well rehearsed in the literature. A fundamental principle of children's rights is the right to have their views considered (Article 12 of the UN Convention on the Rights of the Child), which has strongly influenced the childhood literature. This right extends not only to data collection but also to dissemination. If participation were taken seriously, arguably children should be involved in the interpretation of findings, in decisions on how the findings should be disseminated and in the dissemination itself. It is now commonplace to involve children in conferences on issues that affect them – and indeed conferences have been criticised when children are not included. We thus let participating schools and other groups know about the research findings and invited them to the conference.

With the high media interest in the conference, then, we found ourselves acting as 'gatekeepers' to protect girls from others (in this case, the media) in asking their views. A group of girls wanted to present a role play at the conference and they decided they wanted to speak to the media. We were protective of the girls, spending time with them in advance of and on the day to try to highlight the potential disadvantages of speaking to the press so that they could make an informed choice. Journalists were spoken to by the research team and the University press officer before they spoke to the girls, and the press officer and youth worker were with the girls when they were interviewed. Overall, the girls reported that they felt largely positive about how they were represented. However, a few press items named individual girls and the particular neighbourhoods and the girls were not pleased to have these represented as 'violent'. Shortly after the conference, the youth worker left his/her post –making it difficult for us to have follow-up contact with the girls after the conference.

Perhaps we should have protected the girls completely from the media and not have had them interviewed. This, however, would replicate adult control over the girls' right to consent for themselves and would 'silence' them in the way that has been much criticized in the childhood literature. We had refused journalists' requests to 'shadow' us while we were undertaking the research or to facilitate any access to research participants. Was it better to have at least prepared a group of girls (perhaps inadequately) to discuss the subject with the press rather than leave journalists to seek out girls more randomly or, even more worryingly, to try and track down girls who had participated in our research? The media's interest in talking to 'actual people' and not just to researchers is a frequent experience of research teams, particularly on sensitive issues. How to match this with a desire to engage participants in discussions and dissemination, when these involve the media, would benefit from more discussion.

Conclusion

Sieber's conclusion in 1993 (p. 23) remains good advice:

> The lesson for researchers is clear: Think twice about whether socially sensitive research is being conducted in the most responsible manner possible and whether one is ready for the criticism and misrepresentation that may ensue in any case.

With both the sensitive research and childhood literatures recommending certain principles and practices, recent articles have stated the need to test these in practice and to address the realities faced in research (for example, Borland *et al.* 2001; Harden *et al.* 2000). The experience of undertaking 'A View from the Girls' illuminates this. The research combined two areas that are almost inevitably 'sensitive' and newsworthy – children and violence. The chapter rehearses some of the dilemmas and possible solutions, already familiar to those who know the literatures, in relation to gatekeepers, informed consent, researcher 'identity management' and contact with the media. It also raises matters less prominent in the literature, such as researchers themselves acting as 'gatekeepers' to children, finding themselves in a dilemma between promoting children's participation and protecting their 'best interests'. It discusses the particularities of the presentation of 'violence' as a research topic and girls' presentations of self and their neighbourhoods when 'violence' is perceived as almost inevitably negative.

This research would conclude that girl participants did overtly express more control of the research process when accessed in youth groups, than they did when accessed in schools. Systematic information was not gathered on girls to compare those who took part through the different access routes, but access through youth groups allowed targeting of girls with particular experiences whom we did not involve through schools. In the generality of girls' experiences of violence, we did not observe patterned differences in data collected by setting. Differences were more patterned by the local area, the particular school or the particular backgrounds and experiences of girls. As mentioned above, we did gather more examples of violence from girls accessed outwith 'mainstream' schools. Such findings suggest that researchers with children should explore the differences of undertaking research through formal institutions such as schools versus more informal contacts – both for how children experience their participation, for who is included/excluded and for the effects that the institutional setting will have on data collected.

Notes

1 Funded under the ESRC Violence Research Programme, Award Number L133251018. This study was undertaken by Michele Burman, Kay Tisdall, Jane Brown and Susan Batchelor. This chapter was greatly aided by the specific comments of Jane Brown and Susan Batchelor.

2 For more methodological details see research web-site (www.gla.ac.uk/girlsandviolence) and Burman *et al.* 2001.

3 In this chapter, the phrase 'childhood literature' is used to describe this literature. The phrase has the risk of implying there is a single category of childhood, which is not intended.

4 In order to access girls through schools, the research team approached six local authority education department directors, for their permission to approach schools. One director refused because of extensive other research being undertaken in that authority's schools. The research team then went through departmental procedures as required and subsequently began to approach individual schools based on a variety of characteristics of their student group (e.g. geography, socio-economic background, ethnicity, etc.). While the process was time-consuming, virtually all schools did eventually agree to support our possible access to girl participants.

5 This group was not representative of the wider research population; rather they were a naturally formed friendship group recruited through a Community Education youth group.

6 Equally, if issues of 'significant harm' for girls had arisen, perhaps Hey would have not met this test.
7 Researchers had prompted girls to talk about violence in relation to geography and space: something they did not tend to do spontaneously.

References

Alderson, P. (1995) *Listening to Children: Children, Social Research and Ethics*. Ilford, Essex: Barnardos.

Alderson, P. (2000) 'School Students' Views on School Councils and Daily Life at school', *Children and Society* 14, 1: 10–120.

Anderson, S. (1999) 'Crime Statistics and the "Problem of Crime" in Scotland', in P. Duff and N. Hutton (eds) *Criminal Justice in Scotland*. Aldershot: Ashgate.

Artz, S. (1998) *Sex, Power and the Violent School Girl*. Toronto: Trifolium Books.

Baskin, D. and Sommers, I. (1993) 'Females' Initiation into Violent Street Crime', in *Justice Quarterly* 10, 4: 559–81.

Baskin, D. and Sommers, I. (1998) *Casualties of Community Disorder: Women's Careers in Violent Crime*. Oxford: Westview Press.

Batchelor, S. (2001) 'The Myth of Girl Gangs', in *Criminal Justice Matters* 43: 26–7. Reprinted in Y. Jewkes and G. Letherby (eds) (2002) *Criminology: A Reader*. London: Sage.

Batchelor, S., Burman, M. and Brown, J. (2001) 'Discussing Violence: Let's Hear it for the Girls', *Probation Journal* 48, 2: 125–34.

Borland, M., Hill, M., Laybourn, A. and Stafford, A. (2001) *Improving Consultation with Children and Young People in Relevant Aspects of Policy-making and Legislation in Scotland*. www.scottish.parliament.uk/official_report/cttee/educ01/edconstultrep.htm

Bradby, H. (1996) 'Introduction', in H. Bradby (ed.) *Defining Violence: Understanding the Causes and Effects of Violence*. Aldershot: Avebury.

Burman, M., Batchelor, S., and Brown, J. (2001) 'Researching Girls and Violence: Facing the Dilemmas of Fieldwork', *British Journal of Criminology* 41, 3: 443–59.

Campbell, A. (1984) *The Girls in the Gang*. Cambridge, MA: Blackwell.

Campbell, A. (1990) 'Female Participation in Gangs', in C. P. Huff (ed.) *Gangs in America*. Newbury Park, CA: Sage.

Channels, N. L. (1993) 'Anticipating Media Coverage: Methodological Decisions in Criminal Justice Research', in C. M. Renzetti and R. M. Lee (eds) *Researching Sensitive Topics*. London: Sage.

Chesney-Lind, M. (1997) *The Female Offender: Girls, Women and Crime*. Thousand Oaks, CA: Sage.

Christensen, P. and James, A. (eds) (2000) *Research with Children: Perspectives and Practices*. London: Falmer Press.

Dingwall, R. (1980) 'Ethics and Ethnography', *Sociological Review* 28, 4: 871–91.

Fenton, N., Bryman, A. and Deacon, D. with Birmingham, P. (1998) *Mediating Social Science*. London: Sage.

Frith, H. and Kitzinger, C. (1998) '"Emotion Work" as a Participant Resource: A Feminist Analysis of Young Women's Talk-in-Interaction', *Sociology* 32, 2: 299–320.

Green, David R. (1999) 'Political Participation of Youth in the United Kingdom', in B. Riepl and H. Wintersberger (eds) *Political Participation of Youth below Voting Age*. Vienna: European Centre.

Greig, A. and Taylor, J. (1999) *Doing Research with Children*. London: Sage.

Griffiths, V. (1995) *Adolescent Girls and Their Friends: A Feminist Ethnography*. Aldershot: Avebury.

Harden, J., Scott, S., Backett-Milburn, K. and Jackson, S. (2000) ' "Can't Talk, Won't Talk?" Methodological Issues in Researching Children', *Sociological Research Online*, 5, 2, www.socresoline.org.uk/5/2harden.html

Hazekamp, J. L. (2000) 'Young People Active in Youth Research: An Innovative Approach', *Social Work in Europe* 6, 3: 2–9.

Hey, V. (1997) *The Company She Keeps: An Ethnography of Girls' Friendships*. Buckingham: Open University Press.

Hill, M. and Tisdall, K. (1997) *Children and Society*. London: Longman.

Hogan, D. (1998) 'Valuing the Child in Research: Historical and Current Influences on Research Methodology with Children', in D. Hogan and R. Gilligan (eds) *Researching Children's Experiences: Qualitative Approaches*. Dublin: Trinity College.

http://www.scottish.parliament.uk/official_report/cttee/educ-01/edconsultrep.htm

James, A., Jenks, C. and Prout, A. (1998) *Theorizing Childhood*. Cambridge: Polity Press.

James, T. and Platzer, H. (1999) 'Ethical Considerations in Qualitative Research with Vulnerable Groups: Exploring Lesbians' and Gay Men's Experiences of Health Care – A Personal Perspective', *Nursing Ethics* 6, 1: 73–81.

Klein, M. and Maxson, C. (1989) 'Street Gang Violence', in M. E. Wolfgang and N. A. Weiner (eds) *Violent Crime, Violent Criminals*. Newbury Park, CA: Sage.

Lee, R. (1993) *Doing Research on Sensitive Topics*. London: Sage.

Lee, R. M. and Renzetti, C. M. (eds) (1993) *Researching Sensitive Topics*. London: Sage.

Maguire, R. and Marshall, K. (1998) *Values Education and the Rights of the Child*. Glasgow: Centre for the Child and Society, University of Glasgow.

Maguire, R. and Marshall, K. (2001) *Education and the Rights of the Child*. Glasgow: Centre for the Child & Society, University of Glasgow.

Mandell, N. (1991) 'The Least-adult Role in Studying Children', in F. C. Waksler (ed.) *Studying the Social Worlds of Children: Sociological Readings*. London: Falmer Press.

Mauthner, M. (1997) 'Methodological Aspects of Collecting Data from Children: Lessons from Three Research Projects', *Children and Society* 11: 16–28.

Miller, J. (2001) *One of the Guys: Girls, Gangs and Gender*. New York: Oxford University Press.

Morrow, V. (1999) 'It's Cool … 'Cos You Can't Give Detentions and Things, Can You?!', in P. Milner and B. Carolin (eds) *Time to Listen to Children: Personal and Professional Communication*. London: Routledge.

Qvortrup, J. (1994) 'Childhood Matters: An Introduction', in J. Qvortrup, M. Bardy, G. Sgritta and H. Wintersberger (eds) *Childhood Matters: Social Theory, Practice and Politics*, European Centre, Vienna. Aldershot: Avebury.

Scottish Executive (2001) *Report of the Youth Summit 2000*, http://www.scotland.gov.uk/library3/education/rsys-00.asp

Sieber, J. E. (1993) 'The Ethics and Politics of Sensitive Research', in C. M. Renzetti and R. M. Lee (eds) *Researching Sensitive Topics*. London: Sage.

Tewksbury, R. and Gagne, P. (1997) 'Assumed and Presumed Identities: Problems of Self-Presentation in Field Research', *Sociological Spectrum* 17: 127–55.

The Young Researchers (1998) *Young Opinions, Great Ideas*. London: National Children's Bureau.

Wyness, M. G. (2000) *Contesting Childhood*. London: Falmer Press.

Part III

The impact of institutional contexts for the study of violence

9 Fear of reprisal

Researching intra-communal violence in Northern Ireland and South Africa[1]

Colin Knox and Rachel Monaghan

Introduction

Measuring the impact of violence is fraught with problems, not least because of the definitional problems around what constitutes violence and how this might be quantified. If one considers violence perpetrated by paramilitaries in Northern Ireland or vigilante groups in South Africa then the task becomes even more difficult. This chapter will examine methodological problems associated with gaining access to, and undertaking research in, the dangerous arena of paramilitary violence in Northern Ireland and vigilante violence in South Africa. It will consider the difficulties in obtaining reliable information on the levels of violence, particularly from official police sources, and the way in which this type of crime is classified. Other statistical sources such as pressure group data will be examined and problems highlighted with the use of documentation gleaned from tendentious organisations. Data about the impact of violence from primary research are also fraught with problems. Victims, for example, can be reluctant interviewees for fear of paramilitary/vigilante reprisal. A 'victim' of paramilitary/vigilante 'punishment' may be an erstwhile perpetrator of violence. Should one treat internecine turf wars between paramilitaries in Northern Ireland in a similar way to violence meted out in pursuit of their political goals? These and other issues make the measurement of the impact of violence difficult methodological questions. This chapter will therefore highlight these problems and examine how we managed them within this study of intra-communal violence.

The research context

South Africa

South Africa and, more tentatively, Northern Ireland are emerging from bitter ethno-national conflicts in which violence and crime characterised the transition to peaceful political settlements. The collapse of apartheid in 1989, lifting the 30-year ban on the African National Congress (ANC), and the subsequent release of Nelson Mandela, created a climate for political negotiation and change in South

Africa. This paved the way for an interim constitution and the first multi-racial democratic elections in 1994 and led to the Government of National Unity. The ANC's success in the June 1999 elections gave the party an overwhelming mandate to accelerate Thabo Mbeki's programme of 'transformation' aimed at tackling the significant socio-economic problems facing South Africa: unemployment, AIDS, crime and education. The legacy of political resistance, often violent, deployed to make the townships ungovernable during apartheid has created a culture tolerant of citizens taking the law into their own hands. Although the number of political killings dropped sharply from about 2,500 in 1994 to fewer than 240 in 1999 (South African Institute for Race Relations 2000), Mbeki in his inauguration speech regretted that some South Africans were 'forced to beg, rob and murder to ensure that they and their own do not perish from hunger'. This is reflected in a rising tide of other kinds of violent crimes. Rape, car-jacking, serious assault, housebreaking and common robbery have been increasing since 1996, and the trend has been sharply upwards since 1998. About one-third of all reported crimes in 1999 were violent, and the number increased by over 9 per cent on 1998. The savagery of the crime wave is captured in reports that one in every two South African women will be raped during their lifetime, the average South African is eight times more likely to be murdered than the average American, and one policeman is killed each day – 1,400 have died since the ANC came to power (*Weekly Mail and Guardian* 2000). Accordingly, the public response is that 'brutality should be met with brutality. The rich surround themselves with razor wire and private security guards, and the poor resort to vigilantism' (*The Economist* 1999: 23).

Vigilantism is undertaken by organised groups such as Mapogo a Mathamaga[2] in the Northern Province, People against Gangsterism and Drugs[3] (PAGAD) and the Peninsula Anti-Crime Agency[4] (PEACA) in the Western Cape. In addition, taxi associations in some townships have become involved in 'crime solving' for a fee. All of these groups stand accused of using corporal punishment and violence in responding to crime. Indeed Mapogo's leader, John Magolego, asserts that public flogging 'is the African way of stopping crime. The criminal must lie on the ground, and we must work on his buttocks and put him right' (quoted in Soggot and Ngobeni 1999). Alleged suspects are usually beaten until they confess or provide information as to the whereabouts of stolen goods or moneys. Mapogo has also been accused of throwing suspects into crocodile-infested waters, while taxi-drivers in Guguletu (a township in Cape Town) are implicated in dragging alleged criminals behind vehicles. Further to its crime-solving activities, Mapogo has moved into the area of crime prevention by offering services usually provided by private security firms such as the protection of property and patrolling; takers have included schools and churches.

Furthermore, in some cases spontaneous mobs form to mete out justice to alleged criminals. In some instances, those present convene kangaroo courts[5] but this is not always the case. The justice meted out is often of an extremely brutal nature and deaths are common. Examples in the townships include the stoning to death of three youths found stealing chairs from a church in Pimville, Soweto

(Khangale 2001); the severe beating of an alleged rapist by women in Chatsworth, Durban (Williams 1999); and the near necklacing[6] of a man accused of armed robbery in Orange Farm, Johannesburg (Ndaba 2001). In some cases, members of the family of a suspected criminal or the family home are targeted. The houses are either destroyed or burnt and often the families subsequently leave the area as a result of intimidation (Ntabazalila 1997 and interview with the mother of an alleged rapist and murderer, November 1999). In February 1997, the mother of an alleged criminal was stoned to death for the deeds of her son by a crowd of 4,000 in the township of Mamelodi, near Pretoria (Amupadhi 1997).

Northern Ireland

Northern Ireland's transition to 'peace' has been more recent and capricious. The signing of the Belfast Agreement in April 1998 and its subsequent endorsement in referenda by its electorate (71.2 per cent) and by voters in the Irish Republic (94 per cent) heralded a political solution to the seemingly intractable problems that bedevilled the province for 30 years. The British and Irish Governments formally resolved their historical differences through the general and mutual acceptance of the principle of consent – Northern Ireland is part of the United Kingdom, and will remain so, as long as the majority wishes. Signatories to the Agreement affirmed their 'total and absolute commitment to exclusively democratic and peaceful means of resolving differences'. This has created the impression that violence has been eschewed in Northern Ireland. Over four years later the evidence suggests that this is far from true. It is the case that the worst manifestations of the conflict, sectarian killings and bombings, are declining. In 1999/2000, for example, seven civilians were murdered, the lowest figure since the 'Troubles' began, and the first year in which there were no security force fatalities (Royal Ulster Constabulary[7] 2000). This, however, ignores an insidious and ongoing level of paramilitary violence inflicted on working-class communities and referred to as 'punishment' beatings and shootings or the informal criminal justice system. Paramilitary groups see themselves as community protectors; their actions aimed ostensibly at maintaining 'law and order' through tackling petty crime such as car theft, joyriding,[8] burglary and drug dealing. Up to the end of 2001, Police Service of Northern Ireland (PSNI) statistics show that there have been 2,564 shootings (an average of 88 per year) and 1,802 beatings (an average of 90 per year) since 1973 and since 1982 respectively, when figures were first recorded.[9]

Paramilitaries exact community 'justice' using baseball bats, hammers, hockey and hurley sticks, iron bars, pickaxe handles and steel rods. Other forms of 'punishment' include dropping heavy concrete blocks on limbs and using power tools on bones. Surgeons in the fracture clinic at the Royal Victoria Hospital in Belfast, for example, report that 'following the cessation of violence there has been an increase in the level of injuries occurring in those undergoing paramilitary punishment' (Nolan *et al.* 1999: 8). Their study of treating victims showed that those who had been shot with pistols, resulting in open injuries, suffered much less damage to soft tissue and bones than those who had been beaten. The brutal reality is that it is 'better' to be shot than beaten.

Informal criminal 'justice' and vigilantism

Three principal reasons are advanced for the existence of the informal criminal justice system in Northern Ireland and of vigilantism in South Africa (Knox 2002). First, in both countries there is no adequate policing service. In Northern Ireland, particularly in republican areas, the Police Service of Northern Ireland has no legitimacy, and these communities would not normally involve the police in dealing with crime in their areas. Republicans claim that the PSNI are prepared to tolerate at best, or encourage at worst, crime in their communities as a way of undermining the 'republican struggle'. Police are therefore willing to 'trade' dropping charges of joyriding, drug dealing or burglary in return for low-level intelligence gathering on so-called known republicans. In loyalist areas, objections to involving the police are more to do with keeping the PSNI out of communities where drug dealing, racketeering and illegal drinking dens and clubs are commonplace. In South Africa, the police are seen as ineffective, not only lacking basic literacy skills but with an estimated 25 per cent of force members unable to read and write (Randall 2000). Their crime-solving capabilities are also unimpressive, not least because experienced personnel were trained in the policing methods of the old apartheid regime. For example, of the 2.2 million crimes reported to the police in 1998, almost half were considered 'undetected' because evidence was insufficient or the suspect had disappeared. Half a million more were withdrawn, leaving 524,000 cases that reached court (*The Economist* 2001).

Second, in Northern Ireland there is a rising level of crime including 'anti-social behaviour', petty and violent crime. This is evidenced in crime and victimisation statistics, which show that those from an unskilled social class background are most vulnerable and feel their quality of life is particularly affected by fear of crime (Northern Ireland Office 2000; Louw and Shaw 1997). In 1998/9 the number of violent crimes (defined as offences against the person, sexual offences and robberies) increased by 21.2 per cent (to 21,452) and in 1999/2000 by a further 12.6 per cent (Royal Ulster Constabulary 2000: 75). A Home Office report on international crime statistics showed Northern Ireland's percentage increase in recorded crime (28 per cent) as second only to that in South Africa where it rose by 37 per cent in 1998 (Barclay and Tavares 2000: 3). In the absence, therefore, of an adequate/legitimate police service and/or because people are discouraged from seeking police involvement, some people in communities turn to paramilitaries or vigilantes to secure a prompt, visible and effective response to crime in their areas. Hence, a proportion of local people living in fear of crime endorse paramilitary 'punishment' beatings and shootings and vigilante stoning or sjambokking (whipping) of alleged criminals or 'anti-social' elements.

Third, the formal criminal justice system within both countries is perceived as slow, ineffectual, and soft on crime. The view of a focus group participant in a loyalist community illustrates this:

> I know young lads who were put on probation for stealing cars. The first week they went to the Probation Board they talked about the consequences of their actions for victims. The next week they were taken go-karting, then deep-sea fishing. The average mother cannot afford to send her kids to these activities. I then heard one young fella who hadn't been involved in crime ask 'how do you join the probation club for week-ends away?' People see these young lads who have committed quite serious crime being taken by the hand without punishment for their actions against the community.
>
> (Interview with focus group, Shankill – Belfast, November 1999)

The formal justice system is perceived as failing not only the victims of crime but also those involved in criminal activities. The case of Brian Connolly, a deceased joyrider, provides an example of this failure of the formal system of justice. Brian was a passenger in a stolen car (allegedly travelling at 100mph) that crashed into the family car of Charmaine and Justin Watson killing the young couple in July 1999 and orphaning their two children. Brian's mother believes the formal system let her son down badly in that if he 'got into trouble, he never seemed to be really punished. He'd often get bail or maybe just a three-month sentence. He also became very good at working the system. He knew what he'd get away with' (Carmel Donnelly quoted in Walker 1999: 5) and had 109 prior convictions, many of them for motoring offences (Harper 2001). South Africa's criminal justice system can also be said to be under-performing in that, on average, fewer than 9 per cent of recorded crimes result in the conviction of the perpetrators. For more serious offences the conviction rate is even lower. For example, in 1999 the rate for car hijacking was 2 per cent, for aggravated robbery 3 per cent and for rape 8 per cent (Schönteich and Louw 2001). Thus in societies where violent conflict has been the norm, it is not surprising that the time taken to process offenders, the safeguards necessary in the legal system, and the standard of proof required for conviction are seen as no match for summary justice meted out by paramilitaries and vigilantes.

Researching paramilitary violence and vigilantism

Commentaries on political violence in Northern Ireland and South Africa concentrate on two broad levels – first, trying to establish the facts or data about the levels, distribution and sources of violence (Murray 1982; Poole 1993; Jefferey 1997; Coleman 1998; Minnaar *et al.* 1998; Truth and Reconciliation Commission 1998; Fay *et al.* 1999) and second, examining the causes of, or motivation for, violence (White 1993; O'Duffy 1995; Patel 1997; and Bornmann 1998). What is largely absent, however, is research on the nature of the relationship between paramilitary or vigilante groups and the communities over which they exert social control. Kennedy, for example, points out that although the 'brute facts of communal violence are well known ... what is less well known is the degree of "internal" paramilitary repression (in the form of beatings, shootings and mutilations) which developed in the shadows of the larger conflict' (Kennedy 1995: 67). The same can also be said of our understanding of vigilantism in South Africa.

There are, however, exceptions including Cavanaugh's (1997) ethnographic study undertaken in loyalist and republican communities in Belfast and the study by Brewer *et al.* (1998) of the role played by local communities in civil unrest and crime management. In terms of post-apartheid South Africa, much of the literature deals with popular justice or community courts (utilising non-violent methods of punishment such as community service) as opposed to vigilantism or kangaroo courts. Examples would include the work of Nina (1995) and his examination of popular justice and civil society, especially within the context of street committees in Guguletu (Cape Town), and the work of Schärf (1992), which explores how community courts can best be adapted to the formal justice system.

These issues combined to frame the research upon which this chapter is based. Our discussions here centre on methodological conundrums associated with conducting qualitative research involving victims of 'punishment' beatings (n = 40), focus groups within communities (n = four) 'controlled' by the paramilitaries in Northern Ireland; victims of vigilante attacks (n = six) and focus groups within communities (n = six) where vigilantes operate in South Africa. Of the four focus groups conducted in Northern Ireland, two took place in loyalist areas and two in republican areas. Furthermore, an area containing a restorative justice project was chosen and also an area without such a project (one of each in a loyalist and republican area respectively). This allowed comparisons to be made at inter- and intra-community levels. We offer these personal reflections on researching paramilitary and vigilante violence in the hope that they have lessons for those undertaking 'sensitive fieldwork' elsewhere. We are mindful of Brewer's conclusions on police research in Northern Ireland. He argued that sensitivity is highly situational and researchers need to consider 'what *they* believe to be controversial and sensitive but also what their respondents, potential gatekeepers, and the community at large might consider to be sensitive about the research' (Brewer 1993: 143). Similarly, Alty and Rodham (1998) suggest that research within sensitive areas requires flexibility and demands practical solutions that are not always linked to traditionally recognised ethical dilemmas. We consider these issues in no particular priority under four key headings: reliable and valid information, accessing victims, personal security, and dissemination and engagement with stakeholders.

The search for reliable and valid information on violence

In Northern Ireland the PSNI collates statistics on the number of paramilitary-style shootings and assaults that are reported to them. These statistics are thought to underestimate the magnitude of the problem by as much as 30–50 per cent, according to one former pressure group (Families Against Intimidation and Terror – FAIT), not least because those who have been subjected to beatings are reluctant to go to the police through fear of reprisal. There is also no information available on charges brought against perpetrators. Detection rates are subsumed within 'violence against the person' statistics but are described by the Police Authority for Northern Ireland[10] (PANI) as 'relatively low'.

Other statistical sources collated by pressure groups such as the former FAIT and the Northern Ireland Human Rights Bureau (NIHRB) are also problematic. FAIT was formed in 1990 by individuals affected or concerned by the continuation of 'punishment' attacks on those allegedly involved in 'anti-social behaviour' or petty crime. The organisation, self-described as anti-sectarian and non-political, sought to 'heighten political and public awareness of intimidation and mutilation within Northern Ireland's controlled communities, to provide support for primary and secondary victims, and to speak out on behalf of those unable or afraid to voice their own objections' (FAIT 1999: 1). As part of its activities it established a database on paramilitary violence including 'punishment' beatings, shootings, intimidation, exiling and petrol bombings. Its figures for the number of shootings and beatings, however, were obtained from the PSNI, merely replicating the official statistics. On examination of the database which we were able to obtain, it is not clear from the data if any distinction was made between 'punishment' and other sectarian or racial attacks. The numbers of individuals exiled or driven out of their homes by intimidation, as counted by FAIT, show a total number of people forced to be re-housed. The organisation counted each person in a household as an individual exiled or intimidated. A family of four therefore counts as four intimidations or exiles although, in effect, only one family member may have been intimidated or told to leave the area by a paramilitary group.

FAIT also experienced internal divisions that resulted in questions being asked about the group's credibility (Oldham 1998; Clarke 1998). For example, Vincent McKenna, a self-proclaimed former member of the Provisional Irish Republican Army (PIRA), who became the group's development officer, named publicly at the UK Unionist Party's annual conference two individuals allegedly involved in the Omagh bombing[11] (Murphy 1999; Fergus 1999). A short while later McKenna left FAIT and formed a new human rights group, the Northern Ireland Human Rights Bureau, in May 1999. The reliability and validity of the figures gathered by the Bureau have been questioned by the Northern Ireland Association for the Care and Resettlement of Offenders[12] (Campbell 1999) as has the credibility of the organisation following reports that McKenna had been investigated in connection with child sex abuse allegations. McKenna claimed that the PIRA was waging a campaign of intimidation against him, including two bomb attacks at his home and the vilification of his character by accusations of child sex abuse. However, McKenna was later arrested and found guilty of 32 charges of sexually abusing his daughter in the Republic of Ireland and received a three-year custodial sentence (Harper 2000). The overall credibility of an organisation affects the credibility of its 'numbers'. As a consequence of the controversy surrounding FAIT, the research team used official PSNI statistics alongside developing its own comprehensive database compiled from daily newspaper reports of paramilitary attacks. The database was subsequently used to analyse the frequency, nature and geographical concentration of attacks over a two-year period using GIS mapping techniques. It also acted as a source of qualitative data, in that each incident recorded brief details of the attack/assault.

During the research project, the best known pressure/support groups in this area of violence, FAIT and the Northern Ireland Human Rights Bureau, lost credibility. Yet the information they generated played a key role in the public debate on the issue. The Conservative Party, for example, drew heavily in a House of Commons debate on information provided by FAIT. This was at a juncture in the Belfast Agreement when the early release of paramilitary prisoners was the focus of heated discussion. The Conservative Party spokesperson on Northern Ireland (Andrew MacKay) set the scene for the debate on

> mutilations, torture and beatings by giving some statistics that have been prepared by Families Against Intimidation and Terror, a non-sectarian organisation that is doing marvellous work to help the victims of such mutilations and beatings, giving them hope, succour and, at times, protection and, sadly, at other times spiriting them out of the country to safety ... FAIT has more accurate and up-to-date figures, than, sadly, the Royal Ulster Constabulary can possibly have.
>
> (MacKay 1999)

This illustrates how the multiple layers of 'counting' and recording violence are ignored in a partisan political agenda. The credibility of statistics gathered by self-appointed spokespeople may be enhanced through publicity in official (*Hansard*) and media sources.

Like Northern Ireland, South Africa collates crime statistics. Unfortunately, the South African Police Service (SAPS) does not maintain separate records for vigilante attacks, and therefore no official statistics are available. Even if they were, it is unlikely that they would be valid and reliable. As the Institute of Security Studies notes, 'crime statistics are usually regarded with caution: in South Africa they are treated with outright scepticism' (Louw 1998: 11). A Committee of Inquiry into the Collection, Processing and Publication of Crime Statistics was appointed in May 1997 by the Minister of Safety and Security and found that there was an absence of an 'information culture' within the SAPS, which highlights the problems affecting crime statistics. The committee found, for example, that many SAPS officials did not make optimal use of crime statistics in their daily policing activities, which in turn affected data input and the quality of the output statistics accordingly. Furthermore, there was insufficient training, a high turnover of skilled personnel and inadequate physical and human resources (Louw 1998). In light of these findings the Minister placed a year-long moratorium (June 2000–June 2001) on the release of crime statistics on the grounds that they were unreliable and inaccurate. Critics suggest that the ban had more to do with masking rising levels of violent crime and the government's poor performance in fighting crime.

Clearly, with the absence of national crime statistics it is difficult to assess the scale of vigilante attacks in South Africa. Having said this, a small amount of information has been compiled by the Human Rights Committee (HRC). The HRC is an independent human rights non-governmental organisation that has been monitoring and reporting on human rights abuses and political violence in South Africa since 1988. In its monthly publication *Human Rights Report* instances of vigilante attacks were detailed in the Political Rights section. These data, although providing some information, are not a comprehensive survey of vigilante activities. In addition the *Report* is no longer published.

Given the nature of the crimes under review here, it is impossible to obtain accurate data on the scale of the problem. Official sources underestimate the level of paramilitary/vigilante crime either because of victims' fears of reporting incidents to the police (in the case of Northern Ireland) or because of systemic data collection problems which provide a useful excuse for politicians embarrassed by lawlessness (in the case of South Africa). When this is overlaid with an overt political agenda to discredit, for example, the outworking of the Belfast Agreement or to criticise the ANC Government, there is no incentive for state bodies (police or criminal justice) to improve the quality of their data and provide their opponents with information to use against them.

Speaking with victims of violence

One major difficulty in the present study was securing access to those who have been subjected to paramilitary 'punishment' or vigilante attacks. Making contact with community organisations with which the researchers had previous experience seemed a useful starting point. While community workers knew victims of such attacks, their role in brokering contact met with limited success. What became clear during the course of this work in Northern Ireland were the contradictions within communities. The very same community organisations may have intentionally or unintentionally referred victims to paramilitaries. It should not have been especially surprising therefore that 'punishment' victims felt unwilling to co-operate with community organisations which they suspected of 'running to paramilitaries' about them. This was not wholly unproductive. We did interview, for example, a father and son who had been beaten in a mistaken identity case and other community volunteers/workers who had themselves been beaten or shot.

A typical account given by a victim illustrates the sensitivity of the topic:

> I was walking down the road and I heard a screech of brakes and I looked behind me, and I knew right away because of the big figures in the car. So I tried to run down an entry (alley) way and they ran on down the front of the street and got to the bottom of the entry before I had. I ran into them and

they hit me a punch and I went on my back and they just pointed the gun at me and told me to lie there. Well they didn't shoot me there, they took me away in a car ... to the area I lived in. They took me into a house there, I was tied up, put a hood over my head and I was made to stand facing the wall. I asked could I sit down and there was no answer so I was going to try and sit down myself. I tried to get down like that and they just laid in and booted me all over the fucking show and pulled me back up onto my feet. They took me out, made me wait for another wee short while in the entry way, brought me out onto a wee grass verge, told me to lie down and kneecapped me. After a couple of weeks I got out of hospital and went home. Two days after I got out of hospital they came to the door and said 'you've got 'til 12 o'clock the next day to get out of the country'.

(Interview with victim of 'punishment' shooting, December 1999)

Other problems arose even if victims agreed to talk to us. Some interviewees expressed concern over who might see interview transcripts. For example, one victim who had received three 'punishment' beatings and been told to leave his local area said 'I'm scared. I don't know what to say, or who's going to hear it. I'm scared in case anybody hears it and knows [my story]'. We assured our interviewees that the audio tapes would be wiped and the interview transcripts anonymised and kept in a secure location. This was not always convincing to interviewees nervous about their security, despite their willingness to participate. In some cases we knew victims' obvious reluctance to reveal stories in too much detail.

When access was proving particularly difficult and slow, however, one suggestion was to visit victims admitted to hospital for injuries resulting from paramilitary 'punishment' attacks, the researcher's equivalent of ambulance chasing. Media coverage of these incidents often carried footage of victims in hospital beds. While this had the clear potential to raise awareness of the horrific nature of these incidents on a scale beyond the capacity of our research, there was also the danger of sensationalism. Our own predisposition was therefore to reject this possibility for access, on the grounds that the victim's distress could be exacerbated by recounting the incident so soon after the event, and we suspected that payments were made for the interviews and that these may have influenced the motivations of the respondents.[13]

The most productive source of access, however, proved to be via the Probation Board for Northern Ireland, an executive non-departmental public body whose aim is to help prevent re-offending. Their day-to-day business brought them into contact with young people, a number of whom had been 'disciplined' by the paramilitaries for 'anti-social behaviour'. Support for the research was secured at the senior level of the organisation and a letter of endorsement sent to area probation managers. Thereafter, the researchers made contact with local probation officers for referrals. Their professional interest in the topic and access to a 'captive' client base proved fruitful. A number of probation officers had to deal with the consequences of paramilitary violence for young people and were keen to assist with research that could help to address its causes. Their brokerage role also carried certain credibility and cultivated trust with those willing to be interviewed which would have been difficult for us as researchers to secure.

Gaining access to victims in South Africa also proved difficult. To this end an informal working relationship was entered into with the Centre for the Study of Violence and Reconciliation (CSVR), a Johannesburg-based non-governmental organisation. CSVR were engaged in a programme of research examining the nature and extent of violence during South Africa's transition from apartheid rule to democracy. One strand of this research focused on revenge violence and vigilantism. Even with this relationship only six interviews were secured with individuals who had been victims of vigilantism. This may in part be explained by reluctance on behalf of victims to come forward through fear of further attacks. Indeed there have been cases of community members paying the bail of alleged criminals so that they are released from police custody into the community and subsequently killed. One interviewee who was abducted from his home by a crowd of 50 community members and taken to a local school hall to appear before a kangaroo court explains:

> The fact of the matter is you either plead guilty or not guilty and then if you plead not guilty you are not given the opportunity to state why you are pleading not guilty. And they say 'but you did this' and whilst you are busy trying to explain something, somebody will come from nowhere and start slapping you and saying 'but tell the truth'. So there is a lot of intimidation, harassment and complete abuse of your personal dignity and esteem so that you end up cowering in a corner. The guys have guns, AK–47s, sjamboks, knobkieries, pangas.[14] You are defenceless in that type of situation. You are completely at their mercy.
>
> (Interview with victim of vigilantism, October 1999)

The brokerage roles of organisations with which victims have had prior contact and where a relationship of trust had been established, help in gaining access. The credibility of intermediary bodies, not seen as organs of the state, was of prime importance. When the state itself is integral to the nature of the conflict and its various manifestations such as communal violence, these prerequisites are all the more significant. Given the problems of accessing victims, the 46 interviewees in the research emerged through a process of snowball sampling, intermediary agencies and personal contacts with community organisations. This is clearly a non-probability sample and it is legitimate to question the quality of data arising from this methodological approach. The research did, however, triangulate victims' stories through focus group work within communities, interviews with statutory and voluntary bodies dealing with paramilitary/vigilante violence, feedback from political parties and secondary data sources (newspapers, periodicals and community-based newsheets). The nature of the attacks, the interrogation processes and the violence used were independently repeated in the accounts of a number of the interviewees. An 'ideal-type' sampling framework simply isn't available to researchers in areas of high sensitivity – being mindful of the consequences of using alternative strategies on data quality and finding ways to validate findings are essential in these circumstances.

Personal security of researchers studying political violence

The personal security risks associated with this type of research are high. Lee (1993), referring to Yancey and Rainwater (1970), described two kinds of danger that may arise during the research process: the 'presentational' and the 'anonymous'. The former occurs when the researcher's presence or actions evoke aggression, hostility or violence within the setting. The latter comes about when the researcher is exposed to otherwise avoidable danger simply because of the dangerous research environment. Both kinds of dangers apply to studying paramilitary violence and vigilantism. Paramilitaries in Northern Ireland are well practised in dealing with 'touts' or those passing information, alleged or otherwise, to the PSNI. This extends to those 'speaking out' against them. Suspected informers are shot, and there are no exemption clauses for academic researchers. For example, a former member of the PIRA, Eamon Collins, was murdered in January 1999 following his evidence against former PIRA colleagues in court and a book, revealing their operations and depicting the members as 'a sadistic conspiracy of ageing, pot-bellied drink-induced egos'. Likewise in South Africa, University of Cape Town academic Dr Ebrahim Moosa had his home bombed after criticising the vigilante activities of PAGAD. Of more direct relevance to this research was the attempted assassination of Queen's University Belfast Professor of Comparative Politics, Adrian Guelke, in September 1991. The Ulster Freedom Fighters (UFF)[15] broke into his home and shot him in the side but failed to kill him because their guns jammed. The terrorists claimed that he was an intelligence officer for the IRA and involved in importing arms from the Middle East. It subsequently transpired from a journalist's investigation that Professor Guelke's South African background and research on violence there had led to loyalist paramilitaries being approached. He was, he suspects, set up by an outsider. Guelke explained:

> How or why I fell foul of some person in South Africa to the extent that I became a target for assassination, I do not know. Perhaps my writing about South Africa's supply of arms to Loyalist paramilitary organisations gave offence, or a brief investigation I carried out into extreme right-wing violence in South Africa may have been the cause. There were a number of possibilities. From my experience of Northern Ireland I know how utterly trivial the reasons someone becomes a target can be. In general, campaigns of violence are rarely conducted with precision, whatever their ultimate purpose.
>
> (Guelke 1998: 196)

Guelke's first-hand experience provides an ominous warning against complacency in undertaking fieldwork into paramilitary violence. A surveillance network operates on behalf of the paramilitaries tasked with 'keeping their eyes open' for unusual activity. As a precautionary measure we 'informed' political representatives of the paramilitaries (Sinn Féin, the Progressive Unionist Party and the Ulster Democratic Party) about our research so that they were aware of its authenticity. In essence this amounted to securing their 'approval' in the event of questions being asked about its precise purpose. A key aspect of convincing the political representatives of our *bona fides* was the source of funding for the research. Had the research received government funding, particularly from the Northern Ireland Office,[16] political/paramilitary 'endorsement' for the fieldwork would have been impossible. Researchers would be seen by republicans, for example, as part of the 'British establishment' and therefore, by definition, engaged in intelligence gathering under the guise of academic research. This would undoubtedly have put us at risk in undertaking fieldwork on such a sensitive topic. The fact that the research had been funded through the Economic and Social Research Council (ESRC) attributed significant independence to our motives and we offered this information to participants as part of negotiating access. Suspicion of the researchers' motives may not arise solely from paramilitaries. The security forces may have concerns about researchers (without a police record) being spies on behalf of paramilitary organisations.

In South Africa, we sought the support of respected community members in the townships we wished to study. These local residents provided invaluable assistance with our fieldwork, acting not only as guides and 'gatekeepers' but also as 'sponsors' and thereby ensuring safe passage in the townships. In most cases, 'gatekeepers' arranged to meet us at the edge of the township and travelled with us in the car. Meetings and interviews were held during the day, so that travelling to and from the townships in darkness was avoided.

Suspicion of 'outsiders' is intense in this type of research. In Northern Ireland, the perceived religion of the researcher is likely to be a key factor in the minds of interviewees. Respondents look for 'clues' to religious affiliation that has become intrinsic to social interaction in Northern Ireland. The most obvious, although not fail-safe, is the researcher's name. Beyond that, area of residence, birthplace, accent/language, appearance, school attended, interest in particular sports and, somewhat bizarrely, whether one is 'Catholic- or Protestant-looking'. Coming from the 'other' community may condition the response of interviewees or put the researcher at some risk given the sensitive topic under review and the nature of the questions posed. In South Africa, this was less of a consideration given that we were non-South African researchers interested in a South African phenomenon. To understand paramilitary 'policing' in Northern Ireland or vigilantism in South Africa requires probing questions about motives, methods, support for paramilitaries'/vigilante actions within their communities, and the exploration of alternative ways of dealing with 'anti-social behaviour'. To the suspicious interviewee this may smack of information gathering reinforced by our preference to tape-record the interview for the purposes of data analysis. For the interviewer in these circumstances, Lee contends that 'complete neutrality is probably impossible' and when researchers proclaim their neutrality 'they are, in fact, concealing their own sympathies' (Lee 1995: 23). This is a difficult and sometimes dangerous balancing act.

It is only sensible in undertaking fieldwork to observe cautious security protocol. Being aware of the constituency in which one is interviewing is crucial – staunchly loyalist and republican enclaves are dotted throughout most towns/cities in Northern Ireland while South African townships tend to be on the fringes of urban areas. Sensible security planning can involve working out entry and exit routes, opting, where possible, for safe(ish) locations to conduct interviews (for example, administrative headquarters of political parties linked to paramilitaries and the offices of non-governmental organisations), taking taxis to venues as opposed to using personal transport with car registration details, doing fieldwork in pairs, informing other members of the research team of your schedule. The venue for conducting interviews is particularly important. Participants and researchers must feel safe. There are areas in Northern Ireland, for example, where one community or the other feels threatened, given the territorial nature of segregated space. Finding 'neutral' venues isn't always easy and hence the use of Probation Board offices, where a number of the interviewees had official appointments, provided secure settings. While highlighting the importance of sensible personal security measures, these must be kept in perspective. Here we concur with Punch, that researchers of controversial topics must not 'become over-sensitive so as to avoid dubbing the setting or topic virtually unresearchable' (Punch 1989: 181).

Feeding back findings: dissemination and engagement with stakeholders

Our final heading concerns the dissemination of the research findings and the extent to which one engages with stakeholders. One month prior to the release of the findings, separate seminars were held in two of the four focus group areas (one in a republican area and the other in a loyalist area). The research team considered it important to give something back to participants in the project and to the communities studied. In both seminars the findings of the research were well received. A findings leaflet was produced and sent to everyone who had participated in the research (copies of the leaflet were sent to Probation Board officers to pass on to those individuals who had been referred to us) and to other interested parties. The project website also contained a summary of the research and its findings.

We did not anticipate how the media would portray the findings. Their reaction was generally supportive of the research but honed in on criticism levelled at the Northern Ireland Office (NIO) with headline items such as 'NIO slammed over punishment attacks' and 'NIO lacking courage on thug menace'. The NIO reacted angrily and denied it was 'indifferent' to paramilitary attacks and refused to 'comment in detail on a report officials were not given the opportunity to see before publication' (Graham 2000: 7). This raises the interesting question as to whether organisations, particularly those which have been criticised in research, should be afforded a prior 'right to reply'. If so, how should this feature in the findings and dissemination process, or how might this be anticipated in advance to give the organisation time to prepare their 'press release'? Furthermore the NIO stated 'What we have seen amounts to a series of unsubstantiated, generalised and politically tendentious assertions' (*Irish News* 2000: 5). What they had 'seen' at the time of issuing this statement were newspaper accounts of the research and not the final report. In fact, the NIO were interviewed as part of the research and the project team also briefed the NIO on 'punishment' attacks prior to a debate on the topic in the House of Commons. In addition, an NIO official attended a research seminar where preliminary findings were presented.

The Northern Ireland Office's response may have been conditioned by their anticipation of how the research could/would be used in the wider political context. Politicians drew selectively on the research to condemn the government and its response (or lack thereof) to the informal criminal justice system. Such was the extent of this public discourse that the report was debated on the floor of the Northern Ireland Assembly. The motion put to the Assembly was:

> The Assembly notes with grave concern the contents of the 'Informal Criminal Justice Systems in Northern Ireland' report on punishment beatings by paramilitary organisations; deplores and condemns the Government's inadequate response to the report; and calls on the Government to bring forward measures to ensure that those responsible are made amenable to the law.
>
> (Northern Ireland Assembly 2001a)

The debate itself highlighted the politicisation of the research findings in which some members of the legislative assembly used the criticisms levelled at the NIO over the issue as a blanket condemnation of the outworking of the Belfast Agreement. One contributor argued that the research report 'has presented cogent evidence that the Good Friday Agreement is failing' (Northern Ireland Assembly 2001b: 47). This enormous extrapolation from a research report which dealt with a single (but significant) issue of criminal justice to a declaration that the Belfast Agreement had failed demonstrates the way in which the findings were manipulated for political purposes. The motion was passed on a strictly partisan vote – the Ulster Unionists, Democratic Unionists and Alliance parties voted in favour; Sinn Féin, the Progressive Unionist Party (PUP) and the Northern Ireland Women's Coalition voted against; and the Social Democratic and Labour Party (SDLP) abstained. The findings of the research assumed a degree of political import never intended or anticipated by the researchers. The timing of the report, when the Northern Ireland Assembly was still faltering, may have been unfortunate in that pro- and anti- Belfast Agreement parties attempted to seize the initiative over any issue in which there was political capital. This volatile political milieu would have been difficult to predict and take into account in the dissemination of the research.

Conclusion

Two broad methodological themes are considered in the conclusion to this chapter: first, data inputs and outputs in the form of valid and reliable information sources, their translation into research findings and dissemination, and second, the specific concerns of access and security in conducting fieldwork. In a comparative research project of this type, the political context is an important and influencing factor on the data sources available. In South Africa and Northern Ireland, the state and its organs are protagonists in the conflict and hence 'official' sources of data may not represent an accurate picture of the problem. This may be for reasons that the state is not perceived as a neutral arbiter and hence there is under-reporting by victims of communal violence or it may be that the state attempts to suppress information which would reveal its poor stewardship. Either way, official statistics are not, in themselves, reliable and valid sources of information. When looking for alternatives, however, researchers need to be aware that pressure groups, by definition, have their own agenda and hence information emanating from these sources may be tendentious. The 'politics' of information is not only apparent at the research input stage but also relevant for outputs or at the point of presenting findings and their dissemination. This research took on a life of its own beyond the formal presentations of its findings. One reflective question is the extent to which this process can or should be managed so that political spinning is minimised. Project data had to rely largely on quantitative reporting from official sources, and the development of our own databases expanded on the detail of each paramilitary assault. The problem of under-reporting remains, however, and is a more fundamental issue associated with fear of paramilitary/vigilante reprisal and lack of confidence in the security forces.

In terms of the fieldwork, this chapter draws attention to two specific issues, access and security. In the former, it took much longer than anticipated to establish contacts, convince them of the bona fides of the researchers, and gain access to victims. When brokering organisations or community groups are used to secure access, they too have baggage as gatekeepers, and researchers must be aware of this in terms of the interviewees they assist with. Once access was secured the key problems encountered were suspicion of the researchers' motives, how the information would be utilised and, importantly, who would have access and how it would be stored. In a highly sensitive research topic these are not unusual methodological concerns. Perhaps more unexpectedly for the research team was the potential to re-traumatise interviewees in the course of retelling their stories and possible repercussions of their own exposure to highly distressing accounts of brutal and violent incidents. In one incident the victim of a particularly brutal paramilitary beating became highly emotional in recounting the incident. He had spoken during the course of the interview of his anger at the attack on him, concern at the disfigurement to his limbs and extreme nervousness about the potential for future paramilitary attacks. In his heightened state of anxiety he dropped his trousers to authenticate the injuries sustained to his legs and broke down in a state of emotional distress. As researchers, perhaps naïvely, we were unprepared for and untrained in dealing with the minor number of cases presenting with symptoms of psychological anguish. Although conducting research in two volatile contexts such as Northern Ireland and South Africa presents obvious dangers, our experience was that with sensible precautions and an acute awareness of the political sensitivities, prior planning and attention to potential problems minimised the risk.

A key consideration for this research was the policy implications of its findings. Since those ultimately charged with implementing policy recommendations (the Northern Ireland Office) were the focus of criticism within the research, this presented difficulties. Ultimately this is a balancing act in convincing key stakeholders that the criticism levelled is constructive and trying to gain their ownership of, and endorsement for, changes recommended. Sensationalist press reporting did not help in the pursuit of this goal.

Notes

1 The authors wish to acknowledge the support of ESRC funding (award number L133251003) in carrying out the work for this chapter, and the research assistance of Dermot Feenan in the early stages of the project.
2 Mapogo a Mathamaga was established in 1996 and has some 50,000 members who pay a monthly subscription to the organisation in return for protection against crime.
3 PAGAD was formed towards the end of 1995 and targets drug dealers and gangsters. Between March and July 1998 the organisation targeted 86 alleged drug dealers and succeeded in killing 24.
4 PEACA is based in Khayelitsha, a township near Cape Town. It was established in August 1998 by ex-combatants of the liberation struggle who came together to fight crime; its members number 1,500.
5 Kangaroo courts are characterised by the assumed guilt of the accused, denial of due process, and instant punishments which are usually violent in nature.
6 Necklacing involves placing a petrol-filled tyre around the victim's neck and then setting the tyre alight.
7 On 4 November 2001, as part of the policing reform process, the Royal Ulster Constabulary changed its name to the Police Service of Northern Ireland.
8 Joyriding is a term used, somewhat perversely, to describe the theft of cars subsequently used for reckless, high-speed chases usually by teenage boys in urban areas. It has resulted in a number of fatalities and serious injuries.
9 The figures show that loyalists were responsible for 44.5 per cent of the shootings and 47 per cent of the beatings; republicans carried out the remainder.
10 The Police Authority for Northern Ireland had key responsibility to secure the maintenance of an efficient and effective police service. It held the Chief Constable to account for his actions in certain areas (e.g. objectives, performance targets, and budgets). A new Policing Board replaced it in November 2001.

11 The Omagh bombing of 1998 was the worst terrorist atrocity in Northern Ireland's bloody history where 29 innocent civilians were killed in a busy rural town centre.
12 The Northern Ireland Association for the Care and Resettlement of Offenders is a voluntary organisation operating in the field of criminal justice which is part-funded by government sources.
13 We deliberated over payments-for-access in our project and decided to reimburse interviewees at a standard rate for expenses incurred in attending, such as travel costs, child-minding fees and lost earnings.
14 Sjamboks are whip-like implements, knobkieries are wooden sticks and pangas are large knives.
15 The UFF is a loyalist paramilitary organisation and a cover name used by the Ulster Defence Association (UDA) to claim sectarian killings.
16 The Northern Ireland Office is the department of the Secretary of State for Northern Ireland which remains responsible for matters not devolved to the Northern Ireland Assembly. These include matters such as policing, security policy, prisons, criminal justice, international relations and taxation.

References

Alty, A. and Rodham, K. (1998) 'Pearls, pith and provocation. The ouch! factor: Problems in conducting sensitive research', *Qualitative Health Research* 8, 2: 275–82.
Amupadhi, T. (1997) 'Police worried about the rise in mob action', *Weekly Mail and Guardian* (Johannesburg), 14 February.
Barclay, G.C. and Tavares, C. (2000) *International Comparisons of Criminal Justice Statistics 1998*, London: Home Office.
Bornmann, E. (1998) 'Group membership as a determinant of violence and conflict: The case of South Africa', in E. Bornmann, R. van Eeden and M. Wentzel (eds) *Violence in South Africa: A Variety of Perspectives*, Pretoria: HSRC Publishers.
Brewer, J.D. (1993) 'Sensitivity as a problem in field research: a study of routine policing in Northern Ireland', in C. Renzetti and R. Lee (eds) *Researching Sensitive Topics*, London: Sage.
Brewer, J.D., Lockhart, B. and Rodgers, P. (1998) 'Informal social control and crime management in Belfast', *British Journal of Sociology* 49, 4: 570–85.
Campbell, B. (1999) 'The dark secrets of a peace hero', *The Independent on Sunday* (London), 26 September.
Cavanaugh, K.A. (1997) 'Interpretations of political violence in ethnically divided societies', *Terrorism and Political Violence* 9, 3: 33–54.
Clarke, L. (1998) 'Terror victim group's head quits in row', *The Sunday Times* (London), 27 September.
Coleman, M. (1998) *A Crime against Humanity: Analysing the Repression of the Apartheid State*, Cape Town: David Philip Publishers.
The Economist (1999) 'Mandela's heir', 29 May.
—— (2001) 'Africa's great black hope – a survey of South Africa', 24 February.
Families Against Intimidation and Terror (1999) *Media Information Package*, Belfast: FAIT.
Fay, M.T., Morrissey, M. and Smyth, M. (1999) *Northern Ireland's Troubles: The Human Costs*, London: Pluto Press.
Fergus, L. (1999) 'Fait "naming" furore', *News Letter* (Belfast), 9 February.
Graham, I. (2000) 'NIO slammed over punishment attacks', *News Letter* (Belfast), 28 November.

Guelke, A. (1998) *The Age of Terrorism and the International Political System*, London: I.B. Tauris.

Harper, S. (2000) 'Self-styled "champion of abused" is a liar and a paedophile', *Belfast Telegraph*, 22 November.

—— (2001) 'Catalogue of tragedy from our spiralling car crime', *Belfast Telegraph*, 24 March.

Irish News (2000) 'NIO "indifferent" to paramilitary attacks', *Irish News* (Belfast), 28 November.

Jeffery, A. (1997) *The Natal Story: 16 Years of Conflict*, Johannesburg: SAIRR.

Kennedy, L. (1995) 'Nightmares within nightmares: paramilitary repression within working-class communities', in L. Kennedy (ed.) *Crime and Punishment in West Belfast*, Belfast: The Summer School, West Belfast.

Khangale, N. (2001) '15 held for mob killings', *Sowetan* (Johannesburg), 5 March.

Knox, C. (2002) '"See no evil, hear no evil": Insidious paramilitary violence in Northern Ireland', *British Journal of Criminology* 42, 1: 164–85.

Lee. R. (1993) *Doing Research on Sensitive Topics*, London: Sage.

—— (1995) *Dangerous Fieldwork*, Thousand Oaks, CA: Sage.

Louw, A. (1998) 'The problem with police statistics', *Nedcor ISS Crime Index* 2, 3: 11–12.

Louw, A. and Shaw, M. (1997) *Stolen Opportunities: The Impact of Crime on South Africa's Poor*, ISS Monograph Series 14: 12–14.

MacKay, A. (1999) 'Terrorist mutilations (Northern Ireland)', *House of Commons Hansard Debates*, 27 January.

Minnaar, A., Pretorius, S. and Wentzel, M. (1998) 'Political conflict and other manifestations of violence in South Africa', in E. Bornmann, R. van Eeden and M. Wentzel (eds) *Violence in South Africa: A Variety of Perspectives*, Pretoria: HSRC Publishers.

Murphy, C. (1999) 'FAIT in internal row over claims on bombing', *Irish Times* (Dublin), 9 February.

Murray, R. (1982) 'Political violence in Northern Ireland 1969–1977', in F.W. Boal and J.N.H. Douglas (eds) *Integration and Division: Geographical Perspectives on the Northern Ireland Problem*, London: Academic Press.

Ndaba, B. (2001) 'Photographer saves suspect from necklacing', *The Star* (Johannesburg), 27 February.

Nina, D. (1995) 'Reflections on the role of state justice and popular justice in post-apartheid South Africa', *Imbizo*, Issue 3/4: 7–14.

Nolan, P.C., McPherson, J., McKeown, R., Diaz, H. and Wilson, D. (1999) 'The price of peace: the personal and financial cost of paramilitary punishments in Northern Ireland', unpublished paper, Belfast: Royal Victoria Hospital.

Northern Ireland Assembly (2001a) *Order Paper OP25/00*. Online. Available HTTP: <www.ni-assembly.gov.uk/order25-00.htm> (accessed 24 January 2001).

—— (2001b) *Official Report (Hansard)*, 23 January. Online. Available HTTP: <www.ni-assembly.gov.ukrecord/010123.htm> (accessed 24 January 2001).

Northern Ireland Office (2000) *Fear of Crime and Victimisation in Northern Ireland*, Belfast: Northern Ireland Office.

Ntabazalila, E. (1997) 'Crowd demolish alleged rapists' shack', *Cape Times* (Cape Town), 30 January.

O'Duffy, B. (1995) 'Violence in Northern Ireland 1969–1994: Sectarian or ethno-national?', *Ethnic and Racial Studies* 18, 4: 740–72.

Oldham, J. (1998) 'Anti-terror spokesman accused of following his own agenda', *News Letter* (Belfast), 5 August.

Patel, D. (1997) 'Taxi wars in South Africa: Can there be peace?', in A. Minnaar and M. Hough (eds) *Conflict, Violence and Conflict Resolution: Where is South Africa Heading?*, Pretoria: HSRC Publishers.

Poole, M. (1993) 'The spatial distribution of political violence in Northern Ireland: an update to 1993', in A. O'Day (ed.) *Terrorism's Laboratory: The Case of Northern Ireland*, Aldershot: Dartmouth.

Punch, M. (1989) 'Researching police deviance', *British Journal of Sociology* 40, 2: 177–204.

Randall, E. (2000) 'Lack of schooled cops plagues SAPS', *The Sunday Independent* (Johannesburg), 19 February. Online. Available HTTP: www.iol.co.za/news (accessed 19 February 2000).

Royal Ulster Constabulary (2000) *Report of the Chief Constable 1999/2000*, Belfast: RUC.

Schärf, W. (1992) *Community Courts*, Cape Town: SJRP/LEAP.

Schönteich, M. and Louw, A. (2001) *Crime in South Africa: A Country and Cities Profile*. Briefing presented at the Institute for Security Studies, Pretoria, 15 March.

Soggot, M. and Ngobeni, E. (1999) 'We must work on their buttocks', *Weekly Mail and Guardian* (Johannesburg), 14 May. Online. Available HTTP: www.sn.apc.org/wmail/issues/990514/NEWS33.html (accessed 14 May 1999).

South African Institute of Race Relations (2000) *South Africa Survey 1999/2000*, Johannesburg: SAIRR.

Truth and Reconciliation Commission (1998) *Truth and Reconciliation Commission of South Africa Report*, Cape Town: CTP Book Printers.

Walker, G. (1999) 'A mother torn by grief and anger', *Belfast Telegraph*, 4 August.

Weekly Mail and Guardian (Johannesburg) (2000) 'A society of rapists'. Online. Available HTTP: www.mg.co.za/mg/news/2000apr1/7apr-rape.html (accessed 7 April 2000).

White, R.W. (1993) 'On measuring political violence: Northern Ireland, 1969 to 1980', *American Sociological Review* 58: 575–85.

Williams, M. (1999) 'Police release kangaroo court victim', *The Mercury* (Durban), 23 February.

Yancey, W. and Rainwater, L. (1970) 'Problems in the ethnography of urban underclasses', in R.W. Habenstein (ed.) *Pathways to Data*, Chicago: Aldine.

10 Veiling violence

The impacts of professional and personal identities on the disclosure of work-related violence

Maria O'Beirne, David Denney, Jonathan Gabe, Mary Ann Elston and Raymond M. Lee

Introduction

Although the volume of research on work-related violence is increasing, there is a paucity of studies on the ways in which professionals talk about the violence they have experienced. Existing research on violence generally assumes that the participants will 'disclose' any or all of the details about these events (Hollway and Jefferson 2000). Most researchers will be somewhat reluctant to take at face value accounts of sensitive topics that can be censored by the respondent. Researchers, either during the fieldwork or in the course of its analysis, will probe the perceptions, experiences and emotions underpinning the respondents' account (Brannen 1988; Lee 1993). Just as researchers consider the content of interviews, so too do participants edit what they might include in or exclude from their accounts. The result may see respondents and researchers bartering for access to more or fewer details.

From the respondents' position, particularly when their words carry currency or responsibility, the scope for disclosing sensitive information is likely to be regulated by the risks associated with imparting this information (Sieber 1993). The risk of being vulnerable to blame or ridicule may inhibit what a person includes in the account, thus muting any desire to disclose (Goodey 1997). Therefore a professional might be willing to talk with the researchers, but what he or she might say may be curtailed.

In this chapter we will examine some of the methodological challenges encountered during our study of work-related violence experienced by General Practitioners, Anglican Clergy and Probation Staff. We focus specifically on the processes and dilemmas associated with professional reports of violence during the qualitative phase of our research. Disclosure about violence, as both a process and a product, has emerged as an important issue in our study, not simply because it was the corner-stone of our research inquiry, but because it was elaborated upon in considerable detail by the professionals we interviewed. Professionals working in cognate professional areas frequently fail to make formal reports to colleagues and management about the violence they encounter. Others, exploring violence experienced by social care staff also note that:

The absence of a supportive work culture has led to under reporting and has prevented the sector from developing an integrated strategy against violence.
(Brockman and McLean 2000)

Through the use of specific examples, we will show how the professionals grappled with the matter of talking about violent behaviour of those service users who were abusive towards them. We examine how the process of disclosure incorporates both personal and professional ways of talking about violence, that sometimes may veil its presence. We also examine how disclosure of violence has an impact on a vocabulary of explaining motives for violence, which emerged during our interviews.

Disclosing violence: setting the methodological scene

Between June 1998 and December 2000, through a self-administered postal questionnaire of 3,500 professionals, and 75 interviews with professionals willing to be interviewed, we set about examining how respondents defined and experienced violence as part of their routine work. The survey was adapted from a standard victimisation survey (such as the British Crime Survey). We defined violence as a continuum of behaviours from verbal through to physical and sexual assault, while bearing in mind the impacts of these behaviours on the professional in terms of emotional and physical injury.

Through a 16-page, 72-question schedule we sought professional disclosure about specific details associated with the most recent incidents of two forms of violence – threats and assaults. In all, 62 per cent of GPs, 72 per cent of clergy and 79 per cent of probation officers completed and returned their questionnaires. Their survey responses provided us with a snapshot of the nature of violence experienced by professionals of different ethnicity, age, gender and place of work. We assumed that most professionals would understand the terms we used in the survey and the associated behaviours but it was impossible to capture the professionals' own meanings of violence within the parameters of the survey. To address this matter we were keen to explore what violence meant to the professional who had been assaulted, by examining the ways it was described in their accounts. As a result of the 75 interviews, patterns emerged which suggested that understandings of violence were consistent with those we included in the survey, but also extended to other forms of expression including body language and intonation of voice, rather than actual words. Violence was described not just as an act but in terms of the impacts of those acts. Professionals also described the negative emotional outcomes from violence, including feelings of powerlessness, distress and fear. Together these experiences were discussed in detail in the course of one-off interviews usually in the professional's place of work or their home.

Selecting 75 participants from our sample was a challenge, in as much as we had the choice of interviewing any of 400 professionals. Consequently we chose to contact first those who had experienced physical assaults and then those who had been threatened with violence. We recognised that this sampling strategy would affect the scope of our inquiry, in as much as we would not be including professionals who had experienced verbal abuse solely or those who reported that they had avoided violence, to compare and contrast their experiences. But the strategy would enable us to look at how forms of violence considered serious would be described.

In our survey we and, to some extent, the respondents made assumptions that each of us understood the other's questions and responses. There was limited scope to validate these assumptions given the demands made of the survey. In contrast through the semi-structured and in-depth interviews, the negotiation of meaning and experiences of violence could take place. It is these qualitative discussions with professionals that the remainder of the chapter describes.

Preparing to discuss experiences of violence

Interviewing people about personally sensitive experiences is not the easiest kind of fieldwork for any researcher to undertake. Researchers who have interviewed people about their experiences of violence regard this type of fieldwork as challenging (Kelly 1989; Stanko 1990; Moran-Ellis 1996). Our interviews with professionals provided an arena for probing emotionally sensitive topics which had a social significance for both researchers and participants. We also sought to understand how the nature of safety, of risk and of violence was constructed and deconstructed during the interviews.

As in any inquiry into sensitive subjects, careful consideration was given to the choice of words used and the ways these were expressed during each interview. Choices arose which required immediate resolution, as to who should be included or excluded from interviews, the topics to include, the wording of questions and the flexibility allowed to stray from well-made plans as the interview progresses. Furthermore, we were mindful that one could ask whether we as researchers inadvertently 'talked-up' violence or 'minimised' it through the words we use and our line of inquiry.

The demands made upon some of us during the interviews were concentrated and immediate. The topic guide, although carefully designed, was often sidelined as the interview progressed. It is understandable that researchers must think on their feet when, for instance, participants ask their own questions about our experiences of violence and our attitudes to the topic covered. Kelly (1989) considered it important that she question her own experiences and perceptions of violence before she could ask others to do so on her request. Even if it is a difficult exercise, Edwards (1993) has argued that researchers should locate themselves and the respondent within the interview situation. In other words the researcher needs to be 'self-aware' and 'other-aware' throughout the interview. Such close attention to the researcher–participant relationship is important because of the assumptions being made about the outcomes and outputs of that once-off encounter. While these issues are more than likely standard features of research planning, they are sometimes sidelined especially when the study is large-scale, yet the implications of these preparations are important in shaping how the researchers respond and engage with the respondent and their accounts.

At almost every phase of the interview process there is scope for the researchers to question their own skills, the underlying motivations for their inquiry and their feelings about the topic and the participants. Emotional detachment can diminish as the discourse unfolds. As Moran-Ellis (1996) notes, while reflecting upon her interviews with professionals in referral services:

> Recapturing a sense of shock and outrage through hearing or reading accounts of abuse had reduced this professional distance from the subject and hopefully prevented me from becoming totally immune to the realities of sexual abuse.
>
> (Moran-Ellis 1996: 184)

To fulfil one of the objectives, we encouraged respondents to present both personal and professional feelings and perceptions about their experiences of violence. The result of this at times triggered emotions such as concern or empathy among some of the researchers. While trying to retain a professional detachment as an interviewer, the interplay between formal and personal emotions and responses was something which some of the researchers also managed.

One of the authors (Maria) presents her reflections about preparing for the interviews undertaken with clergy and probation officers.

> I found preparing for the interviews quite a challenge. All of my previous interviewing experiences were in another country with people who are perceived to have little power/authority in society (young people, people who are unemployed, disabled or chronically ill). The participants of these studies volunteered to take part so that their experiences of vulnerability and exclusion would be highlighted. The research process was of bi-lateral benefit – in exchange for a snap shot of their perceptions and experiences I could provide a platform to raise their issues that erstwhile, had been sidelined and ignored. Preparing to interview professionals – who in relative terms (to those I had previously interviewed) have some authority in society – prompted me to reflect upon how they might explain and rationalise their feelings and experiences about a violent event within the context of our interview. I thought about why someone with relative authority would seek to disclose to me their experiences of vulnerability at the hands of clients or public? Given the demographic differences between us, I wondered if my gender, nationality and age and our mutual cultural idiosyncrasies might impact upon the process and if so with what effect? In the end I decided to employ a tactic I used in other interview situations. My starting point was to engage with the respondents as women or men firstly and then to incorporate the other aspects of their identity, including their professional status, age, ethnicity, etc. While this precaution helped me achieve some consistency between the

different interview contexts, it did not completely reduce the concentration required to interpret and further probe the often emotional accounts of violence that unfolded.

To some extent we thought that the interviews would follow the sequence of the topic guide that we had spent considerable time developing. However, through the course of approximately 50 interviews, we found that although a topic guide was useful to promote consistency between interviews, its original structure was not always easy to follow in every interview. In those interviews where the professional 'directed' the discussion, there was greater fluency in their descriptions of the violence they had encountered – the accounts flowed with a clear beginning, middle and end. In these instances the professionals had more scope to alternate between and elaborate on conceptual meanings and feelings associated with the incident than if we had prompted them to do so. In the interviews where we stuck rigidly to the topic guide – for example, when the accounts were short and the professional was not keen to elaborate – the narrative was more fragmented and guarded in nature.

Although the two interview styles influenced the organisation of the accounts of violence, nevertheless the professionals were equally willing to discuss their experiences of violence in both types of interview.

How professionals talk about violence

We present examples of professional accounts of violence, focusing upon the reports of two of the three professional groups in this study – Anglican clergy and probation officers. We have focused upon these two groups of professionals because of the distinction between their organisational structures and cultures, which undoubtedly affect their experiences of violence. While clergy tend to be self-employed and for the most part lone workers, probation officers are part of a large organisational hierarchy that deals with risky behaviours and clients as part of its routine work. From these two groups one might expect to find differentiated accounts of work-related violence, and perhaps a different form of disclosure to us and to colleagues.

Professional disclosure about violence is context specific. The content of professionals' accounts, in terms of descriptions, feelings, facts and those they choose to impart this information to will vary. For the most part we inquired about professionals' disclosure to five significant groups: family, peers/friends, employers/management, police, and professional associations/community/society.

These five significant groups relate to the informal and formal support systems upon which professionals draw for their emotional and occupational welfare. While family, peers and friends provide the emotional support for the professional, the issues that professionals choose to disclose to these groups are often regulated by what they think these supports are able to 'cope with'. On the other hand, talking about violence to employers, managers and other professionals and services is often contextualised within the parameters of employee rights and employer responsibilities regarding occupational health and safety. Choices are made specifically in relation to what it is permissible to say, to whom and why. The reasons why professionals choose to talk or not to talk about violence vary considerably. In the following accounts, we focus on the ways in which professionals report violence to those associated with their work. We have not covered family members in this instance, although they are clearly a very important 'significant' other.

When do professionals talk about violence?

When the professionals we interviewed talked about their disclosure of violence to colleagues, they described their perceptions and experiences in two 'voices': either in a confident, rationalising voice of the 'survivor' who has learned from past negative experiences, or in a second voice, which hinted at frustration and helplessness. The story of John (a priest) is an example of the former and Ann (a court welfare officer), whose account follows thereafter, is an example of the latter.

Being a vicar who had moved from a northern parish to the south-east, John reflected in the interview upon why he chose to disclose his experiences to colleagues in his current parish rather than in his previous, rural-based community:

> I would disclose anything in my team [in current parish] because I mean we get that support. And of course nowadays we're encouraged, because of insurance purposes for various reasons to immediately report to the Diocese anything, even the smallest burglary or harassment that we get. I think there's a feeling, and it's one I no longer have, I used to have but I no longer have it because of my own training, but there's a feeling that clergy have to be strong to meet all needs. And I think to go to another priest and say 'I can't cope with this' certainly in my younger days in ministry was almost ... you didn't do that and if you did people would come up with some inappropriate solution. Whereas now I think we're much more able to share our experience. But I think it's selective, it depends on the locality. Certainly in [my last parish] I couldn't have done that. The remoteness anyway was a barrier. The nearest priest was 7 miles away. The Bishop was an hour's drive away ... whereas here when you're on the main arteries one can tap into resources much more easily.

When John speaks about disclosing violence, he creates a rationale for selective disclosure to some and not to others. His words and their ordering distance him from the barriers in his profession that impeded disclosure. John also appears to be referring to a form of professional failure. This failure was understandable at two levels. First, there was an implied failure to break down personal barriers necessary to gain support from colleagues. Second, the professional culture, which creates an atmosphere in which disclosure is not routine, has also contributed to the creation of an unsafe working environment.

The solution to the problem is, for this priest, the sharing of experiences, which makes redundant the professional requirement to be strong to meet all needs. Disclosure, therefore, becomes the starting point for the creation of a safer work environment. John's view lends weight to the suggestion that 'For some groups of workers, vulnerability stems not from an incapacity to do the job but from the prejudices and attitudes of others' (Davidson and Earnshaw 1991: 3).

In addition to the real or imagined prejudices, sometimes barriers impinge upon the victimised professional's ability to disclose, but also upon his/her colleagues' ability to offer support following an incident. As Ann, a court welfare officer, suggested:

> I think there can be barriers, those sort of barriers to disclosure. But one would hope being a caring profession that our doors are always open to each other and we will talk about them. Clearly when somebody's had a very bad incident sometimes you don't want to approach them because you don't have anything to say.

While Ann talks easily to us about the constraints on disclosure, it is clear that there are times when such ease of reporting to colleagues is an aspiration.

Why professionals choose not to talk about violence

How do professionals talk about their reticence to speak about their experiences of violence to others? With regard to informing the police, Alan, a vicar in an urban parish, considered the implications of making a 'formal' disclosure about being pushed against a door by an irate parishioner and why he chose not to make a formal report to the police.

> I didn't ring the Police. Whether I was right or wrong I don't know. But you have this dilemma you know. I suppose I thought well if I rang the Police it's going to be his word against mine. I mean there were no marks. I mean I suppose if there'd been cuts. But I mean I was shaken, I was definitely shaken and very upset for certainly two or three days. But I suppose this is also this thing about 'What do we do?' Because we are clergy. And if you start bringing in authority you suddenly … I don't know, people then think that we don't have a forgiving attitude. Or that we're supposed to be compassionate and if somebody's upset or screwed up or getting violent, we're supposed to accept it and understand it. Well I mean yes, to some extent, but I don't think we should ever be allowed to be in that position and actually just say 'Fine, we accept it'.

Alan's words are delivered in quick bursts, his use of 'I mean', 'I suppose', 'I don't know', re-enforcing his need to validate his actions or thoughts. He was not seeking it from the interviewer but perhaps from another significant other, but who that 'other' might be is not exactly clear in his account. He is wavering between what is expected of him and what he expects of himself. Here, we see a choice not to disclose for pragmatic reasons – not to 'worsen' his working experiences. Alan's account is very emotionally charged and his lack of confidence in how he should deal with the incident is vivid. This combination of many signals (arising from the emotionally charged response and the limited confidence therein) did make demands upon the concentration of the researcher. It led the interviewer to question whether they should probe this elusive 'significant other', or whether to probe how this respondent had dealt with the matter.

In much the same way probation officers will disclose experiences of violence to certain colleagues in their immediate team, but will be careful which senior officers they inform apart from that team. As Jane stated,

> So although they might want support, they may talk to colleagues about it but they may not record it or talk to the senior fully in terms of there being a particular incident because they might feel as though in some way they're going to be blamed for it.

Jane's words are not personal, but draw upon a collective 'wisdom' of peers. The choice of what to say to senior probation staff is clear. Jane's statement is delivered concisely, fluently and with 'insider-knowledge'.

Handling personal–professional accounts of violence

As the previous accounts illustrate, just as professionals consider to which significant others they recount their experiences of violence, what they choose to tell us, as researchers, about these disclosures is also a matter of choice. The options about what they say are determined in part by how the researchers will view them and, in part also, by how they will view themselves. We know that professionals who volunteered to be interviewed were willing to discuss their experiences and to some extent the content of the interview was partially shaped by the researchers' questions. But any interview is a negotiated event and certainly the professionals had the scope to introduce or exclude topics, feelings or details as they wished. In much the same way as the professionals discussed factors that prompted them to edit their accounts of violence to peers, it is probable that they considered what to include in or omit from their accounts to us. Indicators of this included some hesitancy in accounts, switching between the professional and personal perceptions about experiences and respondent–interviewer 'connection' or speaking with an emotional voice when recounting something very important to them. An example of the last kind of account was evident in the way with which one priest spoke about his experiences of intervening in a domestic violent incident involving a young parishioner's parents. He spoke in detail of his anxiety for this girl and her mother when he walked in on a very heated argument. His voice and facial expressions were full of emotion when he recounted his instinctive response to the scene – to 'sort the father out' – and how he actively suppressed that urge in case he worsened the mother's and daughter's situation. He also suppressed his instincts in part because he was concerned at how it would look to others to have a priest resort to violence to prevent further violence in the domestic sphere. The tension between official and personal emotions and actions in his account illustrate how his 'professional self' controlled his personal feelings during that incident. Second, from a methodological perspective, his account illustrated the greater ease and forthrightness with which he spoke about interpreting and reacting to violence against others than about understanding violence against him.

Equally important to the interview event are the reactions of the interviewers. The choices made by the interviewer to probe or listen to the account unfold further depend upon the content of the account, the way it is presented and its impact upon the researcher.

This is particularly evident when the professionals discuss the impact of violence on their emotions and their work practices. In many ways, reflecting upon the emotional outcomes of violence is an opportunity for the interviewee to switch from the professional to the personal, as the following quotations suggest. Ann, a probation officer, describes how an incident of intimidation and physical assault by a client at work affected how she went about her daily life in its aftermath. Her account sees her double back over her words to ensure that she is not misunderstood and does not seem to be 'incompetent' to herself or to us.

> Well I smoked a lot which I don't normally do, and I was very, very inefficient which was very … I mean, I don't mean sort of inefficient in terms of work like … the place was a mess and I couldn't get anything together very well. I mean I did keep things together but I mean I … was very much sort of sloppy than I normally am about domestic tasks and I was much more … just mentally less alert really.

The impact of the attack appears to have affected both her private and working lives. She emphasises what might appear to be reflections upon the attack. 'The place was a mess', which underlies the disorder and disorientation in all aspects of the interviewee's life following from the attack. Her sentences are short, fast and emotional. Her words indicate that she does not want to appear completely affected and vulnerable to us, so she selects terms such as 'inefficient' and 'less alert' and 'sort of sloppy' rather than their synonyms – unprofessional, incompetent or chaotic.

In much the same way, Peter, a community service supervisor, talked about how 'nice' it would be if he could be 'honest' about how scared he felt when seeing certain clients instead of appearing as the professional competent and resilient resettlement officer.

> I was very conscious that all through the time I worked as a resettlement officer I lived with a level of fear that was sometimes, you know, not a problem and at other times was a massive problem, because you would have

to see this person regularly and they were terrorising you basically. And I mean my senior was a woman and she was very understanding and very supportive about this, but it doesn't alter the fact that you have got to do it. And no amount of support, you know, gets you sort of past that really and it's just about how you manage that level of fear. And you go through this entire thing, well you mustn't show it because that might make them worse, you know, or you mustn't do anything different. ... And I just wonder about that sometimes, whether we shouldn't just be a lot more up front say, you know, you're scaring the shit out of me and I don't like it ... I would prefer to handle it like that, but it's just kind of not done, not allowed. I don't know.

Peter indicates the need to show vulnerability not just to his manager but to us. His need to indicate 'honestly' how vulnerable he felt is reinforced in his *choice* to say 'shit' in the course of the discussion. Does he swear as a normal part of conversation? Well, not if the rest of his interview is anything to go by, as he does not swear frequently or with the same intonation elsewhere. So, in this instance Peter's words and tone are 'gritty', indicating a 'gut' requirement to voice his emotions and vulnerability to us, if not to his management.

Through the expression of personal emotions associated with the violent incident, a connection between the participant and the interviewer is difficult to avoid. The accompanying cues, from eye contact and body language during these sometimes uncomfortable disclosures permeates our respective professional demeanours during the interviews. There is no doubt in the researchers' mind that when the professionals discussed the impact of and their relationship with violence, the professional and private spheres merged. This is evident in the account of Tony (a priest) of how the 'angry' attitudes of church members about his sexuality undermined his ability to cope with the physical assaults he had experienced.

Violence is anything where you feel a person wants to wipe you out, eliminate you, hurt you. And that's something um ... (pause) ... There are parts of the Church, members of the Church who do get angry, very angry [over gay issues]. I remember one woman screaming at me at a Synod meeting that it was an insult to our Lord's crucifixion that I even brought up the subject for discussion. And she was actually screaming. And a colleague, talking about these bloody 'fags'. ... That is violent ... These people do not even respect, they don't think I should be a priest. They don't think I should be a Christian. As far as they're concerned I have no place here. And that's quite a fundamental attack on me because my identity is formed in part by believing that God created me, that God loves me, that he calls me to be a Christian ... it's quite personal. I've been physically assaulted twice since being an adult and that didn't hurt as much.

Before Tony spoke, he paused and looked at the interviewer (Maria) and looked at the table between them, then started to speak, his eyes moving around the room, only occasionally focusing on her while he recounted his feelings and experiences. Here is the interviewer's interpretation during that disclosure:

> I was sitting in a well worn sofa with missing springs, the sort that you fall into and out of. I felt myself sink uncomfortably fast, further into the sofa as his account unfolded. Tony was becoming more animated as he spoke about his experiences of hearing colleagues talk about 'those bloody fags' – his voice was louder and there was indignation in its tone. While I kept up with his words and gestures my mind kept flagging the anxious questions – 'why didn't he tell me this earlier? – do I re-contextualise all of his previous statements on the basis of this disclosure?' It seemed to me that when he paused before making this disclosure he was making a choice to over-turn a previous decision to retain this information – why he did this, I did not know.

In the remaining time he gave to the interview he talked in detail about his experiences of being a 'gay vicar', and during that time the tone of his voice became softer and his eye contact more steady than during the 'key' disclosure and the sense of methodological panic subsided.

From the interviews we find that violence is not experienced or interpreted solely in terms of the professional's status or role. Instead memories of violence from another time in their life are often interwoven (as the priest illustrated in his account of wanting to intervene in the violent domestic incident) into their accounts of recent aggression, bridging past identities with the present. Margaret describes in her account of childhood experiences how these influenced the way she coped as a vicar working with people who had mental illness:

> I have no basic fear of mental illness. My father was mentally ill all my life and could be very abusive and very aggressive and violent. And I learnt you had to just stick it out and face it out. … There are potentials [for aggression]. And it mainly comes from the mentally ill in the community but I am fairly aware of them. I know not to be afraid of them. … Again experience has taught me that I can cope.

The interviewer (Maria) documented her concern for the vulnerability expressed in this professional's account of her childhood as follows:

> I felt uncomfortable, I wanted to discover the level of her coping and how she had learned it. But I found it difficult to ask her these questions. What would it mean for her to talk through past experiences which still perhaps triggered raw emotion, flashes of which I heard in her account, and moreover, how would I deal with the outcomes in the interview situation. Because I considered any further probing to be bordering on voyeurism and an unnecessary intrusion of my role. Consequently, I did not probe more deeply, because Margaret moved quickly on and the opportunity to connect with her on that issue again had passed.

The personal coping skills to deal with violence were evident in accounts of many professionals we interviewed. Through their disclosure of how they had handled certain violent incidents we heard of how they had been 'let down' by their organisations. This criticism of their organisations was more apparent among probation staff than among clergy and it raised questions as to the role of disclosure in large government-based bureaucracies compared with the looser and more differentiated organisation of the Church of England. Carol, a probation officer who had been attacked, claimed that: 'Support from seniors is hardly existent … It's non-existent.'

Thus few, if any, formal complaints had been made to the probation service by officers who had been attacked. The apparent stoical acceptance of unsafe working conditions suggested that they had not forcefully disclosed the impact of an attack on management. They displayed a professional resilience even if privately they did not subscribe to a 'culture of tolerance'. Probation officers were not as reticent when speaking about their experiences to researchers. During the interviews they complained that they were denied the use of functioning mobile phones, that gates in car parks (places where probation officers appear to feel most threatened) were left unlocked, intercoms were hardly used, and that offenders were frequently unscreened. Some probation officers had asked for one-way mirrors to be installed and for restrictions on the number of clients allowed in a room at any one time. Although the officers discussed this information with us, some whose accounts included names of senior staff double-checked with us that their transcripts would not be seen by another member of the team.

Despite these requests for our reassurance, many of the reports made to us about poor management were calls for change through a neutral third party – us, the researchers. In most instances we were asked what we would do with all of the information that we were gathering in our research and whether this information would be fed back to their employers or organisations. Many interviews ended with the professional saying 'Thank you for listening/talking to me, I hope something useful comes out of this research.' The request that we, as researchers, 'do something' with the research findings was implicit in their participation as it was in the detail of their disclosure.

Discussion

As our account demonstrates, there were clearly advantages in using a multi-method approach to understand the professional discourses of violence in order to map patterns and details of the personal and of some professional accounts of violence. The qualitative methods were needed to capture complex meanings of violence in general and of specific meanings with respect to particular individuals. Professionals utilised different modes of discourse when disclosing violence in an attempt to relay personal and professional justifications for their actions. The examples we have provided indicate that professionals make decisions to disclose certain details and not others to us as they do with colleagues, management and 'significant others'. Underpinning these accounts was the choice of showing their vulnerabilities or not – depending on who was listening and asking the questions. Disclosure about violence in the office, church or hostel sometimes required details of emotions, or previous personal experiences, which may be 'safe' to discuss in the cocoon of our interview, but not to disclose to another with authority over that person. Although the interview event is a common enough situation for the researcher, it is likely to be seen as a novel experience for other professionals – such as those in our study. Talking about violence to us, in the interview situation, may be seen as a means of off-loading, which is relatively unproblematic as there seemed to be no obviously negative consequences to adversely affect the professional's standing within the employing organisation as long as confidentiality was retained. But disclosure at a more formal level to management or other professional groups, as the accounts presented suggest, may be problematic. Despite existing legislation Employment Act 1974, RIDDOR 1995 – which necessitates incident reporting, professionals' accounts indicate the reticence to disclose their experiences of violence for reasons related to their understandings of what constituted 'professional' behaviour. For the clergy, legacies from traditional Christian ministry encourage them to accept all aspects of human behaviour even though it may be personally threatening. Few, if any, formal procedures were available after disclosure for clergy which reduced motivation for formal disclosure, although informal disclosure to selected colleagues occurred. Conversely probation officers working in a large national government bureaucracy which had formal procedures in place indicated that the 'victim blaming' culture and insensitive managerial style dissuaded them from making formal disclosures.

What is important in relation to our methodology is that professionals are often called upon by their organisations to frame their experiences of violence into official categories used for formal risk assessments by employers. Such tasks do not require and often do not permit professionals to disclose the emotional aspects of a violent experience or the possible impacts that violence has had on their lives. Probation officers, for instance, are constantly being called upon to make 'objective' written formal risk assessments, thus suppressing some of their own anxieties about the potential for violence. However fearful for their own personal safety, the clergy are required to present a fearless and caring vocationally based persona to those who might have threatened or abused them.

As we have seen, in-depth interviews can generate accounts that are simultaneously presentations of professional and emotional selves in the discussion of work-related violence. The emotional presentations may be at odds with culturally normative professional accounts, but both co-exist and are negotiated by the professional during the interview situation. One set of accounts may try to silence the other – in this instance we have seen examples of how the professional self which espouses competency and control quashes certain experiences which these individuals might otherwise want to express. Even in the act of disclosing violence there is an attempt to veil some of its less acceptable aspects and ramifications.

We would suggest that a number of strategies might be employed by researchers when seeking the disclosure of sensitive information about professionals and their working lives:

- Try to establish a rapport with professionals that invites them to present more than a professional identity, but also personal and past identities which may underpin their experiences or attitudes. It requires the interviewer to create a relaxed atmosphere akin to 'friends' catching up.
- While professionals are willing to be interviewed, they may not be willing to disclose all aspects of the violent incident or its impact. To encourage a more detailed narrative, allow the professional the scope to direct the discussion. For example, do not start the interview with a discussion about violence unless the professional chooses to do so.
- Try to be mindful of the changes between professional and personal narratives in respondents' accounts of violence – which are sometimes interchanged quickly – and probe these changes wherever possible to look for disagreements and consistencies.
- Try to be aware of the extent to which our own reticence to query and listen to accounts of violence may impact on the interview. Why do we ask certain questions and not others and what impacts have these choices for the understanding of violence that unfolds?
- Ideally, there should be a follow-up interview with the professional to discuss the transcript from the first meeting and to clarify or expand on any points made previously.
- Be prepared and willing to provide information on support for professionals who have experienced trauma as a result of violence.

In this chapter we have tried to present the dilemmas and choices about content and process associated with professional disclosure about violence to researchers and colleagues. The implications of these dilemmas are significant, not only for social research, but for the growing domain of formal audits and risk assessments of violence in professions such as those we studied, that require professional disclosure. The 'safety-net' of the interview situation with its trained non-judgemental listener and a flexible agenda has raised dilemmas for the researchers regarding the types of information that professionals choose to share.

The alternative and mainstream arena for professional disclosure – formal disclosure to colleagues or management via tools such as the incident audit form – will succumb to these same dilemmas at best and create others. We know that professional disclosure is sensitive to context and part of that context is the vocabulary used to prompt disclosure – in short the questions asked. In our view not only is there a lesson for academic researchers studying work-related violence, but also for organisations who are required to audit and respond to violence against their own staff. If such inquiry does not enable respondents to disclose their emotions – particularly 'fear' about disclosure – then the complexity of relationships between professionals, their organisations and their clients will become oversimplified and polarised and effectively silenced.

References

Brannen, J. (1988) 'The study of sensitive subjects', *Sociological Review* (36): 552–63.

Brockman, M. and McLean, J. (2000) *Review paper for national task force: violence against social care staff.* National Institute of Social Work Research Unit: London.

Davidson. M. and Earnshaw J. (eds) (1991) *Vulnerable workers.* John Wiley: Chichester.

Edwards, R. (1993) An education in interviewing – placing the researcher and the research. In *Researching sensitive topics* (eds) Renzetti, C. and Lee, R. M. Sage: London.

Hollway, W. and Jefferson, T. (2000) *Doing qualitative research differently.* Sage: London.

Gabe, J., Denney, D., Lee, R., Elston, M., O'Beirne, M. (2001) Researching professional discourses on violence, *British Journal of Criminology* (41): 460–71.

Goodey, J (1997) Boys don't cry, masculinities, fear of crime and fearlessness, *British Journal of Criminology* (37) 3: 401–18.

Kelly, L. (1989) *Surviving sexual violence.* Polity Press: Oxford.

Lee, R. M. (1992) Nobody said it had to be easy: postgraduate field research in Northern Ireland, *Studies in Qualitative Methodology,* (3): 123–45.

—— (1993) *Doing research on sensitive topics.* Sage: London.

Moran-Ellis, J. (1996) Close to home: the experience of researching child sexual abuse. In *Women, violence and male power* (eds) Hester, M., Kelly, L., Radford, J. Open University Press: Buckingham.

Sieber, J. (1993) The ethics and politics of sensitive research. In *Researching sensitive topics* (eds) Renzetti, C. and Lee, R. M. Sage: London.

Stanko, E. (1990) *Everyday violence. How women and men experience sexual and physical danger.* HarperCollins: Glasgow.

Underdown, A. and Ellis, T. (1997) *Strategies for effective offender supervision.* London: Home Office.

11 Researching domestic violence in a maternity setting

Problems and pitfalls

Loraine Bacchus, Gill Mezey and Susan Bewley

Introduction

Domestic violence is widely recognised as an important public health issue that has serious consequences for women's physical and mental wellbeing (British Medical Association 1998: 29–32). In the United Kingdom domestic violence, defined as the physical, emotional or sexual abuse of an adult woman by a male partner, affects around one in three to four women in their lifetime (Dominy and Radford 1996: 6; Mooney 1993: 26; Mirlees-Black 1999: 18). Similar rates of domestic violence have been reported in surveys from Canada (Johnson and Sacco 1995) and the United States (McFarlane *et al.* 1991).

Evidence suggests that women may be more vulnerable to domestic violence when they become pregnant. The first epidemiological studies on violence during pregnancy were conducted in the United States (Gelles 1975; Helton *et al.* 1987; Hillard 1985; Parker *et al.* 1994). The prevalence of partner perpetrated violence in pregnancy is reported to be between 7 per cent (Campbell *et al.* 1992) and 22 per cent (Purwar *et al.* 1999) with the greatest risk occurring during the postpartum period (Gielen *et al.* 1994). The adverse health outcomes for the mother and her unborn child make domestic violence a major concern for midwives and obstetricians (Dye *et al.* 1995; Bullock and McFarlane 1989; Fernandez and Krueger 1999; Morey *et al.* 1981; Newberger *et al.* 1992; Ribe *et al.* 1993; Pak *et al.* 1998; Stark and Flitcraft 1995). At the extreme end of the spectrum, domestic violence may result in the death of the mother, her unborn child, or both (Dannenberg *et al.* 1995; Department of Health 1998: 159; Harper and Parsons 1997; Maryland Department of Health 2001).

Health professionals have an important role in identifying women who are experiencing domestic violence and ensuring that appropriate advice and support are provided. Women who experience domestic violence make considerable demands on health resources (Campbell *et al.* 1994; Kernic *et al.* 2000). However, although abused women are more likely to seek help from health care settings than from any other social organisation, they rarely disclose the underlying reason for seeking care, namely violence by a partner (Hayden *et al.* 1997). The use of structured screening questions by health professionals has been found to increase significantly the rate of detection of violence in maternity settings (Norton *et al.*

1995), accident and emergency (McLeer and Anwar 1989) and general practice (Hamberger *et al.* 1992). In addition, a number of studies have shown that the majority of women are in favour of health professionals asking routine questions about violence (Bacchus *et al.* 2002; Bradley *et al.* 2002; Friedman *et al.* 1992; McWilliams and Mckiernan 1993: 73).

Despite the existence of guidelines for developing effective responses to domestic violence in health settings (American College of Obstetricians and Gynecologists 1995; American Medical Association 1992; Bewley *et al.* 1997; British Medical Association 1998; Department of Health 2000; Royal College of Midwives 1997) and the growing evidence linking domestic violence to poor physical and mental health status, health professionals have been largely ineffective in addressing domestic violence. Women experiencing domestic violence frequently describe their contacts with health professionals as unhelpful and negative (Gerbert *et al.* 1996; Pahl 1995; Plichta *et al.* 1996; Williamson 2000: 47–66). Many health professionals feel poorly equipped to handle cases of domestic violence because of the lack of education and training on the subject. Fear of offending women, the belief that domestic violence is not a legitimate health issue, and feeling frustrated when women do not act on their advice are other inhibiting factors (Brown *et al.* 1993; Chez and Jones 1995; Parsons *et al.* 1995; Sugg and Inui 1992).

In the literature, health professionals are described as being ideally placed to identify and support women experiencing domestic violence. However, in practice, this appears much more difficult to achieve than one would expect. Health professionals often work under major time constraints, in conditions of pressure characterised by a lack of resources, staff shortages, high staff turnover, and low morale. These structural factors, common to most health care settings, will undoubtedly have an impact on the quality of care that health professionals are able to provide to abused women.

Description of the research study

This chapter will outline some of the methodological challenges encountered while implementing a domestic violence research study within the maternity service of an inner city teaching hospital. We shall also discuss the implications of these findings for developing effective and sustainable domestic violence interventions in health care settings and for future research in this area. The study was funded by the Economic and Social Research Council as part of a Violence Research Programme in the United Kingdom, and provides the first British data on the extent of domestic violence in pregnancy and associated health outcomes. The objectives were as follows.

- To examine the prevalence of domestic violence in pregnancy when midwives are trained to use a screening instrument.
- To examine the impact of domestic violence on maternal health and obstetric outcome by examining women's maternity records.

- To explore midwives' experiences and perceptions of routine enquiry for domestic violence through focus groups and semi-structured interviews.
- To explore women's experiences and perceptions of routine enquiry for domestic violence through semi-structured interviews.

The study design was a cross-sectional survey in which trained midwives screened pregnant women for domestic violence at three specific points: at the first antenatal appointment (booking), at 34 weeks, and within ten days postpartum. The study used trained midwives rather than researchers to screen women for domestic violence. This design was adopted so that the findings could be extrapolated to clinical settings and to examine the feasibility of screening women for domestic violence in a maternity service.

Location and description of the research setting

The study was conducted in the maternity services of Guy's and St Thomas' NHS (National Health Service) Hospital Trust, the largest maternity unit in the London region with approximately 5,800 births a year. The hospital serves a population which is diverse and high-risk in medical, social and mental health terms. Guy's and St Thomas' Hospital Trust is also a tertiary referral centre for women with medical complications of pregnancy, and for problems of fetal cardiology, and the patients may require admission to the High Dependency Unit. At the time of the study the maternity service consisted of eight hospital teams and ten community teams, each consisting of six midwives, including one senior midwife.

The hospital teams looked after pregnant women from booking (the first antenatal appointment) through to delivery. Many of these teams also had a specialist function, such as caring for women with substance misuse problems, with diabetes, or women whose babies had cardiac abnormalities. Hospital teams were also responsible for providing care to women post delivery on the postnatal wards, but not in the community once women returned home. The community teams were based within general practitioner's surgeries and, in liaison with the general practitioner, provided antenatal, intrapartum and postpartum care for women (up to ten days). Women were then discharged to the care of a health visitor. Community teams organised their own workload and tended to provide better continuity of care for women compared with the hospital teams. They were also able to see women in general practitioners' surgeries, health centres or at home according to the woman's need.

Specialist midwives were responsible for the development and co-ordination of services in the areas of HIV screening, bereavement support, female genital mutilation, practice development, and auditing. These midwives were involved in all clinical areas, including bookings, and so became a part of the study.

Finally, core midwifery staff were hospital based and responsible for one particular clinical area (e.g. the antenatal ward and Day Assessment Unit, where women would be assessed or admitted with complications during pregnancy, the delivery suite and the postnatal ward). Core midwifery staff were not required to participate in the screening study, as they were not responsible for providing routine antenatal care to women. However, all medical and non-medical staff in these areas received an adapted domestic violence training session as it was anticipated that the raised awareness created by the presence of the study might lead to an increase in the identification and reporting of domestic violence.

Staff rotation between teams and clinical areas was frequent, with a change list re-allocating a number of staff every three months. Community midwives tended to stay in their teams for longer, but could be requested to work in another team or clinical area if necessary.

Many changes occurred within the service during the period of the study. There were plans to merge the two maternity units and base the new service at the St Thomas' site. This involved a major reorganisation of the midwifery teams. At the start of the study, midwives were working the traditional system of three eight-hour shifts. Six months into the study midwives were required to work two 12-hour shifts. The new shift pattern was introduced as a method of achieving continuity of carer. However, continuity of care was hard to predict, with staff turnover and rotation having an impact on how many midwives a woman might have contact with during her care. In addition, the midwives were required to attend mandatory training for a new computer program for storing women's maternity records.

Development of the screening instrument

The screening questionnaire used was based on the Abuse Assessment Screen (McFarlane *et al.* 1996) which has been used extensively in North American studies of domestic violence in pregnancy (Helton *et al.* 1987; Parker *et al.* 1994). However, during the initial stages of the study several midwives expressed concerns about the directness of the language used in the questionnaire. For example, the original Abuse Assessment Screen asks whether the woman has been 'hit, slapped, kicked, or otherwise physically hurt' during different time periods, or whether she has been 'forced to have sexual activities'. The questions were modified slightly to ensure that midwives felt comfortable with the wording and were not discouraged from using it. For example, in the amended version women were asked whether they had been 'physically hurt', or 'made to engage in sexual activity when they didn't want to'. In order to increase the midwives' comfort with using the screening instrument, it began with general questions about feeling afraid or unsafe and threats of violence, before progressing on to more sensitive questions about actual physical or sexual violence. Women were asked to indicate on a body map picture the location of any injuries they received during pregnancy. They were also asked to refer to a card to indicate the types of injuries they sustained during pregnancy. This method was used to reduce the emotional stress and feelings of embarrassment that may arise from being asked to verbalise information. It is not possible to comment on the validity or reliability of this modified version, although the pilot study showed that it was acceptable to women and midwives. It could be argued that the modified questions were not able to determine abuse status, which may account for the rather low prevalence of domestic violence in pregnancy found in this study (2.5 per cent). However, several other research studies have used similarly phrased questions and have reported higher rates of violence in pregnancy than this study (Amaro *et al.* 1990; Dye *et al.* 1995; Irion *et al.* 2000; Stewart and Cecutti 1993). This is the first study in the UK to examine the prevalence of domestic violence in pregnancy using trained midwives to screen women as part of their maternity care. As such there are no comparative UK data upon which to draw regarding the effectiveness of using domestic violence screening questions in a British population of pregnant women.

The screening questionnaire did not enquire about experiences of psychological or emotional abuse, and therefore women who had experienced only non-physical forms of violence during pregnancy would not have been included in the prevalence figure. Studies that have enquired about a range of abusive behaviours, including less injurious acts such as verbal abuse and controlling behaviours, have generally produced higher rates of domestic violence in pregnancy (Gielen *et al.* 1994; Hedin-Widding *et al.* 1999; Webster *et al.* 1994). The decision to exclude the question 'have you ever felt emotionally abused?' from the original Abuse Assessment Screen was based on the premise that it would be difficult to explain the relationship between emotional abuse and obstetric complications such as antepartum bleeding and low birth weight. In this study, the investigation of the impact of domestic violence on pregnancy outcomes was limited to physical and sexual violence. Experiences of emotional abuse are less tangible and more subjective than acts of physical violence and therefore difficult to establish through a single broad-based question such as the one used in the original Abuse Assessment Screen. It was also necessary to keep the screening questionnaire as brief as possible to enable midwives to incorporate it into limited antenatal appointments. A more in-depth exploration of non-physical forms of abusive behaviour was achieved through a series of semi-structured interviews with women who reported domestic violence in the screening study.

Problems associated with conducting research in clinical settings

Many of the practical problems encountered during the study are related to undertaking research in clinical settings, rather than researching domestic violence itself. There are a number of methodological approaches that can be used to investigate the prevalence of domestic violence in pregnancy. If experienced researchers had conducted the screening study, it is likely that this would have led to higher response rates and would have been less complex to organise. The administration of self-completion questionnaires, given the relative anonymity of this method, may have led to a higher rate of disclosure of domestic violence as demonstrated by two UK studies conducted in primary care settings (Bradley *et al.* 2002; Richardson *et al.* 2002).

However, as with the first approach, the results are not easily translated into effective working practices by health professionals. A third approach involves delegating the collection of data to clinicians, in this case the midwives. This design was adopted to allow the results to be interpreted within the context of clinical practice and examine the feasibility of screening women for domestic violence in maternity settings. However, the use of clinicians to screen for domestic violence generally requires specialised training and support over and above that normally provided to research staff.

Roth (1966) has discussed the problems associated with using 'hired hands' to conduct research. Roth suggests that distortion, cutting of corners and carelessness in the process of data collection are a normal and an inevitable consequence of hiring other people to conduct research. A researcher, working on an area of particular interest, will endeavour to collect and process their data in the most accurate way. Midwives do not primarily envisage themselves as researchers, although there is an increasing trend in midwifery towards delivering evidence-based care. Therefore, they do not fit the profile of the dedicated researcher who has a vested interest in ensuring that their project is conducted to the best of their capabilities. Furthermore they are often required to pursue research questions in which they may have little interest, or which they may perceive as being irrelevant to their clinical practice.

Roth (1966) also states that once the tasks of the research study are divided up and assigned to others, the data collectors may not understand all the complexities and subtleties of the research in the same way as the person who designed the study. The data collector is removed from the final product, in that the research does not belong to them. Even with training, it is difficult to develop the research interests and dedication of those hired to conduct the research. Therefore, it is inevitable that some will fall into a pattern of carrying out the research with the minimum of effort, avoiding inconvenient, embarrassing and time-consuming situations. Roth concludes that the use of 'hired hands' not only causes a study to take longer and cost more, but is also likely to introduce more dubious data and interpretations into the process of analysis.

It is not surprising that some of the highest rates of domestic violence in pregnancy have been reported in studies conducted by trained researchers, as opposed to clinicians. Amaro *et al.* (1990) used a trained bi-lingual interviewer to screen pregnant women, while Gielen *et al.* (1994) used trained interviewers from the same community as the women in the study. Registered nurses with expertise in both counselling and antenatal care were responsible for screening women in a study by Helton *et al.* (1987). Midwives working in a frenetic and understaffed maternity unit are unlikely to regard domestic violence enquiry as high priority. Added to this is the potential risk of hostility or violence to themselves or the woman if a suspicious partner is alerted to the nature of the research.

It is likely that the use of midwives with limited research experience to conduct an investigation of domestic violence in pregnancy contributed to the high attrition rate after the first screening phase, and the low rate of disclosure of domestic violence compared with other studies (Tables 11.1 and 11.2). The alternative would have been to use experienced researchers to screen for domestic violence, but within the limited timeframe and budgetary constraints of the study, there was no possibility of setting up a comparative study of this kind. However, using researchers to screen women for domestic violence also has a number of disadvantages. Although it may increase response rates, the research is conducted in an artificial situation where the problem of domestic violence is separated from the context of the women's health care and their lives. Unless a woman specifically requests it, any disclosure of domestic violence cannot be communicated to other health professionals to allow appropriate care to be provided. The woman can be referred to the relevant agencies, but she has no automatic access to increased support and interventions by maternity staff. In addition, the views and experiences of a researcher screening pregnant women for domestic violence are not necessarily a realistic or valid representation of what a health professional will encounter in the clinical context.

In order to prepare the midwives for the study, the researchers designed a two-and-a-half-hour training programme. This consisted of domestic violence awareness raising, use of a screening instrument, and effective responses to disclosures of violence. Midwives were provided with a training pack and referral information about community resources to offer to women disclosing domestic violence. The researchers trained 116 out of 145 (80 per cent) of the midwives over a seven-month period. The training period was more protracted than initially intended. This was partly due to staff rotation and high staff turnover, but mainly because midwives were unable to find time during their hectic schedules to attend training, particularly if they were working on teams that were short of staff. A number of midwives needed to have individual training sessions to accommodate

Table 11.1 Questionnaires returned by screening phase. Values are given as n (%)

Screening phase	Booking	34 weeks	Postpartum (within 10 days)
Agreed	771	86	140
	(70)	(97)	(43)
Refused	120	0	4
	(11)	(0)	(1)
Inappropriate circumstances*	214	3	185
	(19)	(3)	(56)
Total	1,105	89	329

* One or more of the inclusion criteria could not be met (i.e. private consulting time, use of a female professional interpreter).

Table 11.2 Prevalence of domestic violence by screening phase. Values are given as n (%)

Screening phase	Sample (n)	Lifetime	Last 12 months	Current pregnancy
Booking	771	103 (13.4)	46 (6.0)	14 (1.8)
34 weeks	86	17 (9.8)	5 (5.8)	5 (5.8)
Postnatal	140	16 (11.4)	10 (7.1)	7 (5.0)
Total	892[a]	122 (13.4)	57 (6.4)	22 (2.5)

a Refers to total number of women screened on at least one occasion. n=86 women were screened more than once.

Note: Domestic violence is defined as any adult experience of physical or sexual abuse perpetrated by a current or former partner, or family member.

this, others attended during their days off work or opted to attend two short sessions. While the training may have been sufficient to enable the midwives to screen women for domestic violence and improve their general awareness of the problem, it was not sufficient to incorporate many of the issues that they wanted and needed to be informed about. Most midwives felt that they would have benefited from follow-up training sessions during the course of the study, yet the researchers experienced difficulties getting midwives to attend the basic training. Trying to maintain contact with over 100 midwives, most of whom were based in the community, while co-ordinating training sessions and attending to other research activities was a difficult task. It required monitoring changes in shift patterns and the movement of staff between clinical areas or midwifery teams. It was difficult for the researchers to maintain a visible presence within all of the clinics, as there were around 40 general practitioners and health centres where midwives conducted antenatal clinics, often simultaneously, and in addition to the hospital-based antenatal clinics. The number of midwives who participated in the domestic violence screening dropped dramatically during the study, with 74 per cent of trained midwives screening at booking, 23 per cent at 34 weeks and 40 per cent during the postpartum.

Other researchers have reported on the problem of maintaining the momentum of domestic violence screening and interventions in health settings (Harwell *et al.* 1998; McLeer 1989). In these studies the introduction of protocols for identifying domestic violence and training programmes resulted in an increase in health professionals' knowledge about, and confidence in detecting domestic violence, higher rates of completion of safety assessments and referrals to community resources. However, this improvement was no longer apparent when follow-ups were conducted. It seems that, once the impetus provided by the research team ended, staff reverted to previous practice and women were treated for their injuries without any attempt to explore the cause.

The impact of the domestic violence screening study at Guy's and St Thomas' was also short-lived. For the purposes of this study, a domestic violence protocol and information on community resources was produced for the maternity service and incorporated into the antenatal guidelines for midwives. The information could also be accessed via the hospital intranet. However, follow-up enquiry by one of the researchers, one year after the study was completed, found that very few midwives were aware that the protocol existed and domestic violence training and screening had effectively ceased. No mechanism existed by which midwives could be supported to maintain good practice for enquiring about and responding to women who experience domestic violence. Additionally, many of the midwives who received domestic violence training as part of the study had left the maternity service. Those who remained will have lost many of the skills they acquired as part of the study since there is currently no practice of routine screening and no individual co-ordinating a domestic violence role within the maternity service. It is clear that ongoing training, support and quality assurance monitoring systems are necessary to promote sustained changes in practice and to maintain domestic violence as a priority issue in the minds of health professionals.

Although midwives were required to screen women on three occasions, very few women were screened more than once. In total 892 women were screened for domestic violence, 67 of whom were screened on two occasions and 19 on three occasions. The poor attrition rate can be attributed, in part, to the fact that once the first screening phase ended, domestic violence became less of a priority as the maternity service was going through a period of organisational change. By the 34-week screening phase, some trained midwives had moved to other clinical areas outside the research study or had left the service altogether. A second training session would have helped to maintain the pace of the study, but midwives were overwhelmed by increasing demands on their time and could not get away from clinics to participate in further training sessions. In addition, the screening questionnaires could not be kept in the maternity record for use at the 34-week or postpartum screen as women kept their maternity notes at home after the first antenatal appointment (the booking screen). Since there was no prompt in the maternity record, midwives had to remember to get the questionnaire out.

Another factor that contributed to the attrition rate and consequently the low rate of reported domestic violence was the lack of time during antenatal appointments. Most of the 892 women were screened at the first appointment (booking) which is often the longest routine antenatal appointment a woman will receive during her maternity care, and which involves the taking of a detailed medical and obstetric history. The midwives reported that the domestic violence screening questions were much easier to incorporate into this first appointment compared with the 34-week and postpartum screening phase. When faced with the prospect of a clinic full of women waiting to be seen and not enough time to complete existing tasks, midwives reported that they found it difficult to introduce the issue of domestic violence sensitively and have enough time to deal with any disclosure.

Concerns about lack of time persisted into the postpartum screening phase. Since the end of the 1980s there have been radical changes regarding postnatal visiting by midwives. Routine daily visiting up to the tenth postnatal day has been replaced by selective visiting, allowing midwives to miss some visits before the tenth day if appropriate (Garcia *et al.* 1994). In the domestic violence study there was considerable variation between the community midwifery teams with regard to the number of visits, and the majority of women received only two or three postnatal visits. This may have been exacerbated by problems of staff shortages occurring within the maternity service at the time. Selective visiting considerably reduced the number of opportunities that midwives had to enquire about domestic violence in a safe and confidential setting. Many midwives felt there was insufficient time to identify and deal with social problems in general, which deterred some women from disclosing domestic violence and midwives from raising the issue. In addition, as the postnatal visits were the last opportunity for contact before discharge, the midwives had no opportunity to follow up or arrange ongoing support for women who disclosed abuse. As a result, midwives remained anxious about raising the subject of domestic violence.

The lack of postnatal care was not unique to the maternity service in this study and has also been described in a survey of 960 women who gave birth in 1999 or 2000 (Singh and Newburn 2000: 20). The survey found that 60 per cent of women did not think there were enough midwives available to care for them in the initial days following birth, and a quarter suggested that they received no emotional support from health professionals during this time. These findings suggest that postnatal services currently give greater priority to women's physical care than their need for information and support. As the research evidence suggests that women are at an increased risk of domestic violence after birth, it may be appropriate to extend postnatal care beyond the first ten days after birth, to increase the detection of domestic violence during this period.

Repeated enquiry for domestic violence was used to determine whether this would increase the rate of detection, as suggested by other research studies (Covington *et al.* 1997). However, it is difficult to assess the impact of repeated enquiry in this study because very few women were screened more than once, and a different midwife administered the questionnaire in most of the cases where repeat screening did occur. The lack of continuity of care may also have discouraged midwives from asking about domestic violence, because there were fewer opportunities for offering long-term support to women. Enquiring more than once about domestic violence is beneficial for women as it allows for the detection of violence that begins later in pregnancy, or of changes in the severity of violence that may require additional support and intervention. More importantly, the woman is given the chance to develop a trusting relationship with her midwife, which can facilitate disclosure. Women reported that, having disclosed abuse to a midwife with whom they had developed a good relationship, it was then difficult to repeat these experiences to a completely different midwife at a subsequent appointment. It would appear that the extent to which women will discuss their experiences of violence depends upon the skill and approach of the midwife enquiring.

What became apparent were the considerable differences between midwives in their attitudes towards the study. Support for this argument can be found in women's comments on the way individual midwives approached the questions and responded to disclosures. In spite of the fact that they were trained to follow specific procedures after a disclosure of domestic violence, there were still variations in the way individual midwives responded. In the most positive encounters midwives were described as being relaxed and confident with the issue, caring, empathic and non-judgemental. In direct contrast, others were described as appearing disinterested, hurried, and unresponsive to disclosures of domestic violence. The perfunctory manner in which some midwives approached the screening questions is likely to have deterred some women from disclosing domestic violence. The results of the semi-structured interviews with a sub-sample of women who were screened indicate that the use of standardised questions alone will not guarantee an increase in the detection of domestic violence in health settings. The skill and ability of the health professional to put the woman at ease, and to pose the questions sensitively in a way that conveys a genuine concern with the issue, will also affect the willingness of women to disclose domestic violence.

If routine questions about domestic violence are to be incorporated into maternity care, they cannot be approached in a mechanistic or impersonal way. Many maternity units in the UK use a computerised booking system, whereby the midwife will ask a series of questions relating to the woman's obstetric and medical history and input the information directly on to the computerised maternity record. In the context of a busy clinic it is difficult to imagine how such a system could facilitate rapport building, or sensitive enquiry around commonly asked questions such as history of depressive illness, sexually transmitted infections, and past terminations. How would domestic violence be addressed within this context? Enquiry about domestic violence takes time and if the midwife appears hurried or distracted, the woman will be alerted to this and will be less likely to reveal that she is being abused.

The relative lack of midwives' investment in the research may also explain their dwindling commitment to the study as it progressed. They did not have direct control of the study and so were not in a position to make drastic changes when problems arose. Midwives' concerns about the study were fed back to the researchers who in turn informed the grant applicants, and adjustments were made wherever possible. For example, the midwives felt that the second screen should take place at the 34-week antenatal appointment instead of the originally intended 28-week appointment, during which many other issues needed to be discussed with the woman. The role of the researchers was to support the midwives and obtain data on their views and experiences of screening women through interviews, focus groups and informal contacts. However, it was not possible for the researchers to incorporate all the midwives' suggestions into the study design.

The researchers tried to generate interest and enthusiasm in the midwives by seeking their views and experiences about the study, and emphasising the likely policy-making implications of the study for future care of abused women in maternity settings. By establishing a steering group, which consisted of the research team and a small group of midwives, who were consulted during the development of the research proposal and the pilot study, we aimed to encourage ownership of the research by the midwives. At the end of the study, research results were presented to staff and domestic violence guidelines were developed for the maternity service. However, there was little possibility of the work being sustained in their clinical practice without ongoing training and funding, none of which was made available. Even midwives who initially held the view that the research was an important piece of work eventually came to perceive the study as a cumbersome exercise that had to compete alongside other tasks demanded of them.

In her ethnographic study of community health outreach workers on an AIDS education programme, Fox (1991) also makes reference to the differing and often opposing interests of workers and project directors. Project directors are described as being less involved in the daily management of the project and therefore are more removed from the concerns of those carrying out the work. Their primary aims are to produce work of publishable quality, obtain funding to conduct further research, and disseminate findings through participation in local and national conferences. Fox argues that project directors spend more time networking and devising strategies to gather support for their work from potential funding sources and other powerful bodies, in order to expand the reputation and influence of the project. In comparison, the outreach workers envisaged their role in the study as more altruistic. Similarly, some of the midwives working on the domestic violence screening study defined their role as care-givers rather than researchers, which is not surprising given that they spend an appreciable amount of time with women who are prone to confiding their personal concerns and problems to them. As a result of the close therapeutic relationship that often develops, some midwives saw themselves as a panacea for women's problems. The pressure on the midwives to collect more data under increasingly difficult circumstances, and to meet research objectives that were sometimes regarded as incompatible with other clinical demands, undoubtedly had an impact on their willingness to continue with the study.

One of the objectives of the study was to examine the impact of domestic violence on women's health before and during pregnancy. This was achieved by collecting data from women's maternity notes. Despite strenuous efforts by the research team, maternity notes were obtained for only one-third of women in the screening study. The system for filing and recovering patient records was somewhat chaotic; some maternity notes were not available because they were still being held by the community midwives, and others appeared to be lost. Occasionally the maternal notes were found, but records pertaining to the infant were not attached. In addition, during the middle of the study there was a change in the software program used for computerised storage of maternity information.

Consequently, the details of some women were not on the new system. Relying on clinical databases to meet research objectives has implications for the quality and robustness of the results that it generates. The difficulties that the researchers experienced in obtaining patient data may be inherent in many large-scale, busy NHS settings where storage of and access to medical records are difficult. However, as a result of being able to obtain only one-third of women's maternity notes, this study is limited in its ability to draw definitive conclusions about the association between domestic violence and health outcomes. A recent UK study of domestic violence in primary care settings also reported a low rate of accessing the medical records of women attending GP surgeries because only one-fifth of the women in the study gave permission to have their medical records reviewed by the researchers (Richardson *et al.* 2002).

The methodological problems associated with using clinical databases where information has been collected for purposes other than research have been discussed by Macintyre (1978) who conducted an observational study of record-taking by nurses, obstetricians and health visitors in an antenatal clinic. The study highlights the importance of considering the way in which the data are generated in the first place and the implications for the interpretation of data. Macintyre observed that staff tended to employ various typifications of patients when eliciting information. This was based on the assumption that standardised questions would not elicit standardised responses from patients with differing social and occupational backgrounds. These typifications influenced the vocabulary used and the staff's interpretation of the patients' responses. Questions were often modified or rephrased according to the health professional's perception of the woman's competence to understand or answer them. For example, Macintyre noted that enquiries about whether the patient had a history of nervous disorders were often phrased in such an ambiguous way that most women would answer 'no'. There was also a tendency for nurses to apologise for questions they regarded as intrusive or potentially embarrassing. For example, the question on whether the pregnancy was planned was often rhetorical: 'So you planned on having another baby, did you?' and 'So you were pleased when you fell pregnant, were you?'. These predictions often stemmed from the nurses' assumptions about women from particular social groups and their ability to plan. Therefore, well-educated, married women were perceived as being more likely to plan than less-educated, single women who were often asked 'So I don't expect you planned on this baby, did you?'. Macintyre concludes that the results produced by such record-taking practices are incorporated into sociological or clinical theories about the social world, thereby reinforcing the underlying assumptions and allowing the record maker to use them with greater confidence. Hakim's (1983) study states that research based on secondary data is compromised because it is not possible to determine whether particular information was obtained, and why information is missing, because there is no standard coding frame available to the researcher. In a survey, the researcher has clear instructions about definitions and meanings applied to both the questions and the answers in the survey questionnaire. As is the case with maternity records, there is often little or no equivalent background information held in the record. For example, as demonstrated in the Macintyre (1978) study, the meaning of the question on whether or not a pregnancy was planned is open to interpretation by the interviewer, in this case the midwife, and the respondent. The fixed choice response of 'yes' and 'no' does not accommodate ambiguous answers such as 'we didn't plan not to have a baby'.

The midwives at Guy's and St Thomas' were required to seek information regarding any social problems that a pregnant woman may be experiencing. However, there were no prompts or specific questions in the maternity notes defining social issues or indicating how to elicit such information. The maternity notes simply contained a box entitled 'social issues'. Therefore it was left to the individual midwife to decide whether, how and whom to ask about social issues. The only way of knowing exactly how and why information was recorded in a particular way may be to talk to the individuals asking the questions, in this case midwives and obstetricians. However, this would have been difficult to accomplish within the context of a large study. It is clearly important to acknowledge the problems of reliability and validity when analysing and interpreting data obtained from secondary sources.

The introduction of a new maternity record during the study created further problems for the researchers as they tried to develop a standardised data collection schedule based on three different sets of maternity records; one for each hospital and the newly introduced common maternity record. The information contained within the records varied, which meant that data for some variables had to be recorded as missing.

The practical difficulties described in this section are not unique to the maternity service involved in the study and it is worth considering the likely impact of introducing domestic violence interventions in the wider context of midwifery care. During the period when research was conducted, a report from the English National Board for Nursing, Midwifery and Health Visiting (1999–2000: 12–13) documented chronic shortages in staffing levels. Figures for 1999 show that 39 per cent of maternity units in London had vacancy levels in excess of ten unfilled posts. This increased to 54 per cent in 2000 (English National Board 2000–2001: 13–14). Both of these reports highlight the fact that continuity of carer has been difficult to establish in many maternity units, as staffing levels have been insufficient to provide continuity of carer throughout antenatal, intrapartum and postnatal care. In the study, the combined effects of long hours, low morale and the pressure of working in under-staffed conditions resulted in fewer women being screened for domestic violence and a reduction in midwifery participation rates. The resource implications of screening women for domestic violence in clinical settings should not be underestimated. Without careful consideration of these factors, domestic violence interventions in health settings will not be safe or effective.

Problems associated with researching domestic violence in clinical settings

Research on domestic violence raises important ethical and methodological challenges. Issues of confidentiality, safety, interviewer skills, experience and training are more important than in other areas of investigation. If proper precautions are not taken, the physical safety and emotional wellbeing of both the investigator and the participant may be jeopardised. During the study, the research team encountered a number of difficulties that may be intrinsic to investigating domestic violence in health settings, and which resulted in decreasing midwifery participation. It was necessary for the study design to include systems for protecting the safety of women and midwives, and to ensure that the research was conducted in an ethical and sensitive manner.

The first challenge that the research team faced was convincing the midwives and the midwifery managers that domestic violence was an important and relevant issue to be addressed in maternity care. There had been no domestic violence training for staff in the maternity service prior to the study. During the early stages of the research, midwives asked whether domestic violence was a legitimate health issue worthy of investigation and voiced concerns about 'opening up a can of worms'. Some midwives felt that domestic violence screening represented an extension of their role and that other, more important, aspects of the woman's maternity care would be neglected. There was a tendency for midwives to categorise problems as 'medical', which came within their domain, or as 'social', which were not their concern, rather than recognising the complex interplay between the two. Although the training was designed to address these issues, it was not possible to change such deeply ingrained beliefs in one training session.

The need to ensure the safety of women meant that informed consent was obtained verbally rather than in writing. The research team wanted to avoid situations where consent forms might be taken away by women to read and then discovered by a partner, or left lying around public areas of the antenatal clinics. Women were informed of the study in two ways: a poster campaign in the women's toilets giving information about the study and by the midwives themselves. Midwives had to obtain confidential time with women in order to explain the study to them and obtain verbal consent. The explanation of the study was scripted in the questionnaire to ensure that midwives did not omit any information that might affect a woman's decision to participate. Women were advised, prior to questioning, that all information was confidential unless they indicated that there was a risk of harm to an existing child, in which case this would need to be reported to a social worker. To avoid the misconception that midwives were selecting women they suspected were being abused, it was made clear that all antenatal attendees within a given time period were being approached to participate in the study. Once the midwife had explained the study, women were specifically asked 'may I continue with the questions?' and the response documented on the screening questionnaire. It is highly likely that some of the women who declined to take part in the study, or did not disclose domestic violence, made this choice because of the midwives' obligation to report evidence of harm to a child. Fear of children being taken into care by social services has been given as a reason for not disclosing domestic violence to a health professional (Bacchus *et al.* 2002). However, midwives felt it was important to make women aware of the limitations of confidentiality before getting their consent. Women were occasionally seen by more than one midwife. Therefore midwives used a special coding system in the maternity notes that would indicate to other midwives whether a woman had been introduced to the study, and whether or not she had participated or requested never to be asked again.

The midwives were asked to use only female professional interpreters – and not family or friends – to screen non-English-speaking women. This was done to ensure the women's safety and confidentiality. However, there was a scarcity of female professional interpreters within the service, resulting in a large number of women being excluded from the study. At the booking screen, 88 (8.1%) women needed a female interpreter, but for 65 (75.0%) none was available. Midwives were required to offer women private consulting time during antenatal appointments, so that enquiry about domestic violence could be carried out safely. They were advised to ask about other sensitive topics during the confidential time, such as history of depressive illness, or previous terminations. This was done to provide women with an alibi should a suspicious partner enquire too closely about what was being discussed. However, obtaining confidential time proved to be extremely difficult in practice. In the UK, modern midwifery practices have effectively reduced the opportunity for abused women to disclose these experiences to midwives. There is currently no national policy for offering women confidential time with their midwife. Partners are encouraged to be present during antenatal appointments and labour. This may be a positive experience for many women, for example, educating partners to the woman's needs during and after pregnancy. However, for those women experiencing domestic violence, it may deny them the opportunity to request or be provided with help. In addition, midwives must feel able to enquire about domestic violence without jeopardising their professional relationship with the woman and her partner, or their own safety.

Although some midwives were confident about asking to see women alone, others found it quite challenging. The women themselves welcomed the opportunity for time alone with their midwife and were generally appreciative and positive about this. However, some midwives gave accounts of over-solicitous partners who refused to be excluded from any part of the woman's care, who answered questions directed at the woman during appointments and made decisions about care. Under these circumstances midwives found it difficult to arrange confidential time with women and some reported having to use various subterfuges to achieve this, particularly if they suspected that a woman was being abused.

Failure to obtain the necessary conditions of privacy and confidentiality accounted for most of the women who were not introduced to the study at each screening phase. During the booking screen, midwives managed to obtain confidential consulting time with 117 of the 311 (37.6 per cent) women who were accompanied to the appointment. At 34 weeks, seven out of 12 (58.3 per cent) accompanied women were seen alone. The greatest difficulties occurred during the postpartum screening phase where midwives obtained confidential time with only nine of the 191 (4.7 per cent) women who had a partner, family or friends present at the postnatal visit. In order to carry out the research safely, midwives needed complete privacy without fear of interruptions. However, women were rarely left alone during the immediate postnatal period. There were often visitors to the home, partners were frequently present, as were children, and quite often there was insufficient space in which to conduct a confidential interview. Some midwives felt it was inappropriate to ask for confidential time in the woman's home where they perceived themselves to be a guest and therefore constrained from making enquiries of such a sensitive nature. In comparison, the antenatal clinic was regarded as a legitimate and acceptable place to ask for confidential time. The lack of privacy was compounded by the reduction in postnatal visits, which meant that there were very few opportunities for midwives to conduct the domestic violence screening.

Following on from issues of privacy and confidentiality, were the midwives' concerns for their personal safety when conducting the research. Community midwives were particularly apprehensive about visiting women in their homes late at night, with the knowledge that an abusive partner might be present. Some midwives were concerned that they might be placing women at increased risk of violence or reprisals from partners simply by asking about domestic violence. Every effort was made to ensure that partners were not aware of the study. The poster campaign, used to inform women about the study and sources of help, was displayed in safe areas such as the women's toilets. However, during the course of the study there were a few incidents involving midwives being confronted by angry, hostile partners who had somehow become aware of the study. Occasionally it was felt that women placed both themselves and the midwife in danger by raising the subject of domestic violence in the presence of a partner, even after being advised by the midwife that this would be unsafe. While these incidents were handled appropriately and no one was harmed, they acted as a disincentive to enquiring about domestic violence.

The researchers were sensitive to the possibility that some midwives may have had personal experiences of domestic violence. The prevalence of domestic violence among female health professionals has been found to be equivalent to that in the general population of women. One study reported that 38 per cent of obstetric nurses had suffered partner abuse (Janssen *et al.* 1998). A survey of medical residents found that 31 per cent of female doctors had a history of child abuse or domestic violence, and 73 per cent had been harassed during training (Komaromy *et al.* 1993). During the course of the study many midwives disclosed personal experiences of violence, both work-related and in their personal lives. The training sessions and focus groups with midwives facilitated safe and confidential discussion of personal experiences of domestic violence. Midwives were trained separately from managers and supervisors to allow midwives to express any negative or ambiguous feelings they had about the study. It was made clear that no midwife would be made to engage in the study and that they could withdraw from the project without having to justify the decision and with no need to fear negative repercussions. For some midwives it was the first time they had discussed their experiences of domestic violence and, while many found this empowering, the study provoked feelings of helplessness and inadequacy in others, to the extent that they were unable to participate. For these midwives, the prospect of trying to help women in their care when they were dealing with violence in their own relationships was quite overwhelming. However, midwives who had resolved their personal experiences of violence were able to give very strong, active support to the study, spending considerable amounts of their own time assisting abused women. In many circumstances, their personal experiences enhanced the midwives' interviewing skills and empathy, and there was an impression that this led to increased rates of disclosure of domestic violence.

In order to respond to the needs of the midwives and reduce the stress of the investigation, the research team also provided support and advice to help them deal with difficult disclosures, and any practical or personal difficulties that arose during the study. This was in addition to the focus groups and interviews that were used to collect qualitative data on the midwives' perceptions and experiences of screening women. The research team also offered support and advice to women who needed additional assistance following disclosure of domestic violence. The team established and maintained links with local community agencies via local multi-agency initiatives in order to maximise the support available to abused women.

During the course of the study the research team received around 50 unscheduled contacts from midwives and other maternity staff, requesting assistance or advice regarding women experiencing domestic violence, or wishing to discuss personal difficulties with the study. Some of these cases were detected outside the screening study. On one occasion, for example, a researcher was asked to respond to a very frightened and distressed woman who had attended an antenatal clinic with multiple bruising. The woman voluntarily disclosed that her partner had tried to strangle her before the appointment. On another occasion the same woman failed to attend an antenatal appointment, resulting in one of the researchers and a community midwife paying a home visit. The woman's partner had broken into her home and destroyed her telephone. In some instances it was necessary to advise a midwife to take a break from the study because the emotional impact was affecting her ability to work. These informal contacts with midwives became an important research tool for seeking their views on the study and how it was affecting them. However, the researchers were often faced with the mutually incompatible demands of maintaining a professional detachment and engaging in support activities, which involved a greater investment of their time than the research objectives allowed. On occasion other research tasks had to be put on hold to enable the research team to respond to requests for assistance. Future research studies on domestic violence in health settings should consider budgeting for additional support, such as an on-site domestic violence advocacy worker whose sole responsibility would be to provide support to abused women and health professionals.

Strategies for creating a clearly identifiable and understood support structure are important when implementing domestic violence interventions in health settings. Dealing with disclosures of abuse is stressful and the midwives reported that they would not have felt confident enough to undertake the work without opportunities to discuss their experiences of working with abused women and having support and advice on site. Once the study ended there was no longer any support mechanism in place, which may partly explain why midwives stopped screening women. Midwives were in favour of a specialist domestic violence midwife who could be responsible for training and professional development in the area, but also provide them with the support and encouragement they needed to enable them to screen women with confidence.

Domestic violence screening carries with it the expectation of an appropriate and effective intervention from the health professional. Role clarification and setting limitations was an important part of the domestic violence training. Whether or not women disclosed domestic violence, midwives in the study were required to offer referral information about community resources such as women's refuges, counselling services, and legal remedies. Midwives were encouraged to listen, empathise and offer validation of women's experiences, but to avoid making judgemental remarks or offering directive advice. Most midwives felt that this was a reasonable and realistic level of response and did not wish to do more than this, although the researchers were aware of several midwives who took a more active role by finding refuge provision, and offering women extra antenatal appointments. Although the majority of midwives accepted that they had a limited role to play in terms of offering help to women experiencing domestic violence, some found it difficult to limit the intervention in practice, particularly when confronted with a distressed woman requesting help. The idea of simply providing women with referral information was not acceptable to some midwives. Many described feelings of helplessness and frustration if they were unable to provide women with an effective solution, or if women failed to take action after being given referral information. Although the training focused on respecting and supporting women's decisions, some midwives still felt that the only way to empower women was to get them to leave the violent relationship. Much discontent stemmed from how little they could do to help abused women. As a result, some midwives were reluctant to raise the issue during appointments.

Broadhead and Fox (1990) have explored the difficulties of controlling researchers' involvement and level of intervention in their ethnographic study of an AIDS education programme based in the community. In the study, community health outreach workers were employed to disseminate AIDS prevention materials such as bleach for sterilising injecting paraphernalia and condoms to potential high-risk groups such as intravenous drugs users and sex workers. The primary function of the outreach workers was to establish contact with potential clients to engage them in research to assess risk behaviours, knowledge and attitudes about risk. Outreach workers also provided referrals for counselling, free food, shelter, clothing, employment opportunities, detoxification programmes, and AIDS antibody testing upon request. Some of the outreach workers became inundated with the complexity of the problems experienced by clients. The act of simply dispensing AIDS prevention materials seemed meaningless when considering the totality of problems faced by the clients. Since most of the outreach workers regarded themselves as social service providers rather than researchers, they found it difficult to limit their involvement with clients, particularly when faced with situations that were emotionally draining. As with the midwives in the domestic violence screening study, the outreach workers with the greatest longevity in the field were those who set realistic goals and expectations for themselves. By managing to sustain a professional detachment from the clients and avoid over-identifying with them, outreach workers were able to conduct the research successfully.

Similarly, midwives who acknowledged that they were not responsible for solving women's problems, but only for offering empathic support and referral to specialist agencies, were more likely to continue with the screening study. However, there are ethical issues relating to the use of midwives, whose primary role is to provide health care, education and advice to women during and after pregnancy, to conduct research on an issue that has an undisputed effect on the health and wellbeing of the mother and her unborn child. It may be unrealistic to expect health professionals to be able to distance themselves from a problem that is extremely prevalent in society and has such a profound effect on women's lives.

Freudenberger's (1974) research on burnout syndrome among health care professionals can also be applied to the experiences of midwives in this study. Burnout reflects a dissonance between an individual's internal expectations of the job and the external demands placed on them. When role conflict occurs, symptoms of burnout can include feelings of helplessness and hopelessness, a progressive loss of purpose, and the development of negative attitudes towards the job and towards other people. Opportunities for peer support and debriefing can prevent the risk of burnout and increase staff effectiveness and confidence in working with abused women.

Implications for policy development and future research

The results of the study were widely disseminated and channelled into ongoing local and national advocacy, policy-making, and intervention strategies. Because of the personal, social and health related consequences of domestic violence, there is an ethical obligation on health services to ensure that the research findings are translated into good practice and improved quality of care provided to abused women. Within midwifery, there is an emphasis on investing in research and development to provide evidenced-based care. While the study was ongoing, there was evidence of raised awareness about domestic violence and a greater appreciation of its relevance to health care provision. Midwives and other maternity staff were more alert to the possible signs of abuse and were better equipped to respond to women experiencing domestic violence. This was reflected in the attitudes and behaviour of staff, as well as the number of domestic violence cases that were identified outside of the study. However, the impact of this study was short-lived and since its completion domestic violence training and screening has ceased. Even with the existence of a domestic violence protocol and referral information, without the necessary training, additional resources and organisational support, very few midwives will have the confidence to incorporate this into practice.

Sustainable domestic violence interventions require active monitoring and auditing, identified support systems to deal with the distress that accompanies disclosure, and the time and confidential space to screen safely to provide an effective response. Ideally health professionals should have direct involvement in the development and implementation of domestic violence initiatives to ensure that knowledge and expertise are maintained within the health setting rather than among external researchers who will eventually leave. Future interventions to help women experiencing domestic violence must also be informed by women's views and experiences of seeking help in health care settings.

Strategies for ensuring sustainability and encouraging ownership of domestic violence interventions include training health professionals to become trainers themselves. Ongoing training is necessary if it is to have any effect on the culture of a health setting and the attitudes of staff within it. Training also needs to be flexible in order to accommodate the working practices and procedures of different health settings. This may involve providing a number of short training sessions that staff can access more easily. Managers and supervisors can enable staff to access training, by re-organising resources or providing the necessary cover so that staff can be released from clinical duties. There also needs to be a greater degree of involvement of health professionals in multi-agency initiatives to improve the response to women experiencing domestic violence and their children.

The results of this study show that researching domestic violence in health settings requires a high investment of resources to ensure that issues of safety and confidentiality are given proper consideration. The safety and wellbeing of the investigators, in this case midwives, and the women should be paramount, and this may occasionally compromise the objectives and outcomes of the research.

Acknowledgement

The authors would like to thank all the women and midwives who participated in this study.

References

Amaro, H., Fried, L.E., Cabral, H. and Zuckerman, B. (1990) 'Violence during pregnancy and substance use', *American Journal of Public Health*, 80: 575–621.

American College of Obstetrics and Gynecologists (1995) ACOG Technical Bulletin 209. Domestic Violence. Washington DC: American College of Obstetrics and Gynecologists.

American Medical Association (19920 *Diagnostic and treatment guidelines on domestic violence. Archives of Family Medicine*, 1: 39–47.

Bacchus, L., Mezey, G. and Bewley, S. (2002) 'Women's perceptions and experiences of routine enquiry for domestic violence in a maternity service', *British Journal of Obstetrics and Gynaecology*, 109: 9–16.

Bewley, S., Friend, J. and Mezey, G. (eds) (1997) *Violence against women*, London: Royal College of Obstetricians and Gynaecologists.

Bradley, F., Smith, M., Long, J. and O'Dowd, T. (2002) 'Reported frequency of domestic violence: cross sectional survey of women attending general practice', *British Medical Journal*, 324: 271–4.

British Medical Association (1998) *Domestic violence: a health care issue?*, London: British Medical Association Science Department and the Board of Science and Education.

Broadhead, R.S. and Fox, K.J. (1990) 'Takin' it to the streets. AIDS outreach as ethnography', *Journal of Contemporary Ethnography*, 19: 322–48.

Brown, J.B., Lent, B. and Sas, G. (1993) 'Identifying and treating wife abuse', *The Journal of Family Practice*, 36: 185–91.

Bullock, L.F. and McFarlane, J. (1989) 'Birth-weight/battering connection', *American Journal of Nursing*, 89: 1153–5.

Campbell, J.C. (1999) 'If I can't have you no one can: murder linked to battering during pregnancy', *Reflections*, 25: 8–10, 12, 46.

Campbell, J.C., Pliska, M.J., Taylor, W. and Sheridan, D. (1994) 'Battered women's experiences in the emergency department', *Journal of Emergency Nursing*, 20: 280–8.

Campbell, J.C., Poland, M.L., Waller, J.B. and Ager, J. (1992) 'Correlates of battering during pregnancy', *Research in Nursing and Health*, 15: 219–26.

Chez, R.A. and Jones, R.F. (1995) 'The battered woman', *American Journal of Obstetrics and Gynecology*, 173: 677–9.

Covington, D.L., Diehl, S.J., Wright, B.D. and Piner, M.H. (1997) 'Assessing for violence during pregnancy using a systematic approach', *Maternal and Child Health Journal*, 1: 129–32.

Dannenberg, A.L., Carter, D.M., Lawson, H.W., Ashton, D.M., Dorfman, S.F. and Graham, E.H. (1995) 'Homicide and other injuries as causes of maternal death in New York City, 1987 through 1991', *American Journal of Obstetrics and Gynecology*, 172: 1557–644.

Department of Health (1998) *Why mothers die. Report on confidential enquiries into maternal deaths in the United Kingdom 1994–1996*, London: The Department of Health.

Department of Health (2000) *Domestic violence: A resource manual for health care professionals*, London: Department of Health.

Dominy, N. and Radford, L. (1996) *Domestic violence in Surrey: Developing an effective inter-agency response*, Surrey County Council/London: Roehampton Institute.

Dye, T.D., Tollivert, N.J., Lee, R.V. and Kenney, C.J. (1995) 'Violence, pregnancy and birth outcome in Appalachia', *Paediatric and Perinatal Epidemiology*, 9: 35–47.

English National Board for Nursing, Midwifery and Health Visiting (1999–2000) *Midwifery practice in England. The report of the audit of maternity services and practice visits undertaken by the midwifery officers of the board*, London: English National Board.

English National Board for Nursing, Midwifery and Health Visiting (2000–2001) *Midwifery practice in action. Report of the board's midwifery practice audit*, London: English National Board.

Fernandez, F.M. and Krueger, P.M. (1999) 'Domestic violence: effect on pregnancy outcome', *Journal of the American Osteopathic Association*, 99: 254–6.

Fox, K. (1991) 'The politics of prevention: ethnographers combat AIDS among drug users', in Burawoy, M., Gamson, J., Schiffman, J. *et al.* (eds) *Ethnography Unbound*, California: University of California Press, 227–49.

Freudenberger, H.J. (1974) 'Staff burn out', *Journal of Social Issues*, 20: 159–65.

Friedman, L.S., Sarnet, J.H., Roberts, M.S., Hudlin, M. and Hans, P. (1992) 'Inquiry about victimisation experiences', *Archives of International Medicine*, 152: 1186–90.

Garcia, J., Renfrew, M. and Marchant, S. (1994) 'Postnatal home visiting by midwives', *Midwifery*, 10: 40–3.

Gelles, R.J. (1975) 'Violence and pregnancy: a note on the extent of the problem and needed services', *Family Coordinator*, 24: 81–6.

Gerbert, B., Johnston, K., Caspers, N., Bleecker, T., Woods, A. and Rosenbaum, A. (1996) 'Experiences of battered women in health care settings: a qualitative study', *Women and Health*, 24: 1–17.

Gielen, A., O'Campo, P.J., Faden, R.R., Kass, N.E. and Xue, X. (1994) 'Interpersonal conflict and physical violence during the childbearing year', *Social Science and Medicine*, 39: 781–7.

Hakim, C. (1983) 'Research based on administrative records', *Sociological Review*, 31: 489–519.

Hamberger, L.K., Saunders, D.G. and Hovey, M. (1992) 'Prevalence of domestic violence in community practice and rate of physician inquiry', *Family Medicine*, 24: 283–7.

Harper, M. and Parsons, L. (1997) 'Maternal deaths due to homicide and other injuries in North Carolina: 1992–1994', *Obstetrics and Gynecology*, 90: 920–3.

Harwell, T.S., Casten, R.J., Armstrong, K.A., Dempsey, S., Coons, H.L. and Davis, M. (1998) 'Results of a domestic violence training program offered to staff of urban community health centers', *American Journal of Preventive Medicine*, 15: 235–42.

Hayden S.R., Barton, R.D. and Hayden, M. (1997) 'Domestic violence in the emergency department: how do women prefer to disclose and discuss their issues?', *Journal of Emergency Medicine*, 15: 447–51.

Hedin-Widding, L., Grimstad, H., Moller, A., Schei, B. and Janson, P.O. (1999) 'Prevalence of physical and sexual abuse before and during pregnancy among Swedish couples', *Acta Obstetrica et Gynecologica Scandinavica*, 78: 310–15.

Hedin-Widding, L. (2000) 'Postpartum, also a risk period for domestic violence', *European Journal of Obstetrics and Gynecology*, 89: 41–5.

Helton, A., McFarlane, J. and Anderson, E.T. (1987) 'Battered and pregnant: a prevalence study', *American Journal of Public Health*, 77: 1337–9.

Hillard, P.J. (1985) 'Physical abuse in pregnancy', *Obstetrics and Gynecology*, 66: 185–90.

Irion, O., Boulvain, M., Straccia, A.T. and Bonnet, J. (2000) 'Emotional, physical and sexual violence against women before or during pregnancy', *British Journal of Obstetrics and Gynaecology*, 107: 1306–8.

Janssen, P.A., Basso, M.C. and Costanzo, R.M. (1998) 'The prevalence of domestic violence among obstetric nurses', *Women's Health Issues*, 8: 317–23.

Johnson, H. and Sacco, V.F. (1995) 'Researching violence against women: Statistics Canada's national survey', *Canadian Journal of Criminology*, 37: 281–304.

Kernic, M.A., Wolf, M.E. and Holt, V.L. (2000) 'Rates and relative risk of hospital admission among women in violent intimate partner relationships', *American Journal of Public Health*. 90: 1416–20.

Komaromy, M., Bindman, A.B., Haber, R.J. and Sande, M.A. (1993) 'Sexual harassment in medical training', *New England Journal of Medicine*, 328: 322–6.

Macintyre, S. (1978) 'Some notes on record taking and making in an antenatal clinic', *Sociological Review*, 26: 595–611.

McFarlane, J., Christoffel, K., Bateman, L., Miller, V. and Bullock, L. (1991) 'Assessing for abuse: self-report versus nurse interview', *Public Health Nurse*, 8: 245–50.

McFarlane, J., Parker, B. and Soeken, K. (1996) 'Physical abuse, smoking and substance use during pregnancy: prevalence, interrelationships and effects on birth weight', *Journal of Obstetric, Gynecologic and Neonatal Nursing*, 25: 313–20.

McLeer, S.V. (1989) 'Education is not enough: a systems failure in protecting battered women', *Annals of Emergency Medicine*, 18: 651–3.

McLeer, S.V. and Anwar, R. (1989) 'A study of battered women presenting in an emergency department', *American Journal of Public Health*, 79: 65–6.

McWilliams, M. and McKiernan, J. (1993) *Bringing it out in the open. Domestic violence in Northern Ireland*, Belfast: HMSO.

Maryland Department of Health (2001) 'Pregnancy associated homicide', *Journal of the American Medical Association*, 285: 1455–9.

Mirlees-Black, C. (1999) *Domestic violence: findings from a new British Crime Survey self-completion questionnaire*, Research Study 191, London: Home Office.

Mooney, J. (1993) *The hidden figure: domestic violence in North London*, London: Islington Council.

Morey, M.A., Begletter, M.L. and Harris, D.J. (1981) 'Profile of a battered fetus', *The Lancet*, 2: 1294–5.

Newberger, E.H., Barkan, S.E., Lieberman, W.S., McCormick, M.C., Yllo, K., Gary, L.T. and Schechter, S. (1992) 'Abuse of pregnant women and adverse birth outcome. Current knowledge and implications for practice', *Journal of the American Medical Association*, 7: 2370–2.

Norton, L.B., Peipert, J.F., Zierler, S., Lima, B. and Hume, L. (1995) 'Battering in pregnancy: an assessment of two screening methods', *Obstetrics and Gynecology*, 85: 321–5.

Pahl, J. (1995) 'Health professionals and violence against women', in Kingston, P. and Penhale, B. (eds) *Family violence and the caring professions*, London: Macmillan Press, 127–48.

Pak, L.L., Reece, E.A. and Chan, L. (1998) 'Is adverse pregnancy outcome predictable after blunt abdominal trauma?', *American Journal of Obstetrics and Gynecology*, 179: 1140–4.

Parker, B., McFarlane, J. and Soeken, K. (1994) 'Abuse during pregnancy: effects on maternal complications and birth weight in adult and teenage women', *Obstetrics and Gynecology*, 84: 323–8.

Parsons, L.H., Zaccaro, D., Wells, B. and Stovall, T.G. (1995) 'Methods of and attitudes toward screening obstetrics and gynecology patients for domestic abuse', *American Journal of Obstetrics and Gynecology*, 173: 381–7.

Plichta, S.B., Duncan, M.M. and Plichta, L. (1996) 'Spouse abuse, patient–physician communication, and patient satisfaction', *American Journal of Preventive Medicine*, 12: 297–303.

Purwar, M.B., Jeyaseelan, L., Varhadpande, U., Motghare, V. and Pimplakute, S. (1999) 'Survey of physical abuse during pregnancy GMCH, Nagpur, India', *Journal of Obstetrics and Gynecology Research*, 25: 165–71.

Ribe, J.K., Teggatz, J.R. and Harvey, C.M. (1993) 'Blows to the maternal abdomen causing fetal demise: report of three cases and a review of the literature', *Journal of Forensic Science*, 38: 1092–6.

Richardson, J., Coid, J., Petruckevitch, A., Chung, W.S., Moorey, S. and Feder, G. (2002) 'Identifying domestic violence: cross sectional study in primary care', *British Medical Journal*, 324: 274–7.

Roth, J. (1966) 'Hired hand research', *The American Sociologist*, 1: 190–6.

Royal College of Midwives (1997) *Domestic abuse in pregnancy: a position paper*, London: Royal College of Midwives.

Singh, D. and Newburn, M. (2000) *Women's experiences of postnatal care*, London: National Childbirth Trust Maternity Sales.

Stark, E. and Flitcraft, A. (1995) 'Killing the beast within: woman battering and female suicidality', *International Journal of Health Services*, 25: 43–64.

Stewart, D.E. and Cecutti, A. (1993) 'Physical abuse in pregnancy', *Canadian Medical Association Journal*, 149: 1257–63.

Sugg, N.K. and Inui, T. (1992) 'Primary care physicians' responses to domestic violence. Opening Pandora's box', *Journal of the American Medical Association*, 267: 3157–60.

Webster, J., Sweett, S. and Stolz, T. (1994) 'Domestic violence in pregnancy. A prevalence study', *The Medical Journal of Australia*, 161: 466–70.

Williamson, E. (2000) *Domestic violence and health: the response of the medical profession*, Bristol: The Policy Press.

12 Racist violence from a probation service perspective

Now you see it, now you don't

Larry Ray, David Smith and Liz Wastell

In this chapter we describe and analyse our experience of gaining research access to offenders who had committed acts of racist violence. We relied on the help and co-operation of staff at all levels in what was then the Greater Manchester Probation Service,[1] and we are conscious that in what follows we may seem to be ungrateful and ungraciously critical of the organisation without which we would have had no research data at all. So we should be clear at the outset that we do not mean to imply that the difficulties we encountered in finding interviewees for the research were attributable to deficiencies in practice that were peculiar to the Greater Manchester Probation Service; rather, we wish to emphasise the inherent problems in identifying perpetrators of racist violence and finding effective ways of working with them. We believe that the difficulties recounted in this chapter would have arisen anywhere, and we are convinced that the Greater Manchester service's commitment to taking racist violence seriously was entirely genuine.

The chapter's subtitle is meant to indicate a paradox. The probation service in Greater Manchester, as elsewhere, had developed a strong culture of anti-racist and anti-discriminatory values and practices, including a commitment to challenging offenders who expressed racist attitudes and opinions. But in practice there was no reliable means of identifying racist offenders and no consistent policy on working with them. Like other probation services, Greater Manchester conveyed a clear public message that racist language and behaviour were unacceptable. Sibbitt (1997) suggests that one consequence of this message is to inhibit offenders from talking about their racism. According to Sibbitt (1997, pp. 93–4), probation officers to some extent welcomed this, since they assumed that racist attitudes were common among offenders (as they were in the communities from which they came), and they would not have known what to do if they were expressed 'other than to invoke local disciplinary procedures for failing to respect the Service's equal opportunities policy'. Thus the 'racism of ordinary offenders remained unchallenged', while some officers 'almost demonised racist offenders as extremely violent political extremists', who aroused a fear 'out of all proportion to their likelihood of ever turning up on the Probation Service's doorstep'. Neither of the probation services approached by Sibbitt produced a single racist offender whom she could interview.

Sibbitt (1997, p. 66) compares probation officers' responses to racism with their response to illegal drug use: they discouraged the expression of racist views while encouraging offenders to talk about their drug use, which offenders were reluctant to do, precisely because it was illegal. The paradox therefore is one which is arguably inherent in probation practice: in order to work relevantly and effectively with offenders, probation officers need them to talk about the very topic which they are most likely to wish to avoid – their offending. Sibbitt suggests that in the case of illegal drug use the paradox can be resolved by the explicit adoption of a harm reduction policy (see also Sibbitt, 1996) that recognises that abstinence from drugs is not always feasible, and therefore creates a space in which offenders can talk safely and openly about their use of drugs, without the fear that this may lead to action for breach of their orders. We think that an analogous approach could be used to make sense of working with racist offenders, and indeed that such an approach was used by some probation officers in Greater Manchester at the time of the research. That is, offenders were encouraged to articulate racist ideas and to give accounts of racist behaviour when this was relevant to the programme of work agreed between the supervising officer and the offender. But this was by no means true of all work with racist offenders, and one of the reasons for this variability is that it is far from straightforward to identify who should count as coming into this category. As we suggest in our chapter in the companion volume to this, it is rarely possible to define acts of violence as straightforwardly and unambiguously racist; false negatives are probably more common than false positives, but both occur. The problem of identifying the relevant offenders was also noted by Sibbitt (1997, p. 93), who expressed surprise that one probation service should have been 'drafting a policy on how to respond to racially motivated offenders' without having first addressed the 'fundamental question of how probation officers could identify racial motivation during PSR [pre-sentence report] interviews or supervision'.

Negotiating access

To start our account of the research process with a section on negotiating access risks being misleading, because it may imply that this negotiation is a once and for all activity that is concluded in a rational and definitive manner before the research begins. As anyone who has conducted research that entails gaining access to subjects through an organisational structure will appreciate, however, access in practice has constantly to be renegotiated and re-managed (Pearson *et al.*, 1992). It is a continuous part of the research process, and in itself can be the source of important findings about organisational cultures and practices.

We chose to seek access to the perpetrators of racist violence via the probation service primarily because it was inherent in our thinking about the research that we wanted to obtain data on adult perpetrators of relatively serious acts of violence. The probation service was the obvious organisation to approach for this purpose, because its tasks are such as to bring it into contact, even if only transiently, with all offenders who (a) are convicted of offences serious or problematic enough for the court to request a pre-sentence report; (b) are made subject to a community penalty (at the time of the research this could be a probation order, a community service order, or a combination order); or (c) receive a custodial sentence that entails supervision on licence after release (covering all sentences on offenders under the age of 21, and all sentences of more than 12 months on adults). We hoped thus to be able to identify the majority of convicted racist offenders in Greater Manchester during the period of the research; those whom we would not be able to identify would have been sentenced without pre-sentence reports (and thus generally for less serious offences) or be adults who received custodial sentences of 12 months or less before the research began.

The Greater Manchester service was approached as a site for the research because it seemed likely to be able to produce a sufficient number of offenders for the purposes of the research, and because the research team had existing good relations with staff at all levels in the service. The proposal was developed in consultation with senior probation staff, and we were assured of the support of the Association of Chief Officers of Probation and the local branch of the National Association of Probation Officers (NAPO, the probation officers' professional association and trade union). The discussions we had before the research began suggested that a figure of 100 was a realistic target for research interviews. They also led to our decision, again made with the full agreement of senior probation staff, to appoint a Greater Manchester probation officer as research officer; the person appointed would work on the research as a 'career break', with guaranteed re-employment at the end of the project. There were two main reasons for this decision. First, a probation officer would have skills in interviewing and would be experienced in dealing with disturbing and distasteful material of the kind that was likely to be revealed in the interviews; we considered, and still believe, that the interviewing skills of a good probation officer were as relevant as those of an experienced social researcher, supposing that we could have found one. Second, because we expected that problems of access and the issue of the researcher's credibility would arise at some stage, we thought that there were advantages in appointing someone with knowledge both of the local area and of organisational culture and practices. Despite the difficulties that arose in gaining access to research subjects, we believe that someone without this local knowledge and credibility would have encountered much greater problems.

In retrospect we were naïve to think that it would be relatively easy to identify the perpetrators of racist violence. To some extent we may have shared the 'demonised' image of these offenders that Sibbitt (1997) found among probation officers – of politically motivated practitioners of ruthless violence who might well be specialists in this type of offence. Sibbitt's work should have warned us not only that this was an over-simplified and indeed unreal caricature (as should the work of Webster (1997)) but that even clear-cut instances of racist violence might not be readily identifiable through the probation service. Instead of the 100 interviews we envisaged we conducted 36; and we obtained basic information on another 28 people whose offences were judged to have a racist element. Another ten were identified as potentially relevant subjects, but for various reasons it was not practical to obtain details of them. We concluded that the number of relevant offenders known to the probation service in the research period was in fact lower than we had thought; indeed, a subsequent trawl within the Greater Manchester service suggested that our total of 74 (including those on whom we had no details beyond the fact of an offence) was probably not far from the actual figure during the research period.[2] In the next section we discuss some organisational factors that increased the difficulty for probation officers, and therefore for us, of identifying racist motivation; and in the section following that we discuss aspects of professional practice that had the same effect.

Organisational factors

The ethnicity of victims of offences was not recorded as a matter of routine, unless the case was signalled as racially aggravated. Thus an offence could be recorded simply as an assault, but there might be features of the case that aroused the researcher's interest: for example, that the assault was on a taxi-driver or a shopkeeper, since many of the providers of these services were South Asians. In some such cases, the researcher was able to encourage the supervising probation officer to consider the case in more detail, and thus to identify relevant cases that had been hidden in the system. This was not always straightforward for the supervisor, however, since he or she often had only the barest details of the circumstances of the offence. A relevant factor here was that in Greater Manchester, as in most probation services, the function of report-writing was separated from that of supervision: report writers were normally members of court teams, supervisors of specialist community supervision teams. Whatever the advantages of such specialisation, in terms of skill development and administrative convenience, the separation of functions arguably militates against successful negotiation between offenders and probation staff at the report-writing stage about the content of work in cases where a probation or combination order is being considered (Bottoms and McWilliams, 1979; Raynor and Vanstone, 1994). It can also mean that, however 'offence-focused' the report-writer has tried to be (Smith, 1996), and however good the information available to the report-writer, the focus becomes diffuse and the precise circumstances of the offence become less clear in the passage of the case from one officer (and one team) to another. This may be particularly important in the case of the majority of offenders given probation orders or combination orders, where typically the first 13 weeks of the order were taken up with a groupwork programme thought to be suitable for all 'new' probation cases, and employing the cognitive-behavioural style of offending-centred work authoritatively recommended as good practice (Chapman and Hough, 1998). Supervision in such cases is not individualised until after the initial programme has been completed, so probation officers may feel that there is little need to refer to individual files. Furthermore, the quality of information available even at the report-writing stage is not guaranteed: the probation officer is in the hands of the Crown Prosecution Service for information about the offence from any source other than the offender.

Like most public sector agencies, the probation service in Greater Manchester was undergoing internal reorganisation and coping with external pressure for change at the time of the research. The impact of this on staff morale and professional self-valuation was felt at times by the researcher, who was necessarily asking questions that could only be answered on the basis of close knowledge of individual cases. Probation officers who feel over-burdened and under-valued are less likely to be motivated to probe deeply into offenders' motives and attitudes. And, while some defensiveness about research scrutiny is inevitable, and the probation service is rightly concerned with the confidentiality of the often sensitive information it holds, there were times when the researcher felt that unnecessary difficulties were placed in her way. For example, although everyone knew that she was a probation officer and that the research represented a break in that career, she was required to wait while an application to the Data Protection Registrar[3] was processed before she could access computerised data sources in the service.

Professional factors

One relevant professional factor, that could also be interpreted as an organisational issue, was that identified by Sibbitt (1997) – the culture of equal opportunities and a commitment to anti-racist practice. Notices reading 'Zero tolerance: racist language is unacceptable' were prominent in probation offices, and could obviously have an inhibiting effect on both offenders and probation staff. This clear 'moral opprobrium' (Sibbitt, 1997) is likely both to have facilitated denial by offenders of the racist element in their offences and to have encouraged probation officers to accept or collude with that denial (especially when the pressures of other work acted as a deterrent to close scrutiny of motives). For some (not all) probation officers, racist motivation was a can of worms best left unopened, because of the difficulties it would pose for supervision. In nine instances, probation officers overtly blocked access to relevant subjects on the grounds that the research interview would upset the offender's relationship with the supervisor or jeopardise the progress that had been made on supervision in respect of other problems. These can be taken as examples of the preciousness or protectiveness towards offenders under supervision which was detected by Sibbitt (1997); it is also possible that some officers were anxious that if racist motivation emerged in the research interview their own neglect of it would be interpreted as lack of skill or professional confidence. It is also, of course, reasonable for probation officers to conclude that there is no point in working on racist attitudes if there is no apparent prospect of changing them.

Probation officers have themselves written useful accounts of the issues specific to working with racist offenders, which we will review briefly. In two early contributions, Gill and Marshall (1993) and Fidgett (1993) note the difficulty of identifying racist motivation and the lack of relevant resources and experience in the probation service. Gill and Marshall distinguish between overt and covert racism, viewing the latter as universal in white on black offending. Evidently with the kind of incident in mind that featured prominently in our research, they note the frequency with which whites make off without payment from black-owned restaurants, take-aways and taxis. They also remark on organisational and professional responses which deny or minimise the problem. Gill and Marshall (1993, pp. 58–9) produced a set of questionnaires and exercises for probation officers working with racist offenders, which had a public airing, but we have found no evidence of their use. The three stages of their approach covered race awareness, challenging myths, and empowerment ('to attempt to make sure that the client…is not left with a set of negative feelings').

At the time of Sibbitt's (1997) research, racist violence was clearly a live issue in the probation service. Reflecting on developments from the mid-1990s, Edwards (1999, p. 38) asks: 'Can we refuse to work with active committed racists on health and safety grounds whilst we continue to see those clients with convictions for murder, sexual assault and other forms of violence?' The reference is to a policy adopted in 1995 by the National Association of Probation Officers (NAPO, 1995) that – confusingly, according to Edwards – called for probation staff to challenge racist attitudes while refusing to work with members of racist organisations. This policy was in the process of being drafted at the time of Sibbitt's (1997) research, and reflects the demonisation and fear of violent racists which she found among some officers: members of racist organisations are seen as posing a risk to staff health and safety apparently not posed, as Edwards notes, by murderers not known to be racist. NAPO had later committed itself to support for 'dedicated and evaluated programmes' in all areas for racially motivated offenders (Edwards, 1999, p. 39).

Dixon and Okitikpi (1999) wrote in support of Edwards' arguments, and noted (p. 157) that 'there currently exists a clear public mandate to engage in work with racially motivated offenders', making NAPO's policy of 1995 untenable. Noting (p. 158) the 'anxiety and apprehension' that probation officers often feel in considering this area of work, they review the educational and training resources available to probation staff for work with such offenders, and particularly *From Murmur to Murder* (Gast and Kay, 1998). Later in the same year, Ledger (1999), who was at the time Vice-Chair of NAPO, wrote to the *Probation Journal* to explain that the previous contributors had misunderstood NAPO policy, and that the 1995 statement was specifically intended to address the issue of the safety of black and white staff threatened by 'politically motivated' racist offenders. Its primary purpose was to encourage 'challenging and confrontative work with racist offenders' while providing safety for staff at risk (Ledger, 1999, p. 288).

We discuss the risks and limitations of challenge and confrontation elsewhere, in the companion to this collection and in Ray et al. (2002), where we express anxiety that after being 'chastised' (Dixon and Okitikpi, 1999) offenders may indeed be left with a set of negative feelings. A practice account that is clearly sensitive to this issue, while also written from a perspective sympathetic to NAPO's concerns, is that by McDonald (2000). The worker's safety is a prominent theme in McDonald's account of intensive (24 sessions of two hours) individual work with a prisoner who had pleaded guilty to racist murders and sought help from the probation service in prison eight years into his life sentence. *From Murmur to Murder* was a key resource, after McDonald rescued it from the office where it had been 'gathering dust' for six months (p. 207). It was supplemented by other material, including a dramatic representation of racism in the context of an industrial dispute and academic and documentary sources, but McDonald also stresses (p. 209) that a 'strong professional relationship' was crucial in sustaining the work. Anxieties about safety, uncertainty about professional competence, and a recognition of how easy it is for racist motivation to disappear as a result of how crimes are defined and processed in their passage through the criminal justice system, and of professional ambivalence, are common themes in these practitioner accounts.

McDonald's differs from the rest, however, in that in this case the offender took the initiative in seeking help, and, as a prisoner, his whereabouts were not hard to determine. This was not the case with several offenders identified as potential subjects for our research. In 13 instances the reason for failure to gain interviews with ostensibly suitable subjects was that offenders who were supposed to be in contact with the probation service were not so in fact, making this a more common cause of failure than probation officers' inaction or resistance. The issue of enforcement of orders and post-custodial licences is a sensitive one for the probation service (Smith, 2000), although in practice the enforcement power lies with other agencies (at the time of the research, with the police). Probation officers can obtain warrants for offenders to be arrested for breach of requirements of orders or licences, but have no means of ensuring that these warrants are executed. Thus at times it seemed to the researcher that, apart from those who were interviewed in custody, the only offenders under probation supervision whom she could contact were either near the beginning of their orders or licences or had recently appeared in court for breaching them, thus being reminded of the importance of compliance. It is, of course, possible that racist offenders are more likely than others to refuse to comply with the requirements of orders, since they may resent the imputation of racism in the first place, or they may become more defiant in the face of manifest disapproval by probation staff. But our data on the perpetrators of racist violence do suggest that as a group they are not markedly different from the overall population of those on probation, and in any case their racist motivation was often not on their supervisors' agenda. A tentative and unexpected finding from our efforts to gain access to interview subjects is, then, that the extent of non-compliance with orders and licences may be greater than official figures suggest.[4]

Refusal to be interviewed

There were only six cases in which potential interview subjects refused to be interviewed. In three of these the refusal was conveyed by the supervising probation officer, and in one the subject (in prison) refused to see the researcher when she arrived for an arranged interview. In two cases offenders declined to be interviewed after meeting the researcher, on the grounds that they wanted 'to put it behind me' and to 'forget it all'. This kind of response was rare: generally, once offenders had met the researcher, they appeared happy to be interviewed, and several used the interview as an opportunity to explain how they had been unjustly treated or misunderstood by the criminal justice system. But those who did refuse to be interviewed should remind us of ethical questions which seem to be little mentioned in criminological research. Not only, and obviously, should potential research subjects be in a position to give fully informed consent; researchers also need to be aware of how an interview about a past offence can revive painful emotions and produce unhappiness. Both criminal justice practitioners and academics are more overtly sensitive to these issues in relation to victims (see, for example, Crawford and Goodey, 2000) than they are when the research subjects are offenders; but offenders too may be damaged by reminders of pain.

The complexity of criminal justice

The final point we want to make about the difficulties of obtaining research subjects relates to the sheer complexity and messiness of the criminal justice process. This is mentioned in some of the practitioner accounts discussed above, and efforts to render the system (if it is a system) more efficient, manageable and controllable have preoccupied policy-makers and academic commentators (e.g. Raine and Willson, 1993). Complexity is inherent in a system that brings together a variety of organisations and interests and, by design, provides for checks and balances so that no one set of interests comes to dominate it; additional complications arise when, for instance, witnesses (or defendants) cannot be contacted or fail to attend when required, prosecution or defence lawyers are unable to proceed, information from the police has failed to reach the Crown Prosecution Service (and so on). In 16 instances contact with potential research subjects was judged to be impractical as a result of such complications. Cases might be dropped because of lack of evidence, at any stage from just after charging to the final court hearing. Offences originally prosecuted as racially aggravated might lead to guilty pleas at the last minute provided that the element of racial aggravation was dropped, thus avoiding costly trials (this was demoralising not only for the researcher but more importantly for those involved in bringing the case forward, and presumably for some of the victims and members of their communities). Delays are normal in the criminal justice process, and have been the subject of continued efforts to increase efficiency on the part of the Lord Chancellor's Department, the government department responsible for the management of courts. O'Brien and Peacock (2001), in the latest of a series of regular reports, found that the average interval between the commission of an offence and the completion of the case in a magistrates' court was 137 days. This refers only to cases which are not committed for trial or sentence to the Crown Court, which lengthens the process considerably; even in magistrates' courts, the average time from the first listing of a case to its completion was 56 days. The average figures, of course, conceal huge variations, and cases where the defendant intends to plead not guilty routinely take many months to be completed. It is not surprising, then, that some interview subjects were 'lost' when cases were withdrawn for lack of evidence after several months, or led to acquittals when they went to trial without all the evidence on which the prosecution intended to rely. A final reason why some potential interviewees were not pursued is that they were no longer accessible from Greater Manchester, having either disappeared or been imprisoned in another part of the country. The criminal justice process is full of such unpredictabilities.

Negotiating the act

These experiences, along with the frequently deployed neutralisation strategies of our subjects (see e.g. Ray and Smith, 2001) raised further methodological issues. In some ways the very status of our object, 'racist violence', became elusive and problematic, but in ways that revealed much about the way the problem is often constructed. Back *et al.* (1999) argue in relation to football racism that the formulation of the sporting person, 'racist hooligan', is an effect of a certain kind of knowledge-practice. It is the product of governmentality in which football supporters are subjected to strategies for maintaining order and establishing codes of behaviour. Similarly, the category of the 'racist violent offender' makes it possible to establish a moral pariah and contrast his behaviour with the ideal subject of anti-racist discourses. However, these categories are often resisted and re-negotiated by those to whom they are applied and the researcher is inevitably caught up in these processes of negotiation. This in turn has a number of consequences.

One consequence of this is that rather than take for granted the categories provided by institutional and public discourses as 'researchable' topics, we need to understand how these objects of knowledge have been produced and constituted by institutional forms of governance. Not only that, but they are unstable and contested categories that become the site of competing claims and projects. Neither the offenders nor the probation service would necessarily acknowledge the object – 'racist violence' or 'racist offender' – since this framing of the behaviour in question was subject to personal and institutional re-negotiation. The institutional processes of negotiation have been outlined above. We have described elsewhere the ways in which offenders often denied or neutralised the racist intent of their actions (Ray and Smith, 2001). This posed a methodological issue in that these ways of talking about violence and racism often became themselves topics of the research and objects of further interpretative practices rather than the putative acts themselves. We found, as have others (Back *et al.* 1998; and Bowling and Phillips, 2002), that racism is not a fixed but a mutable and changing phenomenon in which available stereotypes and markers of cultural difference are deployed and utilised in a multiplicity of institutional and public contexts. It was these forms of deployment and the multiple forms of contestation that accompanied them that often became the object of our study rather than the putative object of the racist offender.

A further consequence of these processes was that the researcher became involved in the interpersonal politics of denial and moral blame. The very constitution of a violent act involves attributions of blameworthiness in that violence is regarded as the illegitimate and intentional use (or threat) of force. Central to the evaluation of an act as 'violent' are judgements as to whether the harm was caused intentionally, recklessly or accidentally (Jones, 2000, p. 4). Accounts of violence among violent offenders become embroiled in attempts to avoid attributions of blame. The researcher can be drawn into attempts at collusion with these denials of both violent and racist intent. On the issue of possible complicity with racism or violence it was important to establish and maintain the trust of the interviewees in order to elicit attitudes or information that were sensitive and likely to evoke public condemnation. But the interviewer had to avoid her non-judgemental stance being interpreted as approval so firmly but politely resisted by indicating disagreement if asked directly for agreement or approval. However, the process of interviewing is itself a social encounter marked by plays of moral attribution, techniques of disengagement and avoidance of blame and displays of self-justification.

Conclusions: for criminal justice agencies and for research

As Sibbitt (1997) remarked, there is little point in the probation service having a policy for working with racist offenders without having some means of identifying them first. But this is not an issue for the probation service alone. The probation service receives offenders who have already been subject to processes of definition and classification – first by the police, then by the Crown Prosecution Service. The probation service can only become involved when people have been convicted (assuming that the illogicality of preparing pre-sentence reports on defendants who are pleading not guilty is accepted). Even now, when the Crown Prosecution Service can decide to charge people with a wide range of offences that are specified as being aggravated by racial motivation, there is, as we have seen, no certainty that even if defendants are convicted it will be for racially aggravated offences. The erosion of the evidential base of prosecution cases, doubts as to the likelihood of conviction, and changes of plea, sometimes at the last minute, on the basis of informal negotiation between prosecution and defence, all create the possibility that racist offenders will be convicted for offences that disguise racist motives. None of this is surprising, given the inherent difficulty of establishing motivation. The classic conception of 'hate crime' (Ray and Smith, 2001) entails that the victim is selected by the offender because of his or her perceived membership of a particular social group, but, as we show in the companion volume to this collection, very few, if any, of the offences of which we learned in interviews conformed in a clear-cut way to the 'hate crime' image of racist violence.[5] Typically, there was some pre-existing relationship – and not always one of overt hostility – between the offender and the victim, and even when there was not, the violent incident tended to be triggered by a dispute about something other than racist hatred – payment of a bus or taxi fare, for instance.

The probation service cannot, then, rely solely on conviction for a racially aggravated offence in determining racist motivation among the offenders with whom it has contact. Conviction for a racially aggravated offence, of course, should signal that racism is a relevant issue on which to engage offenders, from the first assessment in the course of preparing a pre-sentence report to the planning and implementation, where relevant, of a probation order. But probation officers will continue to miss racist elements in motivation and the opportunity to work on these if they do not make their own assessment of the circumstances and contexts of offences. In order to do this more effectively, we suggest, first, that they need the support of better information. A probation service-based system that routinely recorded the ethnicity of victims (which would itself depend on the availability of this information in Crown Prosecution Service papers) would be a start, since ethnicity could be overlooked even at the stage of the pre-sentence report, and is, we have suggested, quite likely to have become invisible by the time the case is transferred to another team for supervision. The risk of this would be reduced if the PSR writer and the supervising officer were the same person, as is rarely the case at present, and if the supervision of community sentences and licences were individualised from the outset; the practice of requiring everyone to attend the same programme at the start of their supervision increases the likelihood that the offence itself will become lost, in the sense of being unavailable as a focus for work. Probation staff could also be helped by being made aware of the areas that tend to produce the highest incidence of racist violence, and of the circumstances in which such violence is most likely to erupt. The distribution of racist offenders is not random, and the contexts in which racism's potential for violence is most likely to be expressed are also, to an extent, predictable.

We can, then, imagine organisational changes and improvements in the flow of information that would increase the proportion of acts of racist violence that become available for the attention of probation officers. But the officers will then need to feel competent to tackle offenders' racism in ways that might make a productive difference. In Greater Manchester we found examples of what we regarded as constructive engagement with the issue as well as instances of anxiety and avoidance, and perhaps of the fear and concern with safety that have been dominant issues in much of the practitioner literature on racist offenders. One important message to the probation service from our research is that perpetrators of racist violence are no more (or less) to be feared than the perpetrators of other violence; their similarities with the rest of the population on probation are far more striking than their differences from it. *From Murmur to Murder* (Gast and Kay, 1998) provided for the first time a national resource intended less as a prescriptive model for practice with racist offenders than as a means of enabling probation staff to feel more confident about the possibility of helpful intervention. As well as summarising theories and research on racist violence, it offers specimen programmes and strategies for working with racially motivated offenders that draw on the same kind of thinking that has provided the model for much contemporary probation practice (Chapman and Hough, 1998). The methods of work it proposes are thus ones which will be familiar to probation officers from other contexts, while the content is racism-specific. This approach could be helpful in reducing unnecessary anxieties consequent on the 'demonisation' of violent racists, since it suggests that what may work with other types of offender may also work with them. The same can be said of the programme for racially motivated offenders produced by the probation service in Merseyside in 2001, *Against Human Dignity* (Hamilton *et al.*, undated). The programme proposed consists of 15 sessions covering all stages of the process of change from initial assessment to 'relapse prevention', a term drawn from work on the treatment of addictions within a harm reduction framework (Prochaska and DiClemente, 1984; Sibbitt, 1996) and again likely to be reassuringly familiar to probation staff. If the programme were delivered as its designers appear to have intended, it is our strong impression that racist offenders would not be treated as a specially dangerous and menacing group, but much as other offenders are treated, and with an emphasis on respecting them as persons while conveying the unacceptability of their actions.

Thus far we have been exploring the reasons for the paradox we noted at the outset: that an organisation with a strong commitment at all levels to anti-racism should have been unable to identify racist offenders with any consistency or predictability, or to devise consistent means of working with them. We have proposed some ideas on how probation practice in this field might be improved, noting that some of the suggested changes require the support of other agencies. We want finally, and unoriginally, to indicate how research on racist violence might be taken forward. First, it is important to remember that our research took place in one area, Greater Manchester. As we have seen, there are indications that probation policy and practice in other areas are unlikely to be very different from what we found, but we are much less confident about claiming that the pattern of racist violence – and therefore the nature of the problem that confronts criminal justice agencies – is the same in other parts of the country. While it seems likely that similar findings would emerge from other urban areas in the north of England, with similar economic histories and demographics, it may well be that in areas of the midlands and in London and the south east the nature of racist violence is quite different (and the same may be true, for example, of Liverpool whose demographic make-up is unlike that of the Lancashire towns with substantial non-white populations, or those in Greater Manchester or West Yorkshire). Research could usefully investigate how far patterns of racist violence differ across areas and how differences are associated with patterns of socio-economic development, restructuring of local economies and housing, and the nature of racialised discourses (for example, in comparing small towns and rural areas with larger conurbations). There are also specific regional issues that deserve to be researched, such as harassment and violence against asylum-seekers in the south east of England. International comparisons could also be made, in terms both of the volume and nature of racist violence (how far it is politicised, for example) and of the response of state and other agencies. We hope that our experience of research in Greater Manchester will be useful in informing subsequent work, if only by warning future researchers of what they ought to avoid.

Secondly, and on a very different theme, our finding that perpetrators of racist violence are rarely specialists in this type of offence ought to be tested. This could be done by examining the criminal careers of people convicted of racially aggravated offences, using the Offenders Index. This would have been impossible before the Crime and Disorder Act distinguished these offences from others, but the opportunity now exists for research to test our assumption that most people convicted of racially aggravated offences will also have been convicted, or will acquire convictions, for a range of offences not bearing the racially aggravated label. Geographical variations in criminal careers (the degree to which racist offenders are specialists or generalists) would be an important focus of such a project.

Notes

1 From April 2001 it became known as The National Probation Service – Greater Manchester.
2 The provisions in the 1998 Crime and Disorder Act covering racially aggravated offences were implemented in October 1998. In 1999, according to Home Office (2000, p. 52) figures, 261 people were recorded by the police in Greater Manchester as suspected of having committed racially aggravated offences. Of these 75 were convicted, 43 were committed to the Crown Court for trial, and four were committed for sentence. Assuming a 50 per cent acquittal rate in Crown Court trials (in line with the national figure (Home Office, 2000)), the total number of convicted offenders who were charged in 1999 was about 100. For the reasons given above, the probation service will have had no contact with some of these offenders.
3 This is the official responsible for ensuring that the confidentiality requirements of the Data Protection Act, which covers computerised data on individuals, are maintained.
4 The Home Office (2001, pp. 30–1) figures show that 6 per cent of probation orders and 13 per cent of community service orders were terminated early for failure to comply with requirements. The figures for combination orders are 10 per cent for the probation element of the order and 15 per cent for the community service element. Action is supposed to be taken after a second unacceptable failure to comply with an order's requirements.
5 The publication of the Macpherson Report (Macpherson, 1999) on the murder in 1993 of the black teenager Stephen Lawrence contributed to the enormously increased public and political salience of racist violence which took place during the period of our research. It presented the murder as a classic case of 'hate crime' – which no doubt it was – and thus promoted an image of racist violence in the media that was very different from what we found in Greater Manchester.

References

Back, L., Crabbe, T. and Solomos, J. (1998) *Reading Race and Racism*. London: Routledge.

Back, L., Crabbe, T. and Solomos, J. (1999) 'Beyond the racist/hooligan couplet: race, social theory and football culture', *British Journal of Sociology*, 50, 3, 419–42.

Bottoms, A.E. and McWilliams, W. (1979) 'A non-treatment paradigm for probation practice', *British Journal of Social Work*, 9, 2, 159–202.

Bowling, B. and Phillips, C. (2002) *Race, Crime and Justice*. Harlow, Longman.

Chapman, T. and Hough, M. (1998) *Evidence-based Practice*. London, HM Inspectorate of Probation.

Crawford, A. and Goodey, J. (eds) (2000) *Integrating a Victim Perspective within Criminal Justice: International Perspectives*. Aldershot, Ashgate.

Dixon, L. and Okitikpi, T. (1999) 'Working with racially motivated offenders: practice issues', *Probation Journal*, 46, 3, 157–63.

Edwards, R. (1999) 'Working with racially motivated offenders', *Probation Journal*, 46, 1, 37–9.

Fidgett, P. (1993) 'Responding to racial violence', *Probation Journal*, 40, 2, 88–90.

Gast, L. and Kay, J. (1998) *From Murmur to Murder: Working with Racist Offenders*. Birmingham, West Midlands Training Consortium.

Gill, A. and Marshall, T. (1993) 'Working with racist offenders: an anti-racist response', *Probation Journal*, 40, 2, 54–9.

Hamilton, E., Lyness, F. and Stelman, A. (undated, 2001) *Against Human Dignity: A Programme for Racially Motivated Offenders*. Liverpool, National Probation Service, Merseyside.

Home Office (2000) *Statistics on Race and the Criminal Justice System: A Publication under Section 95 of the Criminal Justice Act 1991*. London, Home Office.

Home Office (2001) *Probation Statistics England and Wales 1999*. London, Home Office.

Jones, S. (2000) *Understanding Violent Crime*. Buckingham, Open University Press.

Ledger, J. (1999) 'Misunderstanding of racially motivated offenders policy' (letter, *Probation Journal*, 46, 4, 288).

Macpherson, W. (1999) *The Stephen Lawrence Inquiry. Report of an Inquiry by Sir William Macpherson of Cluny* (Cm 4262). London, The Stationery Office.

McDonald, C. (2000) 'Some relevant questions for work with racist and racially motivated offenders', *Probation Journal*, 47, 3, 206–9.

NAPO (National Association of Probation Officers) (1995) *Probation Work with Racist Offenders and those whose Offences are Motivated by Racism* (Policy Document PD3–95). London, NAPO.

O'Brien, J. and Peacock, J. (2001) *Time Intervals for Criminal Proceedings in Magistrates' Courts* (Information Bulletin 5/2001). London, Lord Chancellor's Department.

Pearson, G., Blagg, H., Smith, D., Sampson, A. and Stubbs, P. (1992) 'Crime, community and conflict: the multi-agency approach', in Downes, D. (ed.) *Unravelling Criminal Justice*. Basingstoke, Macmillan, 46–72.

Prochaska, J.O. and DiClemente, C.C. (1984) *The Transtheoretical Approach Crossing the Traditional Boundaries of Therapy*. Homewood, IL, Dow Jones/Irwin.

Raine, J.W. and Willson, M.J. (1993) *Managing Criminal Justice*. Hemel Hempstead, Harvester-Wheatsheaf.

Ray, L. and Smith, D. (2001) 'Racist offenders and the politics of "hate crime"', *Law and Critique*, 12, 203–21.

Ray, L., Smith, D. and Wastell, L. (2002) 'Racist violence and probation practice', *Probation Journal*, March.

Raynor, P. and Vanstone, M. (1994) 'Probation practice, effectiveness and the non-treatment paradigm', *British Journal of Social Work*, 24, 4, 387–404.

Sibbitt, R. (1996) *The ILPS Methadone Prescribing Project* (Home Office Research Study 148). London, Home Office.

Sibbitt, R. (1997) *The Perpetrators of Racial Harassment and Racial Violence* (Home Office Research Study 176). London, Home Office.

Smith, D. (1996) 'Pre-sentence reports', in May, T. and Vass, A.A. (eds) *Working with Offenders: Issues, Contexts and Outcomes*. London, Sage, 134–56.

Smith, D. (2000) 'The logic of practice in the probation service today', *Vista: Perspectives on Probation*, 5, 3, 210–18.

Stanko, E.A. (ed.) *The Meanings of Violence*, forthcoming. London, Routledge.

Webster, C. (1997) 'Inverting racism'. Paper presented to the British Criminology Conference, Queen's University, Belfast.

Index